THE STORY OF
LEEDS

THE STORY OF
LEEDS

DAVID THORNTON

To Sheila Gaunt, Doreen Holdsworth, Joan Parker

First published 2013

The History Press
The Mill, Brimscombe Port
Stroud, Gloucestershire, GL5 2QG
www.thehistorypress.co.uk

© David Thornton, 2013

The right of David Thornton to be identified as the Author
of this work has been asserted in accordance with the
Copyright, Designs and Patents Act 1988.

British Library Cataloguing in Publication Data.
A catalogue record for this book is available from the British Library.

ISBN 978 0 7524 9957 4

Typesetting and origination by The History Press
Printed in Great Britain

CONTENTS

INTRODUCTION AND ACKNOWLEDGEMENTS

In 1906, when Rupert Brooke wrote 'History repeats itself; historians repeat each other', he probably had his tongue in his cheek. But anyone writing the history of Leeds is bound to mention 1626 when Leeds was given its first royal charter, or 1858 when Queen Victoria opened the new Town Hall. A Leeds historian is bound to repeat what previous historians have said. True a historian will always try to unearth new facts even if it is nothing more earth-shattering than that James Henry of Leeds patented the first flat-bed mouse-trap with spring-activated neck-breaker in 1909!

Historians must decide from which point of view they are writing history, bearing in mind what A.J.P. Taylor said in his *Politicians, Socialism and Historians* (1980): 'When I write history I have no loyalty except to historical truth as I see it.' When I write a history of Leeds I have to admit I do so from the point of view of someone who was born in the town, was educated there, spent my professional life in the city and am enjoying my retirement living within half a mile of where I was born. When I write about Leeds, in some ways I write of my own family. The wool textile industry was the bedrock of the Leeds economy: my great-grandfather helped build the local mills in the 1840s, my aunt wove khaki cloth for the Boer War in a West Leeds mill in the 1890s. For centuries coal-mining was another vital part of that local economy: my maternal grandfather was a Leeds miner. When Edward VII and Queen Alexandra drove round City Square on their way to the university my paternal grandfather watched them. When wounded German prisoners were held in Leeds Infirmary my father was one of the Leeds Home Guard supervising them. Like many other Leeds head-teachers, when the Yorkshire Ripper presented such a dangerous threat, I was forced to suspend after-school activities as a precaution.

For me it would be easy to approach the history of the city from a rather parochial point of view; but the history of Leeds is a microcosm of the history of Britain. No-one writing a history of the city can ignore the Norman Conquest and the ultimate devastation it brought to Leeds and its surrounding villages in the shape of the Harrying of the North. When the Black Death struck Britain, the people of Leeds suffered. When civil war tore the nation apart, Briggate echoed to the thunder of cannon, the crack of muskets and the clash of swords. When the eighteenth- and nineteenth-century wars with America and France disrupted trade, hundreds of Leeds people starved as a result. When the First World War took its toll, the young men of Leeds paid the price, and nowhere more emphatically than on that bloody first day of the Battle of the Somme. So a history of Leeds must inevitably be painted against a background of British history; to do less is to deny the city's part in that great story.

Inevitably in writing a history such as this I have been fortunate in the help I have been given, and none more so than from the Thoresby Society, which has kindly given me full access to their extensive archive and library. I am also grateful to have received the permission of Her Majesty Queen Elizabeth II for the use of material from Queen Victoria's diary, to both Armley Local History Society and the Wortley Local History Group, the Leeds Library, the Brotherton Library at the University of Leeds, Special Collections at the University of Leeds, the Leeds Local and Family History Library, Armley Library and the West Yorkshire Archive Service. Various individuals have given me help and advice, including Ann Alexander, Colin Broadbent, Steven Burt, Ann Clark, Don Cole, Janet Douglas, Geoffrey Forster, Sheila Gaunt, Kevin Grady, Michael Meadowcroft, Greta and Peter Meredith, Margaret Pullan, Mick Rainford, Alan and Pat Scott, and Andrew Thornton and Katy Thornton. Needless to say any mistakes in this work are mine and mine alone.

I have tried to use a variety of visual material including photographs, line drawings, prints, paintings, maps and even cartoons. The illustrations are mainly taken from the archive of the Thoresby Society, to whom I am most grateful, as I am to the *Yorkshire Evening Post* for permission to use Thack's cartoon. Other illustrations are from the Wortley Society and my own collection. Some maps I have specifically created for this book, and photographs I have specifically taken. Others I have used are inevitably old, and I must thank Brian Chippendale for his expertise in helping to enhance them and make them more usable.

Finally, I must once again thank my wife, June, and our family for their support, encouragement and sense of humour while I was writing this.

Leeds 2013

one

A PLACE CALLED LOIDIS

Leeds: the fastest growing city in the United Kingdom. It is a metropolitan borough in West Yorkshire that sprawls across the landscape from Otley in the north-west to Rothwell in the south-east; from Wetherby in the north-east to Morley and Pudsey in the south-west. By 2011 its population was estimated to be 726,090. It is the cultural heart of the region and the largest centre for business, legal services and financial activities outside London.

But it was not always so. The reason why it grew as it did, and where it did, begins hundreds of thousands of years ago, long before people settled in the valley of the slow-moving waters of the river Aire or inhabited the rolling hills around it.

There was a point in the valley of the river Aire where, at times, its waters could be forded. That crossing would see the birth of what was to become one of Europe's greatest cities. The Aire is the very lifeline of Leeds, for without it there would have been no city. From the earliest times it has flowed south-east from the bleak, inhospitable Pennines. Ever eastwards, it makes its meandering way to the Humber and the sea. At some time in the future it would provide a ready-made waterway to transport goods from the burgeoning town's industries. In that same valley other smaller streams or becks flowed into it. To the north they passed over layers of millstone grit, which softened and purified the water and which in the distant future would be ideal for its use in the fledgling woollen industry that would eventually develop here.[1] From the south the waters flowed over layers of sandstone and shale, water-bearing rocks which millennia ahead would provide invaluable water supplies when the Aire became polluted and the population grew.

Lurking beneath the surface of the land lay the wealth of the future. To the north of the river were great deposits of millstone grit, stone that in the centuries ahead would provide the material for the great buildings of the city such as

Kirkstall Abbey, the Town Hall, the Corn Exchange and Holy Trinity church.[2] To the south great carboniferous coal measures lay dormant, ready to be used in some future age to fuel the furnaces, power the mills and factories and heat the countless homes of the men and women who would inhabit the area.

It was a place where in the past great glaciers had swept across the frozen landscape during the various Ice Ages. Then in the last interglacial period, about 120,000 years ago when a warmer climate prevailed, hippopotami wallowed in the river Aire, herds of auroch – wild oxen (now extinct) – roamed across the hillsides, and elephants trundled their way over the landscape. About 12,000 years ago another ice age began, the Great Ice Age as it became known. Once again the area became an Arctic wilderness and mammoths roamed the valley of the Aire.[3] Over the years fossilised remains have been found in West Leeds of an auroch and a mammoth, at Thwaite Mills the tusk of another mammoth was discovered, at Kirkstall the antlers of a red deer were found, and the famous Armley Hippo was unearthed in a field at Wortley in 1852.

Eventually the climate warmed and the valley and its surrounding hills became first a wilderness of sparse tundra, then pine and hazel trees dotted the scene. Later still a dense sprawl of oak and elm trees, of ash and birch flourished. Great tracks of boggy swamp and marsh broke up the heavily forested countryside. 'Carr' originally meant 'a boggy place', and even today the names Hunslet Carr, Sheepscar and Carr Crofts are echoes of that time.

But what of people? Excavations by the East Leeds History and Archaeology Society at Austhorpe Hall have unearthed a round barrow, or burial mound, which is believed to date back to between 2,500BC and 700BC, indicating possible occupation during the late Neolithic Age or the Bronze Age. It was about 2,000BC that the first real evidence of human beings in the Leeds area was found, and the city's story really begins.

These people, known as the Beaker People from the pottery they buried with their dead, were a Bronze Age people. They cleared patches of land, domesticated cattle, sheep, goats and pigs, and

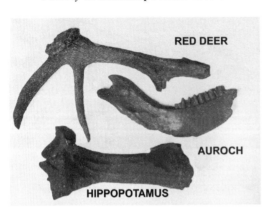

RED DEER

AUROCH

HIPPOPOTAMUS

The antlers of a red deer were found near the junction of Kirkstall Road and Kirkstall Lane in 1858. Both the remains of an auroch or wild ox and those of three hippopotami, two adults and a calf, were found at Wortley in 1852.

grew wheat and barley; but all evidence of their thatched stone huts has long since disappeared. However, artefacts from their period have been found scattered across the area: a beaker was discovered at Tinshill in 1960, four palstaves or bronze chisels at Roundhay, socketed bronze axes both in Kirkstall Road and near Hunslet Moor, and a bronze dagger at Chapel Allerton.[4] They were an industrious people, and as the times were relatively peaceful the Aire valley became a major trade route. Flat bronze axes and gold were transported east from Ireland, while jet from Whitby and amber from as far away as the Baltic were carried westwards.

By about 500BC a new people, the Celts, had arrived in Britain. It was the dawn of the Iron Age. These Celts were a warlike people who organised themselves into tribes. One of the most famous of these was the Iceni of Norfolk, who, under their feisty queen Boudicca (Boadicea), famously rose in revolt against the Roman invaders in AD61. The Parisi tribe dominated the East Yorkshire area, but the greatest of these Celtic tribes was the Brigantes, a federation of clans that occupied Brigantia, the land that stretched from what is today's Derbyshire to Northumberland. The people of the Aire valley were part of that kingdom.

They cleared some of the woodland to grow crops of wheat, barley, oats, rye and flax, but predominantly they reared cattle, sheep, goats and pigs, and were famous horse traders. Some lived in the nine Brigantian towns with their capital Isurium Brigantum, known now as Aldbrough. The vast majority, however, were scattered across the landscape, occupying small isolated settlements and enduring a wetter, colder climate than today's. Such a small cluster of farmers gathered in the Cookridge area. Their homes, circular stone huts with thatched roofs, were about 26ft in diameter. Rectangular walled enclosures provided safe havens for their animals. Remains of these settlements have been found off Iveson Rise and near the site of the old Cookridge Hospital. Here querns, used to hand grind corn, were discovered in 1908 and examples of their pottery in 1923. They were an artistic people, and a stone head discovered near Ireland Wood in 1954 suggests that they may have belonged to some mysterious Celtic cult.[5]

Tribal rivalries led to outbreaks of warfare, and steps had to be taken to guarantee some degree of safety. Defensive enclosures surrounded by ditches and palisades were constructed across the countryside. Both the people and their flocks gathered there for protection when danger threatened and there they remained until the menacing enemy withdrew. Archaeological discoveries show that around the Leeds area such defensive structures were erected at Barwick-in-Elmet, Chapel Allerton, Gipton and Temple Newsam. It has been suggested that Woodhouse Moor may also have been the site of such a stronghold, but any evidence of a structure there has long since disappeared. Certainly its elevated position would have provided an ideal defensive position, and it is possible that the name of the thoroughfare that still runs across it, Rampart Road, is an echo of those long-gone times.

But in AD43 their world would begin to change. That year Emperor Claudius launched the invasion of Britain and Roman legions arrived on these shores. Soon the newcomers' presence was firmly established in the South, but in the North the invaders were happy to establish a diplomatic truce with the Brigantes and their Queen Cartimandua. However, discord grew between the Brigantian tribes. Civil war broke out, and the ensuing chaos was seen as a threat to the Roman occupying forces. In about AD71 the IXth Legion, the Hispana, under the command of Cerialis, was ordered to carry out the invasion of Brigantia and subjugate its peoples.

By AD74 the rebels had been routed and Cerialis was triumphant. Four years later the new governor, Agricola, set about consolidating the occupation. At Eboracum (York) a local legionary fortress had been established, and from there a series of roads were constructed across the region, linking a number of forts built to enforce Roman power in the area. One of these forts, on the Eboracum to Mancunium (Manchester) road, was known as Cambodunum. Historians have long speculated as to its site, some arguing forcibly that is was in Leeds, approximately where the West Yorkshire Playhouse now stands; while the historian, monk and scholar the Venerable Bede makes only the slightest spelling change when in his reference to Leeds, which he called Loidis, he refers to 'the royal residence Campodunum'.

Evidence of Roman occupation of the Leeds area was discovered in 1819 when workmen clearing land just south of Leeds Bridge unearthed a 'compact and hard trajectus', which is believed to have been the remains of a Roman ford. Logically, at some point the Eboracum to Mancunium road would need to cross the river, and here at the ford would have been an ideal strategic site to build a fort to defend such a position. The arguments were further augmented by the fact that 'Cambodunum' means the 'fort by the river bend', and the river does bend not far away.[6]

Another of these roads ran from Eboracum, across a route north of Leeds, to Bremetennacum (Ribchester). It went through Calcaria (Tadcaster), Burgodunum (Adel) and Olicana (Ilkley). In 1966 the Yorkshire Archaeological

Society excavated part of it at Adel between the A660 and the road to Bramhope. With regard to the Roman occupation, Adel is without question a site of some considerable archaeological importance, and excavations there have been carried out at different times from the 1930s. The earliest Leeds historian, the antiquarian Ralph Thoresby, wrote in 1715 that there was a Roman camp there 'pretty entire'. Indeed, he acquired so much material from the site that he required two carts to transport his finds home. A century later Thomas Whitaker wrote of 'A camp, from its form and dimensions, apparently Roman.'[7]

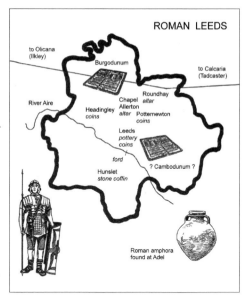

Burgodunum or Adel was a major Roman site but archaeological discoveries have been made across the city indicating that there was a Roman presence in the area.

It was ideally situated as a military site, commanding, as it did, a position above the Aire and Wharfe valleys and from where the occupying auxiliary troops could easily observe the activities of the local inhabitants. Yet, though various Roman objects such as a tombstone, pottery, roof tiles, brooches, coins and coffins have been unearthed there, later academics could not agree whether a fort existed at Adel at all. The argument was finally settled in 1996 when the Department of Archaeological Science of Bradford University proved beyond doubt that a military camp had been built there, though it was not where Thoresby had thought.[8] It was a classic playing-card-shaped fort with entrances on all four sides. To the west of the fort a *vicus*, a typical civilian settlement, also grew up.

In Leeds and its surrounding out-townships, however, though a Roman presence was obvious, no major discoveries have been made. Burials were unearthed at Chapel Allerton and Hunslet; coins have been recovered in Headingley, Osmondthorpe and Burmantofts; pottery has been found near the Headrow; and at Haw-Caster Rigg near Potternewton other evidence of Roman occupation has been unearthed.

At Farnley, James Wardell, the historian, claims there was a Roman site ' of some importance', but unfortunately it has long since disappeared. He also suggests that Street Lane was a Roman road leading to the Calcaria Burgodunum main highway.[9] However, just a few miles east of Leeds at Dalton Parlours, near Wetherby, one of the major Roman sites in the country has been excavated. Here an extensive villa complete with hypocaust, or underfloor central heating system, mosaic floors and a bath-house was built in about AD200.

When the legions were finally recalled to Rome at the beginning of the fifth century, the threat of barbarian invasions became more and more apparent. As Britain was left to defend itself a series of independent kingdoms emerged across the country. One of them, Elmete, stretched from the river Humber to the foothills of the Pennines, and was by now a Christian kingdom. The Leeds area was part of it, and it is during this period that the first mention anywhere is made of Leeds. In his *Ecclesiastical History of the English People* of AD731, Bede refers to the 'region of Loidis', by which he meant Leeds and the area around it. It is possible that it was a subdivision of Elmete or even the capital, for Bede goes on: 'A basilica was built at the royal residence of Campodunum; but this, together with all the buildings of the royal residence, was burned by the pagans who killed King Edwin, and later kings replaced this seat by another in the vicinity of Loidis. The stone altar of this church survived the fire, and is preserved in the monastery in Elmete Wood.'[10]

Now a new threat emerged from pagan Europe as hordes of Germanic tribes, the Angles, Saxons and Jutes, invaded the island. It was a slow process, probably beginning in the fourth century and lasting until the early years of the sixth. The Angles targeted the North, though eventually the whole kingdom would become known as 'the land of the Angles' – England. As a deterrent against the impending assaults, defensive earthworks were dug at Becca Banks, Woodhouse Moor Rein, near Aberford, and Grim's Ditch, about 3 miles east of Leeds. It is also possible that the remains of the fortifications at Adel, which Ralph Thoresby had thought was the Roman fort, were built then. Slowly the invading Angles absorbed one kingdom after another. Elmete, and its capital at Barwick-in-Elmete, was the last outpost of Christianity to fall. Then in AD617 King Edwin absorbed the smaller kingdom into the more powerful Northumbria.

These were brutal and violent times, with the differing kingdoms frequently taking up arms against each other. It is Bede, again, who tells of the great battle fought on Sunday 15 November AD655 to the east of Leeds. An invading army of the pagan King of Mercia, Penda, moved into the area. According to Thoresby it was at Harehills where he gathered his force and engaged in a skirmish on Chapeltown Moor before encountering the army of King Oswy

of Northumbria. They met somewhere near the Cock Beck, where it flows through the Seacroft and Stanks areas. The exact location of the bloody Battle of Winwaed is uncertain, but wherever it took place what followed was a brutal clash of armies.[11]

Weakened by desertions, Penda's force was heavily defeated as it fought in driving rain and struggled against the swollen waters of the beck, which legend has it ran red with blood. Thirty of Penda's leading generals were killed, as was his ally King Aethelwald of Deira. Penda also perished, and the *Anglo-Saxon Chronicle* records triumphantly that 'the Mercians became Christians'. So died the last of the great pagan kings of Britain. Oswy's success was said by some to be his greatest military triumph; yet ironically it is Penda's name that has been perpetuated today in the area, through place names such as Penda's Way and Penda's Walk.

For 150 years the people of Loidis carried on their lives relatively peacefully; then in AD785 the first of the Viking invaders arrived in Britain. Of actual Danish remains in the Leeds area none of any significance has ever been unearthed. Ralph Thoresby wrote of a 'Danish fortification' on Giant's Hill at Armley, but later historians have suggested that the earthworks there may have been a motte-and-bailey or ringwork-and-bailey castle of later date. The ravages of the centuries have destroyed any remaining evidence.

Loidis had grown at a place where the river could be forded, and was the ideal spot for traders to meet and cross the Aire. Consequently it became the focal point for the villages around. Those villages, scattered across the landscape, included what later became known as the out-townships: Allerton, Armley, Beeston, Bramley, Farnley, Gipton, Headingley, Holbeck, Hunslet and Reestones, later known as Wortley.

Falling under the Danelaw, they were subjected to the Viking administration of the area. Yorkshire itself was divided into three parts known as ridings. Leeds was in the West Riding and remained so until 1974, when the area was renamed West Yorkshire to the annoyance of many locals. These ridings were subdivided into wapentakes, similar to the Saxon hundreds. Freemen gathered at the local wapentake to settle any disputes and punish crimes. When they wished to express their approval, members flourished their weapons to indicate agreement; hence the word 'weapon take' or 'wapentake' emerged.

The area around Leeds fell into two such wapentakes, both of which covered a considerable area. Settlements south of the river were part of the Morley Wapentake, which stretched from Hunslet in the east to Todmorden in the

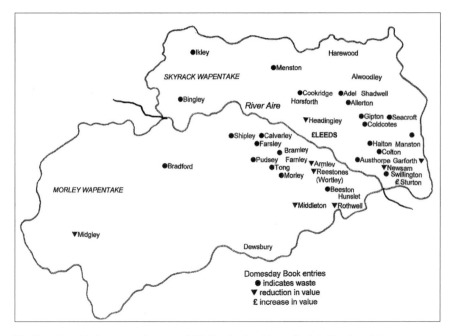

The Skyrack and Morley wapentakes were divided by the river Aire and included Leeds and the out-townships. Other places have been given to indicate the area the wapentakes covered. Note the effect the Harrying of the North and the reduction of value of most places as recorded in Domesday Book.

west and probably met at Tingley. The men from Leeds itself attended the Skyrack Wapentake, which stretched from Arthington and Pool in the north to Aberford in the east and to Bingley in the west. They met in Headingley at the Shire Oak, a massive oak tree probably known as the 'bright oak' or the 'siar-aches', which was corrupted into the word 'Skyrack'. The old tree eventually collapsed in May 1941: 'it gave a sigh and fell forward on the rails surrounding it'. Today the Skyrack Inn, the Original Oak pub, Shire Oak Street and Shire Oak Road perpetuate it.[12]

By now it appears that Leeds had become a religious centre of some note and by the tenth century a place of some political importance, but few details exist. It was, however, significant enough to be mentioned in the eleventh-century *Life of St Cadroë*, which told that when Saint Cadroë visited the King of Strathclyde in about AD842 he was taken to 'the city of Loidis, which is the boundary of the Northmen and the Cumbrians; and there he was taken up by a certain noble-man, Gunderic, by whom he was led to King Eric in the city of York'.

Historians also believe that the five stone crosses, including the famous Leeds parish church cross, which were unearthed when the old parish church was demolished in 1838, prove the significance of Leeds as an important reli-gious centre. But that is conjecture. Apart from Bede's casual references to the area there is little definite known about the town's history up to this time. That was to all change.

It was with the coming of the Normans and the compilation of the Domesday Book that the first detailed and accurate picture can be made of what Leeds and the surrounding villages were actually like. Much of the nearby countryside was woodland pasture intermingled with arable land and rolling meadows. During the reign of the Saxon king Edward the Confessor the vill of Leeds stretched down what is now known as Kirkgate. It was a cluster of wooden buildings, more than likely cruck structures with wattle and daub walls. Probably two bays long, each would have been big enough to accommodate the family in one bay and the animals in the other. There were also smaller settlements at Knostrop, Hillhouse (Richmond Hill), Woodhouse and Buslingthorpe. Seven thanes, men who held a social rank higher than that of a freeman but below that of an hereditary nobleman, owned the seven manors that made up the area. It was a place of some significance, boasting a church and a priest. Surrounded by a considerable amount of arable land and 10 acres of meadow, its most valuable asset was the mill sited on the banks of the Aire; its ancient position is today identified by the name Mill Hill. How valuable an asset a mill was is realised when it is seen that Domesday Book lists only one third of the manors listed as possessing one. At the bottom of Kirkgate was the church where a local priest officiated over the lives of the inhabitants. His duties were not simply restricted to the people of Leeds itself.

By now the parish system had evolved, and he was responsible for the huge parish that rambled from Chapel Allerton in the north to Hunslet and Beeston in the south; from Gipton in the east to Farnley in the west.[13] It was one of the largest parishes in the country covering some 21,000 acres.

Farming was fundamental to the British way of life and would remain so

The Shire Oak at Headingley and the meeting place for the Skyrack Wapentake. Seen here c.1810, the old tree finally collapsed in 1941.

for the next 800 years. The wealth of Leeds was emphasised by the fact that it possessed fourteen plough teams, each made up of eight oxen. The overall value of Leeds itself was put at £6, making it one of the most valuable locations around. Cookridge by contrast was worth 20s, Beeston 40s, and Armley with Reestones (Wortley), Bramley, Chapel Allerton, Alwoodley, Cookridge and Halton were all considered to be worth about 20s.

The rambling parish of Leeds covers 21,000 acres. Plans were made to subdivide it in 1650 but it was not until 1843 and 1844 that changes came about.

It would have seemed to the people of Leeds that theirs was an enduring and unchanging pattern of life. The eternal passage of the seasons was the same for them as it had been for their fathers and as it had been for their fathers' fathers. Then in 1066 and the years that immediately followed the country faced a seismic event that shook their world to its foundations, presenting the men and women of the Aire valley with a catastrophe the like of which would never be seen again in the entire history of Britain.

In September 1066 news would have reached Leeds that a great battle had taken place only 35 miles away at Stamford Bridge. King Harold and his Saxon army had defeated the invading Norwegian army of King Harald Hardrada, and the people of Leeds would have breathed a sigh of relief that the invader had been thwarted and they were safe. Unknown to them it was but temporary relief.

Who were these people of Leeds? In 1086 Domesday Book describes the various social groups who lived in the town. There were four sokemen or freemen, farmers who rented their land from the lord. The four bordars in the manor sometimes worked for wages and performed some duties for the lord of the manor, as well as cultivating land for themselves. The lowest in the social order were the twenty-seven villeins. Neither slaves nor freemen, these men were obliged by law to provide various services to the lord of the manor and in exchange received a cottage and a parcel of land. Including wives and children, Leeds would probably have had a population of about two hundred at the time.

That same September Duke William of Normandy landed at Pevensey and the Norman Conquest had begun. At the Battle of Hastings he famously triumphed over Harold and routed his Saxon army. On Christmas Day 1066 William was crowned king in Westminster Abbey. The South had succumbed. In the North, however, the English were not so easily subdued. By 1068 three revolts had seriously threatened William's grip on the kingdom, and in 1069 the Conqueror marched his army northwards to establish once and for all his power in the region. His army's actions would go down in history as the Harrying of the North.

William's order was simple: turn the land from the Humber to the Tees into a virtual wilderness. The simplicity of the entry in the *Anglo-Saxon Chronicle* graphically captures what happened next: 'King William marched into that shire and completely devastated it.'[14] Peasants were massacred, villages burned, grain stocks ruined and livestock wantonly slaughtered. So it was for the people around Leeds.

When the Domesday Book chroniclers arrived in the area in 1086, their findings reveal the extent of the devastation inflicted. One expression, time and again, is used to sum up what they found in village after village; one word captures the ravages of smouldering ruins, putrefying animal carcases, rotting crops and a distraught people; one sober, simple word: 'waste'. So were described Adel and Beeston, Bramley and Calverley, Farsley and Chapel Allerton, Cookridge and Eccup, Gipton, Colton and Halton, Morley and Pudsey, Seacroft and Tong. Other places were emasculated. Garforth, which had been worth 60s, was now worth 30s. Headingley had been worth 40s and was now worth just 4s. Armley and Reestones (Wortley) had been worth 20s and were now worth 10s. Newsam had been worth 60s and was now worth 6s.[15]

There are, however, some historians who question the extent of the impact of William's actions on the North, arguing that the valuations in Domesday Book are inaccurate and that the term 'waste' may have carried a broader and less damaging implication. But what cannot be disputed is that of the 1,900 settlements recorded in Domesday Book, at least 850 were totally demolished and another 300 seriously reduced in value. Whatever the extent of the disaster, only two places in the district appear to have escaped the punitive wrath of the Norman invaders. Sturton saw its value increase from 30s to 40s and Leeds, which had been valued at £6, was now worth £7.

If the people of Leeds did not undergo the trauma that had beset the surrounding villages, like the rest of the country they nevertheless found them-

In LEDES. x. car̄ træ 7 VI.bo ad gld̄. Tra. VI. car̄.
Septē tainī teneb̄ T.R.E.p.VII.Maner̄.Ibi nc̄.XXVII. ulfi 7 IIII.
fochi 7 IIII.bord hn̄t.x IIII.car̄.Ibi pbr 7 eccla 7 molin̄.IIII.folid̄.7
x.āc p̄ti. Valuit.VI.lib̄.m̄.VII.lib̄.

In LEEDS, 10 carucates of land and 6 bovates taxable. Land
for 6 ploughs. Before 1066, 7 thanes held (it) as 7 manors.
Now there, 27 villagers, 4 Freemen and 4 smallholders who
have 14 ploughs. There, a priest and a church. A mill, 4s;
meadow 10 acres. The value was £6; now £7.

The Domesday Book entry
for Leeds. Top, a drawing of
the original entry; middle, the
original Latin; bottom, the
English translation.

selves in thrall to a new royal family, a new ruling class, a new culture and a
new language. They were now a subjugated people, and Leeds was part of the
huge tract of land William granted to Ilbert de Lacy, the man empowered to
bring order to the area. Ilbert hailed from an estate a few miles east of Rouen
in Normandy. He had loyally supported Duke William during the invasion
and dutifully carried out his punitive orders during the Harrying of the North.
As a reward he was granted 164 manors in Lincolnshire, Nottinghamshire
and Yorkshire. His Yorkshire holdings, known as the Honour of Pontefract,
stretched from the West Riding to Blackburn in Lancashire. Like the other
Norman barons, Ilbert received his lands on condition that when the need
arose he would render specific services to his monarch. In turn he sublet much
of his estate to lesser nobles on the same conditions, and thus the system per-
colated throughout the whole of society, down to the lowliest peasant. This
pattern of landholding and obligation is generally known as the feudal system
(though some historians argue that feudalism related only to the political and
military system of the time and that the arrangements for agricultural labour
should really be called manorialism). The Normans developed feudalism, originally a Saxon concept, and enforced it nationally.

Sometime between 1086 and 1100 Ilbert sublet the manor of Leeds, along
with that of Headingley, to Ralph Paynel, also known as Paganel. A loyal supporter of the Norman king, Paynel found himself endowed with estates across
the newly conquered kingdom. Many were in Yorkshire, with several estates
between the Ouse and the Aire. In Leeds he was an absentee landlord, but possibly established the fortified manor house that occupied a site at the edge of
the wooded manorial park, bordered by today's Boar Lane, Bishopgate Street
and Mill Hill. This would have been the administrative centre of the place. In a

relatively short time, however, Paynel had seriously reduced the economic value of his manor.

Just as the hierarchical structure of society dictated how life would be lived day by day, the Church exerted extreme power over everyone from the mightiest monarch to the meanest peasant, wielding the threats of excommunication and eternal damnation over those who transgressed. To be seen to support the Church was politically pragmatic and could also be a guarantee of a safe and secure place in the hereafter. Ralph Paynel was no exception to this.[16]

In 1089 he founded the Priory of the Holy Trinity on Micklegate in York, a daughter house of the Benedictine abbey of Marmoutier, near Tours. According to the Domesday Book it was 'an unimportant, ruined and poverty stricken church', which had been destroyed during the Harrying of the North. It was Paynel's attempt, as a devout Christian, at some form of reconciliation with the Church, and he granted several rich endowments to the Benedictines

The seal of Ilbert de Lacy, Lord of the Honour of Pontefract. His estate, to which Leeds belonged, stretched from Pontefract to Blackburn in Lancashire.

of Marmoutier that year. He also established within the boundary of the manor of Leeds a small enclave known as the rectory manor of Kirkgate-cum-Holbeck for the new foundation. It included Leeds parish church itself, the local tithe hall and a separate manor house near the church. The tithes from the church and the attendant income were a sizeable amount, which the manor of Leeds could ill afford to lose. In addition, the monks also established a monastic cell in Holbeck and received the income from the church at Adel. Why did Paynel act as he did? The opening words of the charter in which he granted these concessions made it clear: he sought eternal peace in Heaven, stating that 'I, Ralph, surnamed Paynel, inflamed by the fire of divine love, desir[e] to treasure up in heaven what I can after this life ...' The manor was further denuded by gifts to the Knights Hospitaller and the Knights Templar and then, in 1180, the new manor of North Hall was carved out of the old manor. This new establishment stretched roughly from Vicar Lane and Lady Lane to Sheepscar Beck. Then Ralph's granddaughter, Alice Paynel, married first Richard de Courcy and, when he died, Robert de Gant, sometimes referred to as Gaunt; thus the manor of Leeds passed to him by marriage.

In 1838, during the demolition of the medieval parish church, a series of ancient crosses was discovered. The contract of Robert Dennis Chantrell, the architect, allowed him to claim any such finds, and thus he took them and pieced them together in the garden of his home at Headingley. It became clear they were Anglo-Scandinavian in design and dated from the eighth to tenth centuries. One in particular stood out, engraved with interlaced rune-like characters and vine scrolls. The bottom panel featured Wayland the Smith, the mythological Anglo-Saxon hero, while the top of the cross was surmounted with a wheel-head. According to Pevsner it was a 'spectacular piece'. Some historians claim it was a sepulchral monument to Onlaf, the Danish king, and that the crosses indicate Leeds had become an important religious centre.

When Chantrell retired he took the Anglian, or as some people call it the Saxon, Cross, with him, erecting it in his garden at Ivy Cottage, Rottingdean, near Brighton. On his death the news of the cross's existence reached Leeds, and the Vicar of Leeds, Dr John Gott, entered into negotiations to buy it back. Here the story diverges. According to one version, Gott approached the Court of Chancery, which placed a value of £3 on the object. The new owner, a grocer, flatly rejected the offer. Gott then offered £25; the grocer demanded £100. When the vicar pointed out that £25

One of several crosses found when the old parish church was rebuilt. Their discovery possibly indicates Leeds was a place of some religious significance.

was better than nothing and that the cross was of no value to anyone else, the grocer relented, and Gott was finally able to bring the Anglian relic back to Leeds in 1880. However, on 23 October that year the *Leeds Mercury* featured a letter from Mr Washington Teasdale of Headingley, 'an old and intimate friend of the Chantrell family'. He insisted that the cross was never 'sold by order of the High Court of Chancery'; it had been a gift of the Chantrell family to Leeds. Teasdale pointed out that the family were aggrieved that their role had been so ignored. Confusion may have arisen in that permission had to be granted from Sir Richard Malins, vice-chancellor in the Court of Chancery, to authorise the gift.

The cross was finally erected on the altar flat of the parish church in 1880. Teasdale suggested that a plaque should be fitted at its base with the words 'Given to the parish of Leeds by the family of Robert Dennis Chantrell, architect'. The cross still stands there, but no plaque is to be seen.

The manor's continued gradual economic decline took its toll, while the nation found itself plunged into a brutal and devastating civil war as Stephen and Matilda's forces wreaked havoc across the land. 'Never did a country endure greater misery,' wrote the scribe of the *Anglo-Saxon Chronicle*. 'Men said openly that Christ and his saints slept.' Yet even as civil strife ravaged the nation there were some men and women who sought another way of life, and found it in the sanctity of the Church and the tranquillity of the monastery. Thus it was that a small group of monks arrived in the Aire valley to establish a monastery on the outskirts of Leeds.

two

NEWCOMERS TO THE VALLEY

Whate did these newcomers to the Aire valley find? Much of the land around Leeds and its surrounding villages was waste and woodland, though each settlement would have its own great open fields where wheat, oats and rye were grown. One field was left fallow each year and here cattle and sheep were raised. The inhabitants lived in simple cottages with a small plot of land, known as a toft, where they could grow parsnips, peas, lentils, carrots, lettuces, broad beans and onions. Here they reared geese, hens and goats.

Land was vital; agriculture was the foundation on which the whole of medieval society was built. The imposition of feudalism meant that every peasant was obliged to work so many days each year on the lord of the manor's estate, known as the demesne. He was also required to pay certain local taxes. The tenants of the manor fell into three categories. Free tenants or freeholders paid a fixed rent to the lord of the manor, but were not required to give labour or provide services. These free tenants formed about a sixth of the population of Leeds. Below the freemen came the villeins, a social group that consisted of two distinct categories; bondmen and cottars (although some historians argue that the term 'villein' should only be applied to the wealthiest class of peasant, the bondman). A bondman was a fairly substantial member of the community, but 'his son may not be tonsured nor his daughter marry without the lord's licence'.[1] Some bondmen added to their income, and thus William Carpenter and William Shoemaker are listed in Leeds. The other unfree tenants, the lowest in the social strata, were the cottars. These smallholders, who rented simple cottages and small plots of land, worked as farm labourers. Obliged to serve on the lord's land for so many days a year, they also laboured for the freemen and bondmen. Like the bondmen, some cottars supplemented their earnings. In 1258 Leeds cottars engaged in additional activities were Henry Carpenter, Richard Taylor, Simon Forester and Thomas Baker. Unfree tenants had no legal right to leave the estate. Consequently in 1385, when Joan Buslingthorpe wanted to live outside the manor of Leeds, Robert Foster stood security for her.

Medieval manuscripts often portray idyllic scenes of peasants working the fields. The reality was at times vastly different. Crop failures, famine and pestilence regularly occurred, and compounding these disasters were civil disturbances that laid the country waste. Between 1087 and 1135 no fewer than four rebellions disrupted life in England. In addition to these pressures, taxes to pay for various kings' military exploits were imposed. As the *Anglo Saxon Chronicle* said regarding Henry I's war with France, 'England dearly paid for this in numerous taxes from which there was no relief.'[2]

This then was the state of the nation in 1152; the world that the people of Leeds lived in. This was the year that newcomers arrived in the Aire valley and founded Kirkstall Abbey. It was a significant event. Over 850 years later the people of Leeds can still marvel at its magnificent ruins and know that within their city lies one of Europe's finest historic sites.

In the middle of the twelfth century the valley of the river Aire to the north of Leeds was a wilderness of swamp, brushwood and endless tree-covered wastes. Nestling on the eastern river bank was a small cluster of wooden huts where a group of religious hermits had gathered. Seleth, the leader of the group, originated from the south, but a vision of the Virgin Mary had instructed him to travel to Kirkstall in Airedale and there establish a religious community. A friendly cowherd guided him to the place and there he settled, living off roots and herbs. Supported by the generosity of locals, others joined him, and a small community was soon built up. If Seleth's story is as he described, it implies that there was a church in the area, the 'kirk' of Kirkstall, before the hermits built one. Edward Parsons, the nineteenth-century local historian, disputes this, however. He argues that the 'name was unknown until after the foundation of the Abbey'.[3]

Kirkstall Abbey's story began some years earlier in the Benedictine abbey of St Mary's in York. Like other monastic orders the Benedictines were dedicated to a life of simplicity. Their days were spent in worship and work while observing a strict vow of silence. Over the decades, however, the rigorous rules of the order had been eroded. The vow of silence was regularly broken, and their simple diet had given way to what Hugh of Kirkstall described as 'exquisite delicacies' and 'flavoured sauces', producing 'the full and over-gorged belly [with] hardly a scrap of room left in it'. The 'splendid variety of drinks' they enjoyed was equalled by the 'elaborate delicacy of raiment' that had replaced their more

Kirkstall Abbey seen from the river Aire. Although the building was commenced in 1152 and virtually completed within thirty years, the tall belfry was only added between 1509 and 1527.

sombre garments. In 1132 a small rump of half a dozen monks objected to this: this departure from the austere life they had chosen flew in the face of everything to which they had dedicated their lives. The dispute rumbled on through the summer, and eventually Thurstan, the Archbishop of York, was forced to intervene. His arrival at the abbey, however, instead of resolving the dispute, inflamed the situation. Fighting broke out, and the archbishop was forced to herd the recalcitrant monks, now numbering thirteen, into the church and to lock the doors. He then escorted them to his palace, sheltered them over Christmas at Ripon and finally, on 27 December 1132, installed them in a remote part of the valley of the river Skell. It was an uninhabited wilderness, 'a place of horror and vast solitude'. Their only shelter was a large elm tree, but the place abounded with springs. The Latin for 'spring' is *fontis*, and thus the buildings they erected became known as Fountains Abbey.

As the monks struggled to build their home, fighting the ruthless forces of nature and desperately striving to avoid starvation – they even made broth from the elm tree's leaves – they determined they would never again experience the overindulgent laxity they had seen at St Mary's. In 1133 they became members of the strict Cistercian order. It was a way of life that allowed nothing to interfere with their dedication to prayer and work, their commitment to chastity, poverty and obedience. No stained glass windows or elaborate carvings decorated their churches; no paintings graced their walls; no embellished manuscripts were produced; no richly decorated vessels or exquisitely embroidered cloths ornamented their altars. They refused to dye the habits they wore and were thus known as the white monks; the colour of the undyed woollen cloth.[4]

But if they led a limited and secluded existence the monks were still very much part of the real world. They financed their life by rearing great flocks of sheep and selling the wool, and they spread their beliefs by opening daughter houses from the end of the 1130s.

A further opportunity presented itself to the monks when Henry de Lacy, the lord of the Honour of Pontefract, and thus the man in whose domain Leeds was, fell ill. A devout man, he believed that somehow he had offended God, and swore that should he recover he would give land to Fountains for the creation of a Cistercian foundation dedicated to 'the glorious Virgin and Mother of God, Mary'.[5] On recovering he was as good as his word, and offered the Abbot of Fountains, Henry Murdac, land in the desolate Pennines at Barnoldswick. Thus it was that in 1147 Murdac ordered the Prior of Fountains, Alexander, to take with him twelve monks and ten lay-brothers to establish the new foundation at Barnoldswick. It was a bleak and inhospitable place swept by Pennine winds, lashed by incessant rains. Their crops were destroyed and their animals were driven off by marauding brigands, who took advantage of the chaos of the civil war between Stephen and Matilda. Furthermore, constant disputes with the locals led Alexander to accept the inevitable and to recognise in a few short years that their attempt to build a thriving abbey and cultivate the land was doomed to failure.

One day, according to the account of the foundation, Alexander was travelling down a wooded valley when he came upon 'certain brethren in religious garb, leading a hermit's life' at Kirkstall. He realised the potential the site offered. After pointing out to the brothers how much better the Cistercians could develop the area, he made his way immediately to Henry de Lacy to urge his support. With his blessing, the patronage of William de Peitevin and the approval of William de Reinvill (the two men who tenanted the land from de Lacy), the future was agreed. Some of the hermits decided to join the Cistercians; others chose to leave. On Monday 19 May 1152 Alexander and his monks arrived at their new home, leaving a few lay-brothers on the old site to run it as a sheep farm, or grange.[6]

At Kirkstall they cleared the land and prepared the site so that the building of a great monastery could begin. They were fortunate in that a valuable supply of stone was readily available, but historians still argue whether the main source was Bramley's quarries or those at Horsforth. Within thirty years the buildings were be virtually complete. What makes Kirkstall Abbey so special is that the changes which inevitably occurred over the subsequent 400 years were relatively few, and thus it is one of the finest examples of an early Cistercian abbey in Europe.[7]

The other feature of the building that fascinates historians is that it was built at a time of architectural transition. For centuries the round-headed arch had been used in buildings, but in the twelfth century masons began to adopt new techniques, employing the pointed arch as they realised it was structurally far superior. At Kirkstall both types of arch are to be found: the windows and doorways use the traditional round-headed Romanesque or Norman arch, and the pillars of the nave use the Gothic, pointed one. Various skilled masons would have been employed to guide the monks during the building, and the suggestion has been made that the Kirkstall mason who used

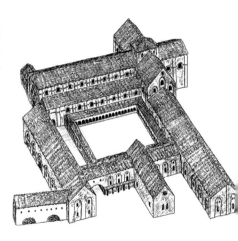

A reconstruction of the main buildings of Kirkstall Abbey as it would have appeared in the twelfth century. The church with its low belfry dominated the site. The long building on the right housed the choir monks' dormitory, the one on the left the lay brothers' quarters.

these very latest building techniques came from France. There is no doubt that the twin entrance to the chapter house is very similar to those used in some parts of Normandy.

Traditionally every Cistercian monastery was dedicated to St Mary the Virgin, but Alexander, perhaps wanting to remember the religious hermits who had occupied the site originally, opted for a different name – and Kirkstall Abbey it became. It would never become as magnificent an abbey as Fountains, nor accumulate the wealth of its mother abbey; neither would it found the numerous daughter houses that Fountains did. But Kirkstall was fortunate in that it acquired generous benefactors in Henry de Lacy and William de Peitevin. The abbey followed the tradition of adapting the coat of arms of one of its major supporters, and used William's heraldic arms.

The monastery's environs, bounded by a stone wall, covered about 40 acres, stretching from the present Morris Lane to the river. Its main entrance was a gatehouse on the lane, but from there the grounds were divided into two courts by a wall. To the north-west lay the outer court, around which were the buildings for day-to-day living: the smithy, stables, farm buildings, a small mill and the guesthouse. The inner court contained the church and monks' living quarters. To reach it, it was necessary to pass through the inner gatehouse, today's Abbey House Museum.

Like all Cistercian monasteries Kirkstall was laid out to the order's traditional design. Dominating the site, quite naturally, was the massive basilica; Henry de Lacy himself is said to have laid the foundation stone of the great church.

Two communities lived side by side in the monastery: the choir monks who worshipped eight times a day and the lay-brothers, or *conversi*, who took similar vows but were illiterate – indeed they were forbidden to learn to read – and spent the bulk of their time in manual pursuits, providing the workforce that generated the abbey's wealth. They worked on the farms where sheep were reared, and Allerton Grange, Breary Grange at Adel, Bar Grange and Moor Grange at Headingley, and Dean Grange at Horsforth are present-day reminders of the extent of the monks' sheep granges around Leeds. These would eventually extend from Accrington in the west to Micklethwaite in the east and Bessacar in the south.

Through the centuries the prosperity or adversity the abbey experienced depended a great deal on the quality of the man chosen to be abbot. Kirkstall was fortunate in that its first abbot, Alexander, was a shrewd, far-sighted individual who oversaw the abbey's building programme. In 1182, when he was 'gathered to his fathers', as the monastery's histories relate, he had lived long enough to see the building almost completed, and knew that the community was at least on a sound financial footing.

The wealth of the abbey came from wool. The grange at Bessacar contained a flock of sheep numbering about 1,000, Seacroft had 700, Bramhope, Cookridge and Potternewton had 300 each, and Beeston 240. After clipping, the wool was brought by pack-horse trains to the abbey, where merchants from Italy, France and the Low Countries came to purchase it.

Kirkstall was not without its disasters. In the latter part of the thirteenth century a series of long hot summers and virulent diseases decimated the abbey's flocks, and by 1278 the abbey was facing a severe financial crisis. In debt to the merchants of Florence, Gilbert Cortles, the abbot,

The main door at Kirkstall Abbey. Compare the lack of decoration on it with Adel church's elaborately carved entrance. By the eighteenth century the main Otley road ran directly through the abbey's church.

a contentious and incompetent administrator, not only saw the debts mount up but even led his monks in open rebellion against their mother abbey of Fountains. Cortles was removed and when, in 1284, black scab wiped out the abbey's entire flock, Hugh de Grimstone was appointed in the hope of turning the abbey's fortunes round. He succeeded. By 1301 the abbey's debts had fallen to £160 from the £5,248 15s 7d he had inherited.

During these troubled times the people of Leeds and the surrounding villages would have had little contact with the abbey, though the monks did occupy certain parts of the area around Leeds, holding land at Adel, Armley, Beeston, Headingley, Horsforth, Roundhay, Allerton, Potternewton and Shadwell, while at Bramley it is said they built a chapel of ease and at Farnley they erected a mill. At Seacroft, from 1200 to 1287, and at Weetwood, from 1287 until c.1400, they operated an ironworks.

There were periods, however, when the Kirkstall Cistercians were forced to supplement their clip by buying wool from local farmers. The poor of Leeds, too, made contact with the monks, for they knew they could always get help and sustenance from the abbey. The almoner was appointed specifically to provide alms to the needy. But the monks owned no land in the village of Leeds itself, so real dealings between the people of the town and the abbey did not develop until later centuries, when Edward III banned the export of wool. It was probably then that the Kirkstall Cistercians began selling their clip locally, and in effect stimulated development of the wool textile industry in the area.[8]

The monks of Kirkstall were not the only monastic order active in Leeds at this time. In the eleventh century a religious/military order known as the Knights Hospitallers was formed in Jerusalem. Sometime between 1166 and 1176 Alice Paynel, who by now had married Robert de Gant, granted them 2 acres of land in the manor of Leeds, along with a building with its adjacent plot and the rights to pasture their flocks. However, it was another order that made a much greater impact on the area east of Leeds, and gave it its present name. In about 1152 the Knights Templar acquired various properties in and around Leeds. In Leeds itself they had holdings on what became the Headrow and Vicar Lane, where Templar Street and Templar Place are reminders of their presence.

They also held land at Seacroft and Horsforth; but it is in East Leeds that their greatest acquisition was to be found – the vast estate at Newsam. The Templars, like the Hospitallers, were a religious/military order, founded in 1118 in Jerusalem to protect visitors to the Holy Land. Over the centuries they accrued enormous wealth, possessing several large holdings in Yorkshire. These included an estate at Copmanthorpe and one near Wetherby, while Cowton, near Northallerton, Hirst, near Selby, and Newsam even absorbed their name – becoming known as Temple Cowton, Temple Hirst and Temple Newsam.

At Temple Newsam the Templars built a monastery known as a preceptory, and archaeologists have been able to establish what it contained. Among its buildings were a chapel, a dormitory, a huge barn, a granary, stables, a dairy, a dovecote, a hall, a watermill for grinding corn and a fulling mill – the first recorded in England, according to a document dated 1185. There were, however, never many knights in residence at Temple Newsam, as the majority were away fulfilling their duties in the Holy Land.

The Cistercians and the Templars were not the only newcomers to the Aire valley. By the end of the twelfth century the gifts of the Paynel family to religious houses and the creation of North Hall Manor had seriously eroded the prosperity of the manor of Leeds. It was left to Maurice de Gant, sometimes using his mother's maiden name of Paynel, to address the problem.

During the twelfth century it began to be realised in Europe that trade and industry could be more profitable than a total commitment to agriculture. Walled towns began to replace villages, while freemen living in them began to develop new businesses and engage in trade. Among the greatest beneficiaries were the lords of the manor, who could now increase rents and impose local taxes and tolls for markets and fairs. Between 1100 and 1300 no fewer than 140 new towns were established in England, the years between 1170 and 1250 seeing the greatest number.[9] To Maurice Paynel, creating such a new town in Leeds offered a possible solution to his financial difficulties. The erosion of the value of the manor over the centuries was compounded by the general economic climate: the early years of the thirteenth century saw taxation increase dramatically as King John imposed new taxes to help build up a war chest large enough to finance a serious challenge to King Philip of France. In 1207 the tax on revenues and properties rose to unprecedented levels,[10] and perhaps it is no coincidence that Paynel decided in that year to act as he did. Determining to create a new town of Leeds, he decided to build it away from the old village centred on Kirkgate, and establish it on the road that ran down to the river. This suggests that a bridge may already have been spanning the waters of the Aire, or that a ferry may have existed there. It is today's Briggate.

Eleven years earlier Roger de Lacy had granted the burgesses of Pontefract a charter, charging them 200 marks to do so. Paynel based his charter on Roger's, but made no charge. Thus is was that on Monday 12 November 1207 Paynel announced to the world his intention of creating a new town. Its strategic position, on the border between the agricultural Vale of York and the emerging textile region of the West Riding, like its position at a river crossing, proved crucial to its success.

The charter was a cautious one. According to Professor John Le Patourel, it was 'modest'.[11] The town's inhabitants would be newcomers, as Paynel would still need his old tenants to work on his land at Woodhouse and Knostrop. In all probability these newcomers were invited immigrants or the sons of the bondmen of Leeds, and they were to be granted personal freedom and fixed rents. A new manorial court was created, better able to adjudicate on industrial and commercial disputes than the old one, although the latter continued – as did trial by duel and ordeal by water. Most importantly provision was made for the men of the new borough, the burgesses, to develop new trades. There was also a limited exemption from tolls when they carried goods by road or river. They held their land freely and were entitled to lease their property, subdivide it or sell it. However, tenants were strictly forbidden from selling any property to the Church or to a monastery, and they were obliged to use the lord of the manor's corn mill and the common oven. Paynel also reserved the right to appoint officials and levy what dues he wished.[12]

Thirty long, narrow tofts were created on either side of the street, large enough to hold a simple cottage, a workshop or an outhouse. The street itself was wide and an ideal location to hold a market, where the newly established tradesmen could sell their wares. The charter did not make provision for markets or fairs, but by 1258 a market had been established and by 1341 two fairs. Through the centuries Briggate would become the town's main thoroughfare, and even today the small yards and arcades that run back from the street are a clear reminder of Paynel's legacy and the tofts originally established there.

Though the success of the new commercial enterprise was vital if Paynel's development was to succeed, land for farming was still essential. To accommodate that demand a further grant of half an acre of land was offered at a rent of 16d a year at a new location known as the 'borough man's tofts', today's Burmantofts.

Paynel's new concept was not the initial success he had hoped. It was slow to come to maturity, and the times were not auspicious for trade or industrial growth. King John's misgovernment and punitive taxation precipitated rebellion among the barons, and Paynel was one of them. The result was Magna Carta, in June 1215, but John had no intention of implementing its contents. Civil war

inevitably followed, with Paynel joining in the insurrection. Pope Innocent III excommunicated the rebels and John ultimately defeated them, depriving them of their land. Paynel was no exception. On 2 January 1216 a royal proclamation announced that 'the good men of Leeds' were to 'be obedient to Philip de Albini'. How effective the king's orders were is not clear. What is known, however, is that Paynel continued to support the dissident barons until, at the Battle of Lincoln in May 1217, their force was vanquished and Paynel was captured. He was forced to pledge his manors of Leeds and Bingley to Ranulph de Blundeville, the Earl of Chester and Lincoln. He would never recover

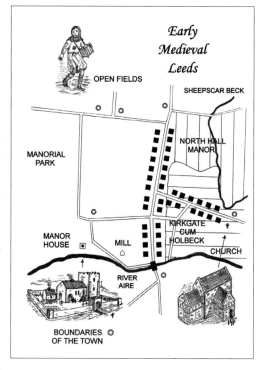

them, and history is silent on his subsequent fate; but existing records leave no doubt what happened to the manor of Leeds.

In 1232 the de Lacy family became the new earls of Lincoln, and in 1294, when Alice, the daughter of Henry, the Earl of Lincoln, married Thomas, Earl of Lancaster, her marriage settlement saw the manor of Leeds become part of Lancaster's vast estate.[13]

National events did not bypass the monks of Kirkstall or the people of Leeds. In 1265, when Simon de Montfort summoned knights and burgesses to his historic parliament, Abbot Simon of Kirkstall was one of the five abbots also ordered there. When Edward I returned from Scotland in 1298, having defeated William Wallace, Kirkstall Abbey was ordered to provide the king with four horses, a cart and two men, to help to transport the royal entourage.

By the beginning of the fourteenth century the Knights Templar had become extremely affluent, possessing numerous wealthy estates across Europe and the Middle East. But their popularity waned, and they were accused of idolatry and other nefarious practices. In October 1307 Pope Clement V dissolved the order. Edward II followed where the pope had led, and in January 1308 he ordered all Templar property to be confiscated in England, Scotland and

About 4½ miles north of Leeds city centre lies what Nikolaus Pevsner, the architectural historian, described as 'one of the best and most complete Norman churches in Yorkshire'. It is dedicated to St John the Baptist, so when people enter the building they step down into it, symbolising stepping down into the river Jordan.

In all probability it was Ralph Paynel, the lord of the manor of Adel, who built the first small wooden church that stood on the site. In 1089 Paynel granted its advowson to the Benedictine monks of the Priory of the Holy Trinity, York. Between 1150 and 1170 they set about erecting a new stone building, using materials from a local quarry.

It is a small church, just a simple nave and chancel. But unlike the Cistercians at Kirkstall, the Benedictines enriched their building with sumptuous decorations. The chancel arch is spectacular, boasting thirty-seven fantastical beakheads. Outside, the corbel frieze running round the building features seventy-eight grotesque heads, but the church's most famous feature is its glorious and elaborately carved south entrance. Here, carefully sculptured above the door, can still be seen (though badly eroded) the Holy Lamb, the four symbols of the Evangelists and scenes depicting the gospel and the fall of man. Around it is a maze of wonderful zig-zag patterns. The eye is drawn to the church's famous closing ring in the centre of the wooden door, the head of a lion-like monster in the process of swallowing a man. Originally made in York in about 1200, it was stolen in 2002 and replaced with a replica.

This Grade I listed building has always been an attraction. When the British Archaeological Association met in Leeds in 1863, its members made a point of visiting St John's. But by mid-Victorian times the church was badly in need of restoration. In 1876 a public meeting was called at Adel, and G.E. Street, the diocesan architect, was called in to carry out a sympathetic and extensive renovation, which included raising the roof. It was a success. Today St John's at Adel is one of Britain's architectural treasures but it is also still a thriving church, a place where people go to worship as they have for almost 1,000 years.

Ireland. The knights at Temple Newsam were disbanded and sent to various monasteries. Richard of Sheffield was dispatched to Kirkstall Abbey, but quickly escaped.[14]

It was not just the Knights Templar who fared badly at this time. For several years, commencing c.1313, crop failures brought untold suffering and famine to the region, and murrain, a highly infectious disease, swept through the local cattle and sheep. Twice Robert the Bruce and his marauding Scots invaded the Leeds area. Historians claim that Adel was pillaged, and Bruce himself wintered at Morley. The Scottish king was an eternal thorn in Edward's side, and the English king's difficulties were further compounded by Thomas, the Earl of Lancaster. By now Thomas had become the wealthiest and most powerful baron in the land, while Edward's popularity waned. The barons grew more and more resentful of the influence of the king's favourites and, as opposition to the king grew, Lancaster called a meeting of disaffected barons and clergy at Sherburn-in-Elmet in June 1321.

The following year, on 16 March, Edward's troops confronted Lancaster's at Boroughbridge. The insurgents may well have had among them men from Leeds and its surrounding villages, who as tenants would have had no option but to support their lord. One such reluctant volunteer was Robert Hood of Wakefield, mentioned in the Wakefield Manor Court Rolls of 1316. The rebel army was heavily defeated and Lancaster was carried back to Pontefract a prisoner. Six days later he was beheaded before a jeering crowd, while Robert Hood became an outlaw, now called Robin. The people of Leeds were also exposed to Edward's vengeance. Three of the king's officers, Robert le Ewer, Sir Andrew Harclay and Oliver Ingham, were dispatched to the district on a punitive expedition. In March 1322 Leeds was handed over to Thomas Deyvill, Keeper of the Rebels' Lands. He reported that the land was 'impoverished and wasted'. So serious was the situation that the tenants felt they were no longer able to farm it, and consequently handed it back.

Opposite, from top

St John the Baptist's at Adel. This mid-twelfth-century church is a Grade I listed building. According to Pevsner it is 'one of the best and most complete Norman churches in Yorkshire'.

Adel church's famous closing ring sometimes referred to as the Sanctuary Ring. Made of bronze c.1200 in York it was stolen in 2002 and was replaced with this replica. Note the man's head protruding from the mouth of a lion.

The elaborate carved doorway at Adel church. The symbols over the door represent Christ in majesty and the symbols of the four Evangelists.

But there were some positive signs economically for Leeds. By now the wool trade was slowly developing in the area. Records show that in 1201 Simon, a dyer, was employed in Leeds (and, as it happens, fined for selling adulterated wine). By 1258 William Webster and John Lister are also known to have been working in wool. As the industry developed the lord of the manor saw its potential, and erected a fulling mill to the east of Leeds Bridge.

It was in the West of England that the wool trade had originally prospered, though by 1300 Beverley and York were both emerging as textile towns. The severe restrictions placed on wool manufacturers there by the guilds saw the industry slowly begin to spread westwards across Yorkshire and, by the middle of the century, the textile trade was becoming established in the West Riding.

Then came one of the most catastrophic disasters ever experienced in world history: bubonic plague swept through Europe. In 1348 it had reached Rouen and Paris, and by June that year it had arrived in Britain. The disease was no newcomer to Europe. Outbreaks were recorded in AD987, 1001, 1046 and 1316–18 and would continue to occur, but the pandemic that devastated Europe between 1346 and 1353 is considered 'the greatest demographic disaster in European history'. By early 1349 it had reached the river Humber and rapidly spread along its tributary waterways.[15] By May it had reached York. For the North of England, the worst months of the outbreak came that summer. It does appear, however, that though the people of Yorkshire suffered appallingly they fared better than those in many other counties.

The inhabitants of Leeds and its surrounding villages were exposed to the pestilence, and it is possible that plague carried off half the manor's population. Even so the town seems to have recovered fairly quickly. Though the manor profits had been reduced from £70–£80 a year to £62–£66, by 1356 business seems to have improved to the extent that a new fulling mill had been opened, and the market made a fairly speedy return to profit.[16]

The reduction of manpower in the area, however, provoked a major change in the way the people of Leeds farmed, and the latter half of the fourteenth century saw the town and its surrounding villages develop its wool textile industry, the industry that would become the basis of Leeds's economy for centuries to come.

three

THE END OF FEUDALISM

The Black Death had come and gone. In the decades that lay ahead the people of Leeds would see the country divided once again by civil war. The ordinary men and women of the town may not have been directly involved in the bloody Wars of the Roses or in shaping the history of the country for the next two centuries, but they would have been exposed to its effects. During the fifteenth and sixteenth centuries they would see the fledgling wool textile industry blossom and flourish to the point where it would become the bedrock of the town's wealth. And the changes they witnessed were not just industrial. Commutation of field services meant that more and more men made cash payments to the lord of the manor rather than fulfil their obligations by working on his land. Commutation had started in the Leeds area by 1341 and in the following century accelerated.

The reeves' accounts for the town give a vivid insight into the everyday lives of the local community, and Leeds historians are fortunate that accounts still exist for many of the years between William Widdowson's record for 1356–57 and William Hargrave's for 1609–10. These detailed documents give graphic information regarding the administration of the manor. For example, the one compiled by Adam Gibbarn, reeve in 1399, recorded that the men at Knostrop and Woodhouse were actively engaged in the commutation of their field services, paying a levy rather than spending their time ploughing and reaping their lord's fields.[1]

Farming was still a vital part of the Leeds economy, but it was the production of wool textiles that would provide the town with its economic mainstay for the next 500 years. Up to the thirteenth century the inhabitants of Leeds and its surrounding villages only produced cloth to make their own simple functional garments. The material was coarse and uneven, its texture open, its colour a buffish grey.[2] The woollen industry proper was concentrated in the Cotswolds, and in Norfolk and Suffolk where Bristol, Gloucester and

Norwich grew wealthy through the trade.[3] By 1300 production had also been established in Beverley and York. However, the restrictive regulations practised by the weavers' guilds there saw the industry gravitate to the West Riding. Around Leeds it took root principally in the townships south of the river: Armley, Wortley, Bramley, Farnley and Hunslet. It was further boosted in 1353 when Edward III prohibited English merchants from being involved in the export of wool.[4] England ceased being a wool exporter and became a wool textile manufacturer.[5]

Demand soared. At the beginning of the fourteenth century it took fifty-four weeks to produce 120 cloths in Leeds, but the industry rapidly developed. By 1468 production had increased to 177 cloths, and that in just forty-two weeks. It went on raising its output to the point that between 1550 and 1600 wool textile production from Leeds and its surrounding villages increased tenfold. The quality of Leeds cloth was recognised as exceptional.

Leeds and its out-townships specialised in producing broadcloths 23 to 25yds long and 1¾ yards wide, and Northern Dozens 12 to 13yds long and a similar width.[6] Its production involved every member of the family. First the wool was cleaned and then the fibres straightened out using teazels and later cards, brush-like tools set with wires; hence it was known as carding. Usually this was done by the younger members of the family. It was then spun by the women of the house, in the early times using a distaff and by the end of the fourteenth century a spinning wheel. It took eight spinners to provide the requirements of one weaver. To help the weaving process grease, often rancid butter, was smeared on the wool fibres.

When completed, the cloth was then sent to a fulling mill. By 1356 Leeds boasted two such mills by the river Aire, on either side of Leeds Bridge. Here the wool was soaked in a solution of fuller's earth powder and stale urine known as weetings. It was then hammered by huge fulling stocks to give it a matted appearance. Finally the finished cloth was stretched on tenter frames. These huge wooden frames, between 12 and 30yds long, were covered with tenter hooks which held the drying cloth in place. By 1477 nine new tenters had been erected by Leeds Bridge. Numerous tenter fields were scattered around Leeds and the out-townships. In the town itself The Calls, Swinegate and Millgarth all had tenter sites, and Armley Moor and Hill Top Moor in West Leeds are but two out-township examples. However, the cloth was left unsupervised, and vandalism such as tenter cutting and outright theft of the drying material became commonplace in the area.

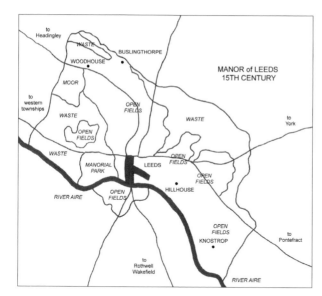

Left The manor in the fifteenth century. Much wasteland had been reclaimed. Woodhouse Moor was common land. Note the manorial park and how it covers the area now occupied by Park Row, Park Square, Park Place and Park Lane.

Below A fifteenth-century manorial barn at Beeston which was used until the 1960s. In the1980s the council carried out significant remedial work but by 2012 it had fallen into disrepair.

After tentering the cloth was sold on for dyeing and finishing. Originally this was carried out in the Low Countries, but later dyeing and finishing shops developed in the town. By 1356 three dye vats had been built. The dyeing and finishing shops were to be found in Briggate, Swinegate, Hunslet Lane and Woodhouse Lane. Finishing the cloth required workers, known as rowers, to raise the nap of the cloth with teazels and then cut it to the required length with croppers. Finally it was taken to the market on Leeds Bridge.[7]

As the woollen industry developed in the Leeds area the fortunes of the Cistercian monks at Kirkstall also blossomed – first by exporting wool to the Low Countries and then, after Edward III's decree of 1353, by selling their

The distaff had been used for spinning from time immemorial. The spinning wheel came into use in the fifteenth century.

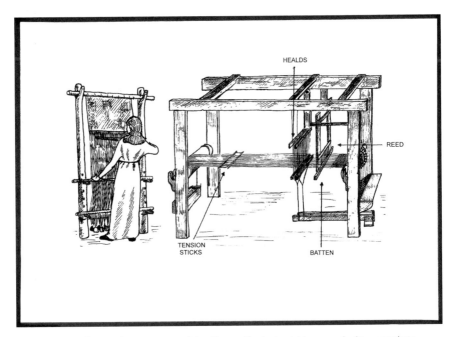

The earliest weaving was done on warp-weighted looms. The horizontal loom required two people to operate it, usually the weaver and his apprentice.

wool to dealers in the West Riding. In 1301 Kirkstall's flock had risen to 4,500. The animals they reared were very probably the breed of long-haired hornless sheep that eventually developed into the Wensleydale. The abbey's flocks produced about 9,000lb of wool or roughly twenty-five sacks a year when a sack contained 364lb, the amount a packhorse could comfortably carry.

As the years passed change was in the air at Kirkstall. Lay-brothers were eventually phased out; the rule of silence no longer prevailed. Meat was allowed on Sundays, Tuesdays and Thursdays, but had to be cooked in a separate kitchen and eaten in a separate dining room. Embellishments to the building that would never have been contemplated in the days of Abbot Alexander were carried out. The roof of the church was lowered and the pantiles were replaced with lead. The three simple windows of the east end were replaced with a single great window. Between 1509 and 1528 William Marshall, the abbot, added a tower to the building, along with pinnacles and corner turrets. Farming methods changed as the monks began to lease their granges to laymen rather than farm them themselves.

Monasticism generally was on the wane, and the monks became more and more unpopular as local communities envied their wealth. While the manor of Leeds earned between £70–80 a year in 1459, the abbey enjoyed an annual income of £354. But if petty local jealousies were apparent, it was the decision of Henry VIII to dissolve the monasteries that made the greatest single impact on monasticism. Historians offer different reasons to explain why the king embarked upon this course. Although there were valuable financial assets to be gained by appropriating monastic properties, the rumblings of discontent within the Roman Catholic Church generally had grown louder and louder. In 1536 the first dissolutions occurred, then in 1539 the dissolution of the larger abbeys began. On Saturday 22 November Richard Layton and the other royal commissioners arrived at Kirkstall with instructions to dissolve the abbey, and drew up the necessary documentation in the chapter house.

The monastery's buildings, farms, granges and moveable goods were confiscated. Lead was stripped from the roofs and windows were removed from their settings. Local people saw the building stone as fair game, and legend has it that the steps built by Leeds Bridge were made from the abbey's walls. Fortunately for posterity, however, the church itself and the cloisters remained, on the whole, untouched.

The monks were treated reasonably, the abbot, sub-prior and remaining twenty-nine monks receiving pensions. Some, like Anthony Jackson, Richard

Bateson, Gabriel Lofthouse and William Lupton, became curates or priests in various parishes in Yorkshire, while Richard Wodd appears to have married.[8] Legend has it that Abbot John Ripley was allowed to take up his lodging in the inner gatehouse and remain there until his death. Ripley had become abbot in 1528. He was a shrewd man. When Catholics in Yorkshire decided to discuss their grievances in 1536 he attended their meeting at Pontefract; but sensing the way the political wind was blowing he refused to join the ill-fated Pilgrimage of Grace. He supervised the closing of the abbey, and his co-operation saw him receive a pension of £66 13s 8d.

Looking back over the abbey's 400-year history, other abbots were not always so circumspect or efficient. Ralph Haget (1182–90) was without doubt a deeply religious man with an overriding sense of justice, but he clashed with King John, and, when he left to become abbot of Fountains Kirkstall, was seriously in debt. Helias de Roche (1203–4), on the other hand, was a pragmatic leader and an efficient administrator. As might be expected, abbots were devout men, and none more so than Turgisius (c.1196–1203). He constantly wore a hair shirt, never used additional winter clothing, refused to eat fish or drink wine, and when he conducted services he was 'never without tears, and so great was the flood of them that he seemed less to weep than to pour them down like rain'. His exact opposite was John de Thornberg (fl.1369–92). An out-and-out villain, he took to terrorising the neighbourhood with a gang of five monks, one lay-brother and four laymen. They even resorted to murder at times.

With the dissolution, the Kirkstall estate passed first to Archbishop Thomas Cranmer, then, from 1583 to 1584, it was bought by the Savile family. It became part of the Brudenell estates by marriage in 1671, and it remained in their ownership until 1888, when the family decided to sell their property in Leeds.

The dissolution also had positive results. It is significant that when the first Leeds corporation was established in 1626, of the twenty-nine families that formed it no less than twenty-four were first- or second-generation newcomers. Several were from families that had begun to farm land which was previously part of the Kirkstall Abbey estate. These newcomers gave an impetus to the local economy and helped the town and its surrounding out-townships to thrive during the following century.

But it was not just monasticism that was losing the people's affection. In the sixteenth century a seismic theological tsunami swept away the old faith of their fathers, the Catholic Church having become more and more unpopular.

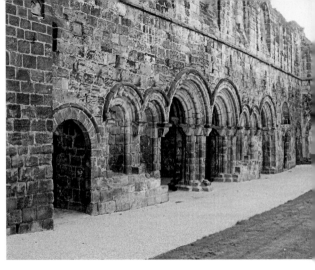

In 1517 the German theologian Martin Luther famously nailed his ninety-five theses to the church door in Wittenburg, his protest generally seen as launching the Reformation. However, discontent about various practices and false doctrines had long been reverberating across Europe.

Kirkstall's Chapter House on the east cloister. The dual entrance indicates that the mason may have come from Normandy where similar entrances are to be found. Here the daily business of the abbey was discussed each day. The door on the immediate left was the library.

Even though opposition and anger were growing against Catholicism, there was bitter antagonism from those who remained loyal to the old faith when Henry imposed the first dissolutions. To counteract these voluble antagonists Henry turned to Thomas Darcy for help. Darcy, the owner of Temple Newsam and the first person to build a house there, had always been a loyal supporter of the king, to the point that when he fought bravely in Spain against the Moors, the king rewarded him in 1512 with land at Roundhay. However, Darcy was a devout Catholic, and consequently when a Northern protest group formed the Pilgrimage of Grace (which John Ripley had diplomatically eschewed) he joined the 30,000 protesters. In 1537 Darcy and the other ringleaders paid for their disloyalty to Henry on the scaffold. The king then granted the Temple Newsam estate to the Lennox family. Their most famous scion, Lord Darnley, the future husband of Mary Queen of Scots, was born there.

It is difficult in the twenty-first century to appreciate the vital part that religion played in the everyday lives of the men, women and children of medieval Leeds. It shaped their thinking and dictated their daily behaviour from the cradle to the grave. The villages of Adel and Whitkirk boasted their own churches, while the great church in Kirkgate catered for Leeds and its out-townships. Holbeck, Beeston and Chapel Allerton each had their own chapels of ease, while Farnley's, built in c.1240, was rebuilt by Sir William Harrington in c.1417 when Henry V granted him the right to replace it, for services he had rendered at the Battle of Agincourt. Though the chapels of ease catered for weekly worship, all parishioners had to attend the parish church itself for marriage and burial ceremonies. There were also other chapels in Leeds, known as chantry chapels. Two were dedicated to St Mary, one at the north-east corner of Leeds Bridge and the other at the junction of Lady Lane and Vicar Lane. Sir William Eure's chapel, dedicated to Mary Magdalene, was at the junction of the Headrow and Briggate. The Revd Thomas Clarell's chapel, dedicated to St Catherine, was at the top of Kirkgate, and boasted a fine chancel decorated with paintings and other adornments.

A church had stood in Kirkgate from Anglian times, and the Domesday Book confirms this. The building was probably rebuilt in the twelfth century, but during the reign of Edward III a serious fire destroyed the structure, and a magnificent new parish church was erected. A 96ft high tower dominated the cruciform basilica and space was created for 3,000 worshippers. By 1420 the church was known as St Peter's. Tragedy again struck in about 1500, when a fire destroyed much of the choir. Restoration work was carried out, and in 1534, when John Leland, Henry VIII's antiquary, visited the town he reported on a 'Paroche Churche reasonably well buildid'.[9]

Henry's actions continued to affect the town. In 1538 he granted the advowson of the parish church to a certain Thomas Culpepper, thus making a stranger to Leeds responsible for the appointment of its vicar. This unsatisfactory state of affairs may well have been responsible for an appointment in 1559 that many considered totally inadequate. The Revd Alexander Fawcett, the first Protestant Vicar of Leeds, lacked any real passion for the new religion, and his preaching was so ineffective that people referred to him as a 'dumb dog'. Thus it was that in 1588 a coterie of parishioners sought to buy the advowson, and eventually did so for £130.

When Fawcett died in 1590, Beeston-born, Leeds Grammar School-educated Oxford academic the Revd Robert Cooke was appointed. He was adept enough to balance his duties as a parish priest with his passion for academic theology. It was claimed that he 'revived a deep Sense of true Religion and Piety', 'true Religion' meaning Protestantism. Most important for Leeds, however, was that he was a Puritan, and Puritans were appointed as incumbents of the parish church for the next century.

As the Reformation, set in motion by Henry VIII and consolidated by Edward VI and Elizabeth I, accelerated, the people of Leeds found themselves torn between the old Roman Catholic tradition and that of the Church of England. In the very early years there appears to have been little eagerness among laypeople of the town to adopt the new faith, which probably explains

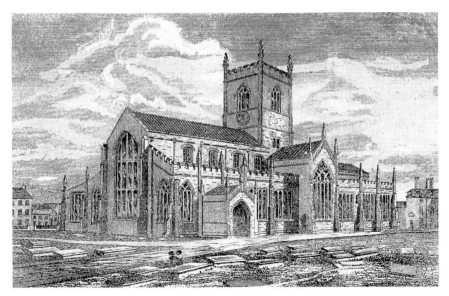

The old medieval parish church seen here in the early nineteenth century. In 1781 John Wesley preached at St Peter's to a congregation of 1,100. The building was demolished and a new one opened in 1841.

the appointment of the lukewarm Protestant Alexander Fawcett. But as Protestantism grew more popular the new Protestant Church itself became divided, as one group sought a more stringent anti-Catholic approach to worship. They tended to wear plain styles of dress and lived strictly moral and pure lives; hence they were abusively referred to as Puritans.

The closing of the chantry chapels during the reigns of Henry VIII and Edward VI had a positive and long-lasting effect on the town. A group of influential men collaborated to rescue certain chantry endowments from confiscation, and these went towards the establishment of Leeds Grammar School in 1552. Sir William Sheafield, the priest attached to the Clarell chantry, at the top of Kirkgate, left £14 13s 4d for payment of a 'Schoolmaister at Leedes'. In all probability the Grammar School was not the first school in the town – documentary evidence in 1341 shows that 'John, master of schools' was already holding land in Leeds – so it may be that Sheafield's endowment was intended to re-establish the existing school as much as establish a new one; but 1552 is the year usually recognised as the date of the Grammar School's foundation.[10]

Inevitably there was still a rump of 'the Parishioners of the towne and paryshe of Leedes' who refused to give up the faith of their fathers and desert the Church of Rome. Refusal to comply with new laws and to accept the doctrines of the Church of England was known as recusancy, and from 1549 legislation was introduced that imposed harsh fines, seizure of property, imprisonment and even death for those who refused to conform. But the seesaw situation between the old and the new faiths continued: during Catholic Queen Mary's troubled reign fourteen Protestant parishioners from Leeds, 'bussy fellowes of the new sorte', were prosecuted in the neighbourhood.

By the reign of Protestant Elizabeth I the majority of Leeds people accepted the new faith, but there were still small pockets of Roman Catholic worshippers in the area. Certainly Catholic families were known to exist at Middleton and Roundhay whilst during the 1580s Richard Hargrave, a Hunslet man, did his best to help those in the Leeds area who still held to the old religion. Such was the bitterness of feeling generated in the town that in 1584 a Catholic family from 'Chappiltoune' was refused permission to bury Richard Lumbye in the parish churchyard. The family and the authorities finally reached a compromise after ten days: the body was allowed to be buried there, but only at night.

But if diverse religious views lurked beneath the surface they did not hamper the economic progress of Leeds. The town was fortunate. Not only was its wool textile industry flourishing, but it also had rich deposits of coal that would serve it well into the twentieth century. In 1715 Ralph Thoresby went so far as to say that 'Coal Mines are now without number' around the town.[11] Coal-mining in the area had been carried out as far back as Roman times and, by the Middle Ages, mines were being operated in The Calls, Kirkgate and Briggate, with coal also being excavated at Roundhay, Allerton, Whinmoor, Woodhouse, Knostrop, Seacroft, Belle Isle, Beeston and Middleton. Most of the pits were beehive or bell pits. These were dug vertically and then widened out, the secret being to know how long to dig before it caved in. Remains of these pits can still be seen in Middleton Woods, and it has been argued that the Belle Isle area of the city derives its name from such workings.

As for the manor itself, the greatest asset was the corn mill sited by the river Aire. Two huge dams, High Dam and Bondman Dam, controlled and diverted the waters. Even men who had commuted their agricultural labours could be forced to help repair the dams, as the mill was vital for the economic success of Leeds. The charter of 1207 had insisted that everyone in the town ground their wheat, oats, and barley at the manorial mill; this obligation was known as the soke. A miller paid the lord of the manor to operate the mill, and was naturally keen to see that the inhabitants fulfilled their obligation by employing his services. In 1483 John Kendall paid £18 3s 4d for the lease.

A medieval bell pit unearthed near Briggate. It had been used to mine iron ore.

Apart from the great mill by the Aire, Leeds boasted other important buildings. The manor house of the Rectory Manor of Kirkgate-cum-Holbeck was near the parish church and quite near the huge tithe barn, while the borough's manor house stood about where Boar Lane meets City Square today. The town's small hospital was sited midway up Kirkgate. At the top of that thoroughfare was the manorial court or Hall of Pleas, occupying the first floor of a building. Here relatively minor offences were dealt with, more serious cases being heard in the nation's higher courts. On the ground floor was the manorial oven. This was not a satisfactory arrangement: the magistrates regularly complained that 'the heate and smoke of the same ovens and furnaces there dayly ascendinge into the said Courthouse, is a very inconvenient, noysom and a great hinderance'. Even so it was another valuable source of income for the lord of the manor. The charter of 1207 reserved the right of the lord to insist that inhabitants of the town bake their bread there or pay for defaulting. One to opt out was Agnes Baxter, who in 1356–57 paid 2s for a special licence to have an oven 'in her house for baking bread during the term of her life'. Like the manorial mill, the manorial oven was leased, and consequently the baker was as keen as the miller to see that the public fulfilled their duty to use the facility. William Nettleton was doubly keen: during the fifteenth century he leased both the oven and the cornmill, and was also involved in the wool textile industry.

It was a dispute regarding the franchise for operating the King's Mills or Queen's Mills, as the mill by the Aire was sometimes known, that saw the first map of Leeds produced. By 1560 Thomas Falkingham had built a mill at Millgarth. Inevitably Thomas Lyndeley and his wife Elizabeth, who were paying for the franchise of the Queen's Mills, took exception to this, and a court case ensued. To determine the rights and wrongs of the issue the judge ordered a map to be drawn. This was the first cartographic representation of the town, and today the 14in by 21in map resides in the National Archives at Kew. For twenty years the case dragged on, until Falkingham was deemed to have broken the law and his mill was demolished.

If Falkingham's was a civil crime, Leeds had its fair share of criminal acts to contend with, from petty larceny to homicide. Probably the most infamous murder committed in the town during the Middle Ages was that of William de Wayte, which occurred in August 1318. It began as a friendly game between William and the son of the wealthiest man in Leeds, Robert of North Hall Manor. The two were gambling before going to church when tempers became frayed. Friends intervened, and it seemed that the men's differences were resolved. When the service ended, William, his servant and a friend, John de Manston, hung around in the churchyard. When Robert

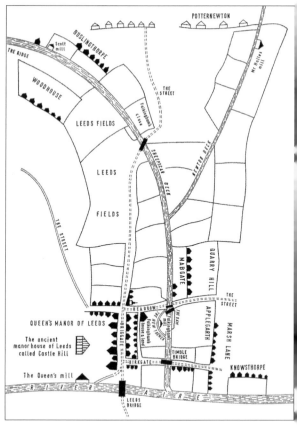

A drawing of the first map of Leeds. It was produced as a result of a dispute between the franchisee of Queen's Mill, bottom left, and the owner of Mr Bailes' Mill, top right.

came out of the building William and his servant were hidden from view, but John began to taunt Robert. The next moment William and his page boy appeared, with drawn swords. Robert turned to retreat into the church but his way was barred. In the mêlée that followed William was fatally wounded, then John de Manston, along with William's servant and two others, Thomas Nesant and the chaplain, manhandled Robert, brutally beating him before dumping him in a ditch, thinking him dead.

Robert's brothers found him, took him to a nearby house and there he eventually recovered. The law had to take its course, so he was accused of murder. The local manorial court was unable to deal with capital crimes, so Robert was arrested and taken to the Marshalsea Prison in Southwark to stand trial. However, sufficient witnesses came forward to testify that Robert had acted in self-defence, and he was released.[12]

CASTLE OR MANOR HOUSE?

One of the eternal questions over which historians have long argued is whether Leeds had a castle. There is no archaeological evidence, but some historians in the past have always insisted that one existed. Ralph Thoresby even recorded that King Stephen had besieged it in 1139 and that Richard II was held as a prisoner there. T.D. Whitaker places its building in the reign of King John, and Edward Parsons claims it was built earlier, 'soon after the Conquest'. John Mayhall is very specific, claiming 1081 as the year. D.H. Atkinson gives no date, but quotes 'a document of the time of Edward III, which speaks of a 'Fulling Mill near the Castle'.

It is fact that in 1828 at the junction of Park Row and Boar Lane, and again in 1836 on land where the Scarborough Hotel now stands, remains of a moat were unearthed by workmen. Disputes about a castle's existence rumbled on in the Leeds press, in particular during the 1880s and 1890s. The c.1560 map of the town identified 'the ancient manor house of Leeds called Castle Hill', and most historians today agree that in all probability a fortified manor house existed on the site. By 1341 the building was a ruin, with only the moat and a few farm buildings visible, but by 1560 it seems the house was once again being used as a residence. In 1765 a larger house was constructed on the site, and this later became the Scarborough Hotel.

Without doubt other manor houses existed in the area. Near the parish church was the manor house of the Rectory Manor of Kirkgate-cum-Holbeck, while the manor house at Cat-Beeston is still standing – a Grade II listed building.

Was there a castle anywhere in the Leeds area? There are claims that one existed at Armley: Thoresby refers to a 'Danish fortification' built on Giant's Hill overlooking the river Aire, and later suggestions have been made that a motte-and-bailey or ringwork-and-bailey castle had been built there. Again, though, all archaeological evidence has long since disappeared, but the area is still called Castleton. There is, of course, a castle-like structure still in Leeds today, but it is Armley Jail – built in 1847!

Remains of the moat of the old fortified medieval manor house was discovered by workmen digging near the Scarborough Hotel in 1836.

One crime in particular threatened the very economic existence of the Leeds area. By the end of the sixteenth century the wool textile trade had developed to the point where John Leland had observed that 'The Toun stondith most by Clothing'. In the last half of the century production had increased enormously, and the town's economic success depended on the pre-eminent place its cloth had achieved in textile markets. This was a success determined by the acknowledged quality of the material that the local industry produced. Consequently merchants and manufacturers grew more and more concerned when nefarious local manufacturers began to produce inferior cloth and claimed it to be the genuine article. By 1590 some producers in the West Riding were stretching pieces of cloth to excessive lengths, thus making it less substantial, or selling Northern Dozens up to 2yds shorter than the law decreed. The authorities acted, and a law was passed in 1597 for 'checking the deceiptfull stretching and taintering of Northerne Cloths'.[13] A further problem developed when some clothiers in the area began making spurious Northern Dozens and dyeing the cloth with logwood.

Meantime, a shadow was cast over the so-called 'golden age' of Elizabeth I's reign by the threat of a Spanish invasion, and the possible reimposition of the Roman Catholic faith should the military assault prove successful. The inhabitants of Leeds were fully aware of the situation. Despite the defeat of the Armada in 1588, further invasion threats still hung heavily over the nation during the 1590s. It was then that Queen Elizabeth demanded a ship money payment from the town: Leeds, in co-operation with Kingston-upon-Hull, Halifax and Wakefield, had to provide money for a ship to be equipped in order to repel any invasion attempt. However, the intended invasion never took place.

When the childless Virgin Queen died and James VI of Scotland occupied the throne of England as James I, a new century had just begun. It was one of the most turbulent centuries the people of Leeds would ever experience as bubonic plague carried off hundreds in the locality, civil war devastated the neighbourhood, warring Parliamentarians and Royalists battled in its streets, and religious differences in the town reached new levels of bitterness.

four

TURBULENCE AND TERROR
1600–1645

O n Saturday 7 May 1603 James VI of Scotland arrived in London to become the monarch who would unite the kingdoms of Scotland and England. He was an astute, perceptive man, observing: 'Although outward peace be a great blessing, yet is it far inferior to peace within, as civil wars are more cruel and unnatural than wars abroad.' Forty years later the people of Leeds and the rest of the nation would find out just how cruel and unnatural civil war was. But this was not the only problem Leeds people would face.

The new reign had hardly commenced when in 1604 bubonic plague struck. It was no stranger to Leeds, having infected the town in 1573, 1575 and 1587; now it struck again with virulence. Lodges were set up on Woodhouse Moor for infected people, and the markets were moved to the moors at Hunslet on Mondays and Chapeltown on Fridays. Special 'tickets or notes' were issued to those wishing to carry wool and cloth in the district, though some refused to comply. Such was William Lawson, who 'having carried himself in a most dissolute and contemptuous manner … [was] imprisoned within the prison of Leeds … and kept fast locked there for three days … [and then] upon his good carriage of time [released]'.

If natural phenomena produced difficulties at various times, religion was a constant source of acrimonious dispute. Bitter religious differences rumbled on from the previous century. While Roman Catholics were viciously condemned, the Church of England itself was bitterly divided between those with leanings towards the High Church and those with Puritan sympathies. Rival factions in Leeds adopted hard-line positions, and the situation was exacerbated when Robert Cooke, the vicar, died in 1615. A considerable number of inhabitants saw in his brother, Alexander, an ideal replacement. Alexander offered what many in the town desired: he was a strict and passionate Puritan ever proclaiming the grace of God and the doctrine of predestination, and he was always a most severe critic of papists. However, a problem emerged over his appointment. Although the advowson of the church had been purchased by a group of Leeds parishioners in 1588, the purchasers had failed to establish a formal trust. A rancorous dispute followed, dragging through the courts until 1617 – when the issue was finally settled in Alexander Cooke's favour.[1] A further group of parishioners, however, were equally furious at the decision to appoint Cooke. They felt threatened by the new incumbent's Calvinistic beliefs and petitioned the queen to replace him with 'some learned and godly divine', as Cooke 'came not in by their consent'.

But Cooke remained in office, and embarked on a zealous pursuit of his puritanical beliefs. He relentlessly attacked those few Catholics still in the town, even though they posed little threat – numbering as they did no more than thirty. He

Pope Joane. A Dialogue Betweene a Protestant and a Papist. One of the diatribes Alexander Cooke published attacking the Catholic Church.

also turned his attention to the church building itself. Anything that evoked memories of Roman Catholicism was removed; the multi-coloured frescoes on the walls were whitewashed over, elaborate religious tapestries were removed and the stained glass windows were dismantled. From the pulpit he launched blistering attacks on Sabbath breakers, 'irreligious atheists, whoremasters, drunkards, epicures, infidels and abbey-lubbers'. Age-old beliefs were cast aside as irrelevant and erroneous. There were those in the town, many of them people of importance, who welcomed Cooke's measures, and endorsed his fervent preaching and undoubted godliness. To others, however, he was no more than a man of 'giddy, brainless, distempered disposition'. So strong was the opposition to him from one faction that Cooke took to walking about his parish carrying a brace of loaded pistols.

But if Leeds was divided by theological differences it was united in its economic expansion. The boom in wool textile manufacture that had blossomed through the closing years of the sixteenth century continued. It was, however, but one town reliant on the wool trade. Leeds, like Halifax, specialised in broad cloths, as did Reading and several Wiltshire towns; Bradford was devoted to rugs and cushions; Witney to blankets; Colchester to coarse cloths. By now

Norwich, which had been the principal wool centre in England, had been displaced by Gloucester.[2]

Beginning in the fourteenth century, certain ports had been designated staple towns to control the export of raw wool, in order to regulate England's most important industry. In 1617 James I introduced twenty-three staple towns in England.[3] To the chagrin of Leeds merchants, Wakefield was one of them. Inevitably the Leeds group protested, and within a year their town had joined the select band. In reality it was a short-lived benefit because of changes in the law.

But Leeds was growing. Its population stood at about 6,000, and a 1612 survey gives a good idea of the extent of the manor. It was a royal manor and consequently King James granted it to his wife, Queen Anne of Denmark. That year Thomas Potts, Deputy Surveyor General, arrived in Leeds to carry out a survey for her of the royal estate. This survey is invaluable, as it graphically describes the extent of the manor in the early years of the seventeenth century.

Without doubt, the most impressive building was the parish church, St Peter's, but between 1615 and 1618 a new building was erected which, if it did not rival the church, was nevertheless most impressive. The Moot Hall dominated the main street, Briggate, which was by now a wide and stone-paved thoroughfare. For years the West Riding magistrates visiting the town had complained that the Hall of Common Pleas in Kirkgate was totally inadequate. In the new hall the magistrates met on the upper floor, while shops were built on the ground floor; the rents from these were used to ease the burdens of the poor. The building itself divided the street into two narrow alleyways, the butchers' shambles on the east and the back shambles on the west side. Above this the street widened out again, and there the market cross was placed.

In its early years the Moot Hall became the source of a criminal dispute that scandalised the town. It involved no less a personage than John Metcalfe, the local

The only three-decker house left in Leeds. Erected c.1600 as a 'little mansion' it was owned for many years by the Lambert family until 1919. The Lamberts were grocers and tea dealers.

bailiff. He administered the new Moot Hall and also the toll dish, a toll imposed on the sale of corn at the local markets. A third of the moneys collected from this went to the poor, a third to repairing the roads and a third was his perquisite. When Metcalfe was accused of misappropriating Moot Hall shop rents and embezzling the toll dish funds,[4] a Royal Commission was set up under Sir John Savile, Yorkshire's MP, and the vicar, Alexander Cooke. Its report appeared in 1620, ordering Metcalfe to repay the money he had stolen. Perhaps more significantly, a new administrative body, known as the Committee of Pious Uses, was established. Its remit was to administer the running of the Moot Hall and to oversee the use of charitable funds in the town. Its first report, *The First Decree for a Committee of Pious-Uses in Leedes*, was published on 5 July 1620.

During this rancorous dispute there was a personality clash between Metcalfe and Cooke. The puritanical vicar accused Metcalfe of what he saw as the cardinal sin of failing to attend church; Metcalfe rejoined that his professional duties prevented him from doing so. The spat continued, and eventually Metcalfe filed a suit for slander and libel in the Court of Star Chamber against the 'perverse, factious sectary and Puritan' Cooke, claiming that the vicar had maligned him both at prayer meetings and from the pulpit. Not only had the churchman accused him of both corruption and immorality, but he had also dramatically brandished a halberd and cried out, 'I wish I had ... Metcalfe here!'

The establishment of the Committee of Pious Uses clearly indicated the need for more centrally organised government of the developing town. Compounding this need was the threat from racketeering manufacturers who, as mentioned above, were producing spurious cloths and selling them as bona fide Leeds Northern Dozens, an act detrimental to local producers. It was felt by the principal manufacturers that a properly constituted corporation would not only be able to counteract such behaviour but would also supervise the growth of the burgeoning town. Not everyone agreed with the move: smaller manufacturers felt that it would place even more power in the hands of those who already dominated the town.

However, the new king, Charles I, ignored their pleas and on 13 July 1626 Leeds received its charter. This enabled the new council to regulate local clothiers and govern not only the town but the out-townships of the entire parish of Leeds. The leader of the new council was to be appointed 'alderman', and the man chosen was Sir John Savile, the MP. As a tribute to him, the owls featured on his coat of arms were incorporated into the new town's insignia. In reality his duties were carried out by John Harrison, one of the newly appointed principal

burgesses. The preamble to the bill explains exactly why it was necessary, and then gives the details of the charter:

> Divers clothiers of the ... town and parish had begun to make ... deceptive cloths, and to dye the same with wood called logwood, to the damage and prejudice ... of the clothiers of the town ...[T]hey most humbly have besought us ... to extend our royal favour and munificence to ... create, for the ... better rule and government and improvement of the town and parish .. a body corporate ...AND ... all houses, buildings, lands, waters, watercourses, soil and ground ... within the town and parish of Leedes ... shall be called and known by the name of the BOROUGH OF LEEDES IN THE COUNTY OF YORK ... and shall be at all times ... able ... to have, purchase, receive and possess lands, tenements ... and also goods and chattels ... and shall be able to ...defend and be defended ... before ... judges and justices ... [O]ne of the more honest and discreet ... inhabitants of the borough ... shall be named the alderman of the borough ... Nine of the more honest and discreet ... inhabitants ... to be elected ... and shall be called the principal burgesses ... [T]wenty other of the more honest and discreet men ... shall be called assistants ... [T]he alderman and common council ... shall be enabled to impose ... penalties and punishments ... [and] fines ... [T]hey shall ... have full power and authority yearly, and every year, on the day of the feast of St Michael the Archangel ... themselves ... be assembled in the common hall ... and there to continue until they ... have nominated and elected one of the principal burgesses ... to be alderman ... AND if ... one or more of the nine ... principal burgesses ... die, or be removed ... it shall ... be lawful for the ... alderman and others of the common council ... to elect, nominate and make one other or others of the assistants ... into the place or places of him or those ... [A] discreet man, and learned in the laws of England ... shall be named, the recorder of the borough ...
>
> [The] alderman, recorder and the principal burgesses ... [shall hold] the office of justice of the peace ... AND FURTHER we will ... grant to the ... alderman and burgesses ... two officers, who shall be ... sergeants-at-mace ... [who] shall ... carry gilt or silver maces ... [T]he alderman and principal burgesses ... from year to year may elect ... one coroner, and also one clerk of the market ... [and] shall have within the borough ... one prison or gaol, for the custody of ... prisoners ... [And] ...shall have the inspection ... of the assize of bread, wine, ale and of all kinds of victuals sold ... within the borough ... WHEREAS in the town of Leedes ...there hath been held and kept one market ... on every monday [sic] in each week ...the inhabitants ... [have] found it better to be holden on a tuesday [sic] ... [T]he borough of Leedes

... shall ... hold ... one, market in every week ... forever on tuesday [*sic*] ... AND FURTHER ... the inhabitants of the borough ... especially the workers and labourers ... shall have reasonable guilds ... WITNESS ourself at Westminster, the thirteenth of July, in the second year of our reign.

The fleece represents the wool trade. The owls are a tribute to Sir John Savile, the first alderman appointed in 1626. The three star-shaped mullets are from the arms of Thomas Danby, the first mayor, appointed in 1661.

Positive as the charter may have been in enabling the town to face the growing problems of the seventeenth century, it also contained the seeds of future discord. It failed to allow the town to elect a Member of Parliament and its arrangements for replacing principal or assistant burgesses would generate endless and resentful dissension through the years. If anyone had to be replaced, the council itself elected the replacement. In the decades to come this would mean that it would eventually be dominated by Tory and Anglican sympathisers, to the mortification of Whigs and Nonconformists.

Charles, acceding to the throne in 1625, had other and more pressing concerns than the effectiveness of a charter for a provincial northern town, finding himself beset with serious financial worries. Compounding this was his ardent belief in the divine right of kings.[5] This set him on a collision course with Parliament, and eventually would see the nation plunged into that very 'cruel and unnatural civil war' his late father had so feared. To ease the pressing financial difficulties and to do so without recourse to Parliament, he turned to, among others, Sir Arthur Ingram, a shrewd and calculating politician with an unrivalled expertise in economics, an unscrupulous financial manipulator and secretary to the Council of the North. Ingram had accumulated vast wealth, which had enabled him to buy several Yorkshire estates.

One of these was Temple Newsam, which he acquired from the Duke of Lennox for £12,000 in 1622. He demolished much of the old house and had a new one erected. In Leeds he became an influential powerbroker, owning the manor of Leeds-Kirkgate-cum-Holbeck and controlling the markets, fairs and the lease of the common oven in the town.

Despite Ingrams's efforts and those of his other advisers Charles's debts continued to rise. In 1628, in order to placate the Corporation of the City of London, one of his major creditors, he granted it several royal manors, one of which was Leeds. Consequently a survey of the town was carried out, leaving for posterity a vivid description of what it was like at the time. Remarking on the 'verie faire church built after a Cathedrall structure', the survey described Briggate as well developed with buildings on either side. Behind these buildings were crammed other dwellings and workshops, many of them 'ancient meane and lowe built; and generallie all of Tymber'. The wealthier inhabitants' homes may have boasted 'large and capacious' frontages, but many of the smaller buildings were 'low and straightened on their backsides'.

Within a year Richard Sykes, a Briggate merchant and one of the biggest property owners in Leeds, led a group, including William Marshall (an influential member of the Committee of Pious Uses and a trustee of the Grammar School), that great Leeds benefactor John Harrison and six other prominent men, that bought the manor from its London owners for £2,710 8*s* 10*d*. Leeds was set to take its destiny into its own hands. Some time later it purchased the control of the markets, fairs and common oven from Sir Arthur Ingram for £700. New buildings arose, including Red Hall, the finest and most impressive house in the town, near the Headrow. Built in 1628 for Thomas Metcalfe, one of the West Riding's most successful merchants, it was said to be the first red-brick house in the town centre.

New public buildings were also raised to answer the needs of the growing town. Between 1636 and 1637 a workhouse was opened on Lady Lane,

Temple Newsam. The Hampton Court of the North. The original house, built between 1488 and 1521, was replaced by Sir Arthur Ingram's new building when he bought the estate in 1622. The house was acquired by the council in 1922 for £35,000.

Said to be the first redbrick house in Leeds, Red Hall was built for Thomas Metcalf in 1628. King Charles I was famously held here in 1647. Its two gardens covered what is now Albion Place and King Charles Croft. The building was demolished in 1967.

described as 'a House of Correction for the Reliefe and setting on Worke the Poor of the said Parish of Leedes'. The belief that poverty was self-induced and could be alleviated by 'correction' and forced labour failed to solve the problems that poverty generated.

Charles's persistent refusal to summon Parliament after 1629 meant he had to seek alternative ways to raise taxes, and in 1634 he revived the unpopular ship money tax. In November 1638 Leeds found itself facing the demand, and no doubt many in the town objected to paying. Relations between Parliament and the king deteriorated to the point that on 22 August 1642 King Charles's standard was defiantly raised at Nottingham. The Civil War had begun. On 19 September a meeting of Parliamentarian supporters was called in Leeds, and they proclaimed Lord Ferdinando Fairfax commander-in-chief of the Parliamentary forces in Yorkshire. Civil war was no comfort to either side: it was clear to everyone that it would dislocate trade, sever life-long friendships and divide families. Thus by the end of September the possibility of peace in the West Riding arose, and a truce was agreed. A group of supporters from both camps met just outside Leeds and signed the Treaty of Rothwell, which stated that all military forces would be disbanded and no more raised. Troops from outside the county would be refused admittance and a 'general amity' would be held.[6] It was not to last. Parliament disapproved, and Leeds and the West Riding were plunged into a conflict that would tear the heart out of the nation and scar it for a generation or more. Generally the North supported the king, but the manufacturing towns of the West Riding, Leeds included, favoured Parliament, and raised loans to support Fairfax's army. The issues that divided the sides were complex, with people in the town torn different ways. Trade was seriously affected, and within a few months Sir Tomas Fairfax, the local Parliamentary commander, wrote to Lord Fairfax, his father, that in Leeds and Wakefield 'All trade and provisions are stopped, so that people in these Clothing towns are not able to subsist.' Many in the town who had known each other and worked together for years found themselves on opposing sides, but some did not let political differences interfere with their friendships. For example, Richard Milner, a supporter of Parliament and a Briggate cloth merchant, remained friendly with John Harrison despite their differing views. Some held apparently contradictory views: despite the Puritans vigorously advocating Parliament's case, the Puritan Vicar of Leeds, Henry Robinson, was a passionate supporter of the king.[7]

It was a time of apprehension for the townspeople of Leeds. They knew that occupation of the town by either side could result in the destruction of property, exorbitant requisitions for supplies and intemperate behaviour by the troops garrisoned there. Added to these concerns were the current shortages of food and the general dislocation of trade. Their fears were justified. First Royalist troops entered the town and then, in October 1642, Sir Thomas Fairfax and a small force dislodged the king's troops and began to recruit and raise funds. In December the small Parliamentarian force withdrew from Leeds as a larger Royalist army advanced on the town. The council, rather than see Leeds wasted in a bloody and destructive encounter, surrendered, and Sir William Savile took control.

Bradford, however, proved a more testing challenge, and Savile, after an abortive attack on the town, withdrew to Leeds and waited to see what his opponent, Sir Thomas Fairfax, would do. 'Black Tom' bided his time, and set about strengthening his force. By the end of January 1643 he was ready. Recruiting in Halifax and Bradford, he had built an army of between 1,200 and 1,300 foot soldiers, 600 musketeers, six troops of horse, three companies of dragoons and 1,000 clubmen. These men were vigilantes who were desperate to protect their families and property from the belligerents of both sides, but were armed only with pitchforks, scythes, sickles and clubs. In Leeds, Bradford and Halifax these ill-equipped volunteers tended to be anti-Royalist, and in the forthcoming battle they made a valuable contribution to the Parliamentarian cause.[8]

Savile anticipated Fairfax's next move, and set to work fortifying Leeds. From Harrison's St John's church at the top of Briggate as far as the river a

2yds-wide trench was dug and a 6ft-high palisade erected. A second trench between Swinegate and the river was dug across the tenterground. Two demi-culverins, brass cannons with an effective range of 1,800ft, were placed in Briggate, one strategically covering the bridge. At Kirkstall the bridge there had been destroyed in an attempt to delay the Parliamentarian army's advance. Savile had at his disposal somewhere between 1,500 and 2,000 men for the defence.[9] Legend has it that on the evening of Sunday 22 January 1643 a small Parliamentary patrol fell upon a party of Royalists camped in the Meanwood area. There was a clash of arms before the Royalists took flight up what is now Stainbeck Lane. Thus ended the so-called Battle of Meanwood or the Battle of Stainbeck. There is little documentary evidence of the event, but musket balls found in Batty Wood could indicate that such a confrontation took place. Of the events the next day there is no doubt, as Sir Thomas Fairfax himself left behind a graphic account of what followed in his memoirs.[10]

On Monday 23 January 1643,[11] as a swirling snowstorm swept across the Aire valley, Fairfax divided his force. Captain Mildmay, commanding about thirty musketeers and 1,000 clubmen, was ordered to move south of the river to Hunslet Moor from where he could launch an attack on Leeds bridge. Fairfax, with the bulk of the force, crossed the swollen waters of the river at Apperley Bridge and then moved south to regroup on Woodhouse Moor. Well aware of the deep religious convictions of many of his men, Fairfax chose 'Emmanuel' as the watchword of the day.[12] As the troops waited on the moor he commended their cause to God, then twice dispatched trumpeters to the town to try to persuade Savile to surrender, thus avoiding bloodshed. The Royalist commander refused. At about one o'clock Fairfax gave the order to advance. With thirty-six banners flying, the army moved forward, lustily singing the sixty-eighth psalm: 'Let God arise, let his enemies be scattered.' In the lead, exhorting them onwards, was Jonathan Scholefield, the minister of Croston chapel, Halifax.

Within two hours it was all over. Fairfax was triumphant. Sir William Savile and Henry Robinson, the vicar, fled by fording the swollen river. In all a dozen Parliamentarians perished in the fight and about thirty Royalist troops. The parish church register of burials recorded 'Eleven soldiers slayne, buried 24 January ... ten unpaid for.' About 500 prisoners were taken. The town was spared any serious damage – and local legend suggests the reason for this was that the Pack Horse Inn in Briggate gave free entertainment for a month to the victorious Parliamentarians!

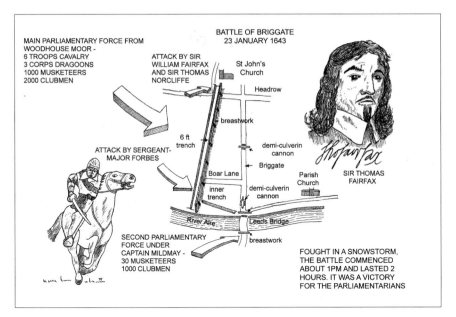

BATTLE OF BRIGGATE
23 JANUARY 1643

MAIN PARLIAMENTARY FORCE FROM
WOODHOUSE MOOR -
6 TROOPS CAVALRY
3 CORPS DRAGOONS
1000 MUSKETEERS
2000 CLUBMEN

ATTACK BY SIR
WILLIAM FAIRFAX
AND SIR THOMAS
NORCLIFFE

St John's
Church

Headrow

breastwork

ATTACK BY SERGEANT-
MAJOR FORBES

6 ft
trench

demi-culverin
cannon

Briggate

Boar Lane

inner
trench

demi-culverin
cannon

Parish
Church

SIR THOMAS
FAIRFAX

River Aire

Leeds Bridge

SECOND PARLIAMENTARY
FORCE UNDER
CAPTAIN MILDMAY -
30 MUSKETEERS
1000 CLUBMEN

breastwork

FOUGHT IN A SNOWSTORM,
THE BATTLE COMMENCED
ABOUT 1PM AND LASTED 2
HOURS. IT WAS A VICTORY
FOR THE PARLIAMENTARIANS

Fairfax offered terms before the battle but the Royalist commander, Sir William Savile, refused. About forty died in the engagement. Savile and the Vicar of Leeds escaped by fording the swollen waters of the river Aire.

In March Lord Ferdinando Fairfax, the commander of Parliament's forces in Yorkshire, decided to consolidate his position in the West Riding and moved his army from Selby to Leeds. To cover this, Sir Thomas Fairfax was ordered to make a feint towards Tadcaster then turn in the direction of Leeds. It was Thursday 30 March 1643 when Sir Thomas decided to move his infantry forward, using his cavalry as the rearguard. Just over 4 miles east of Leeds General George Goring and his Royalists caught up with Fairfax, and thus followed the Battle of Seacroft Moor. Outnumbered, Fairfax's infantry fled. In the region of 200 Parliamentarians were killed; 800 were captured. 'Black Tom' Fairfax claimed that 'This was one of the greatest Losses we ever received'.[13] It was his worst ever military defeat.

In April Queen Henrietta landed at Bridlington with a supply of arms for the king and made her way to the West Riding. Arriving at Leeds she embarked on a siege of the town, probably establishing her main base on what is today Cavalier Hill, approximately the Richmond Hill area. However, the bombardment of the widespread town was ineffective, and the Royalists finally withdrew to Wakefield. Skirmishing around Leeds continued in the following months, with several fatalities recorded. Then on 30 June the two armies met again, this time just outside Leeds on Adwalton Moor at Drighlington. The Earl of

One man who showed compassion to the poor was John Harrison. Born the son of the Leeds merchant, John Harrison, who lived at Pawdmyre, the district at the top of Briggate, he attended Leeds Grammar School, receiving a good classical education. When his father died he took over both the family business and the family home. In 1611 he became the town's under-bailiff and was active in the civic affairs of Leeds.

Harrison was prominent in the campaign to acquire a charter for Leeds, and when this was granted in 1626 he was appointed a principal burgess. He took on the duties of Sir John Savile, the alderman, before being appointed to the position himself. In 1629 he was one of the nine townsmen who purchased the manor of Leeds from the Corporation of the City of London.

A successful businessman, despite some financial misadventures, Harrison was able to build himself an impressive house opposite the east end of Boar Lane where, according to the historian Thoresby, he had cat flaps cut in the wainscot to accommodate his pets. His wealth also enabled him to provide the town with a market cross above the Moot Hall in Briggate in 1619, Harrison's Hospital in 1653 – a group of twenty almshouses for forty poor women, who each received a pension of £80 a year – and two great public buildings. The first of these, in 1624, was a new home for the Grammar School on a thoroughfare he had recently created at the top of Briggate; it was known as New Street or New-kirke-gate, later New Briggate.[14] The school was near the present Grand Theatre, on what today is appropriately called Harrison Street. Seven years later Harrison bestowed on Leeds one of its architectural gems. It is no exaggeration to say that it is one of the country's finest examples of seventeenth-century ecclesiastical architecture,

John Harrison (1579–1656), one of the great benefactors of Leeds, giving the town almshouses, a new grammar school and St John's church.

the church of St John the Evangelist at the top of Briggate, today the oldest church in the city centre.[15] By the 1630s the growing population of Leeds was desperately in need of a second church. It can be seen as a compromise building, emphasising as it does the differing traditions that divided the Anglican community. Its chancel catered for those who supported the Laudian, High Church traditions, while the prominent pulpit stressed the role that preaching the word of God and Holy Scripture played in traditional Protestant worship.

The Archbishop of York, Richard Neile, had grave misgivings about this project. He thought it was too near St Peter's church and also feared that a Puritan incumbent at St John's

Leeds Grammar School. Founded in 1552, it moved to this new building at the top of Briggate in 1624. It was the gift of John Harrison, one of its old boys.

might be appointed to support Henry Robinson, the new Puritan Vicar of Leeds. The new church was still part of the parish of Leeds, so it came under Robinson's jurisdiction. Neile was right to be apprehensive: to his annoyance Harrison opted to appoint the Puritan Robert Todd, Vicar of Ledsham and a lecturer at the parish church, to the post. A deeply religious man, he no doubt knew of Todd's leanings. In reality Todd was a moderate Puritan, a good academic and a passionate preacher, and when bubonic plague later struck the town he showed himself to be a man of considerable courage, remaining at his post to tend his sickening flock when many would have fled.

The building was consecrated on 21 September 1634. What followed is a fascinating example of just how divided the Anglican Church was at that time – assuming the tale is true. There are no ecclesiastical records to confirm it, but it has long been an accepted part of Leeds folklore. The archbishop's chaplain, Archdeacon John Cosin, preached the inaugural sermon at St John's and, as expected, advocated the sentiments of High Church Anglicanism. That afternoon Todd took to the pulpit and launched a puritanical tirade refuting virtually everything Cosin had asserted. An infuriated Neile immediately suspended the new curate, and only after the intercession of Harrison and Sir Arthur Ingram was Todd eventually restored to his post.

Harrison's final years were unhappy. Widowed and bedridden, this tragic, dejected figure found one of his greatest gifts to the town become a source of great anguish and distress. Although he had appointed the Puritan Robert Todd,

Above, left St John's church at the top of Briggate seen in 1816. John Harrison's magnificent building was opened in 1634.

Above, right John Harrison presented the market cross to the town in 1619. It is seen here, appropriately enough, in a stained glass window in Harrison's St John's church.

Harrison was at heart a true Anglican. When Todd goaded his Presbyterian faction into savagely attacking Harrison's commitment to the Church of England, such was the bitterness engendered that when Harrison died in 1656 his funeral service, on 8 November, was not at St John's, the church he had bestowed on the town, but at the parish church. He was buried in his own orchard. Only later were his remains moved to St John's.

Unquestionably John Harrison was one of the town's greatest benefactors, and appropriately his statue now graces City Square.

Newcastle and his stronger Royalist army not only won the day but Fairfax was compelled to withdraw from the West Riding.

The Royalist prisoners in Leeds now broke out of prison, seized arms and ammunition and took over control of the town. Shortly afterwards Newcastle garrisoned the place with a small Royalist detachment. However, on Thursday 7 April 1644 Sir Thomas Fairfax retook Leeds for Parliament. He met no resistance. In July, at the Battle of Marston Moor, Parliament was established once and for all as the dominant force in the county. Major-General Carter was appointed military governor of Leeds and the town remained Parliamentarian thereafter.

Carter soon had to face a far greater challenge than any posed on a battlefield. In August 1644 rumours began to be heard around the town that bubonic plague had returned. On 11 March 1645 Alice Musgrave of Vicar Lane was

buried, and there was no doubt bubonic plague was the cause of her death. Vicar Lane was the worst affected area, but the infection spread rapidly through The Calls, Lower Briggate, Marsh Lane and Mill Hill, ravaging the over-crowded, insanitary areas of the poor before quickly striking in the more open areas of the town and the outlying townships. In July alone over 300 perished. Markets were moved to Woodhouse Moor, Hunslet Moor and Chapeltown Green, while potential cases were accommodated in special cabins erected on Quarry Hill. The overall effect of the outbreak was devastating. Trade came virtually to a halt, grass, it is said, grew in the streets and Ralph Thoresby later wrote that the disease 'so infected the Air, that the Birds fell down dead in their Flight over the Town'.[16] With Henry Robinson, the Royalist vicar, still absent, the parish church was closed, but Robert Todd at St John's remained at his post, preaching on 'Hezekiah's boil': 'Thus saith the Lord, the God of David thy father, I have heard thy prayer, I have seen thy tears: behold, I will heal thee.'

Between March 1645 and the end of December that year almost a fifth of the local population succumbed to the epidemic, a total of 1,325 people. In an attempt to restore some degree of stability houses were fumigated, valuable property was washed and aired, the rest burnt.[17] Even if the crisis was over for the moment, the men and women of Leeds still had to witness a maelstrom of conflict and its aftermath as the 'cruel and unnatural' civil war continued to sweep the land.

five

INTERREGNUM AND RESTORATION

s 1646 dawned it must have seemed to the inhabitants of Leeds that at least three of the Four Horsemen of the Apocalypse had swept through the town. In the past few years War, Conquest and Death had stalked its streets. A fifth of the town's population had perished in the plague, and the pestilence was indiscriminate with regard to its victims, rich and poor suffering alike. Thomas Metcalfe, one of the town's foremost citizens, saw his young wife die; Joseph Hillary, a principal burgess and a pre-eminent merchant, lost both his son and his daughter. Fatalities among Leeds craftsmen and tradesmen not only depleted the workforce but would have destabilised the local economy. It may well have been that in an attempt to bring greater economic stability to the town Major-General Carter, the military governor, decided that year to reinstate the corporation. But it was to be a new corporation and one with a difference.

By now several of the old council had died; other members with Royalist sympathies were discarded. A new council with decided Parliamentarian leanings was appointed.[1] Its members were wealthy, membership being as exclusive as the one it replaced. The new burgesses included Francis Allanson, a Kirkgate clothworker and merchant who in a year or so would unsuccessfully stand in the town's first Parliamentary election; John Dawson, a Mill Hill merchant who would be appointed the first alderman of the new corporation; Martin Iles, a gentleman from Bramley; and John Thoresby, a Kirkgate merchant and grandfather of the historian Ralph.

In June and July 1645 the king's forces had been humiliated by Sir Thomas Fairfax and the New Model Army at Naseby and Langport. Royalist desertions saw the king's army begin to disintegrate. Charles made one last, desperate gamble. If he could exploit the differences that existed between the Presbyterian Scots' army and Parliament it could only be to his advantage. On 5 May 1646 Charles surrendered to the Scots and began negotiations.

Leeds *c.* 1680. William Lodge's engraving shows cloth merchants from Hunslet transporting textiles to the market on Leeds Bridge. Note St John's church on the left and the parish church centre.

It was not to be. At Newcastle on 28 January 1647 the Scots Commissioners took their leave of him. As the Scottish army moved out Major-General Philip Skippon's Parliamentarians moved in. Charles was now a prisoner of Parliament's Commissioners.

On 3 February they began their journey south, and a few days later reached Leeds. They commandeered Red Hall, Thomas Metcalfe's magnificent and newly built house by the Headrow. Gardens rolled away on two of its sides, and its interior with its figured plaster ceilings reflected the wealth and social position of its owner. It was an appropriate place to hold a royal prisoner. There were, no doubt, inquisitive souls standing around the Headrow who would have watched the mounted party arrive. Amongst them Royalist sympathisers saddened by the prospect of seeing their king a captive, and Parliamentarian devotees delighted that the man who had plunged the country into chaos had finally been apprehended. But if political differences divided them, an age-old superstition still united many across the social and political spectrum. Since the days of Edward the Confessor it had been understood that simply by touching the king's person anyone suffering from scrofula,[2] the 'king's evil' as it was called, could be cured. The commissioners were desperate to play down any suggestion of divine attributes to the monarch, and consequently issued a stark warning to the townspeople: 'All persons whatsoever, which are diseased, not to presume hereafter to repair unto the court ... upon pain of being punished severely for their intrusion – Dated at Leeds, 9 February.'

According to legend, however, one person in the town did 'repair unto the court': John Harrison, the town's greatest benefactor, asked permission to take a tankard of ale to the king. Leeds, after all, was famous for its good nut-brown beverage. He was admitted to Charles's presence but when the king opened the top of the tankard he found it full – not with good Leeds ale but with a mass of gold coins. These he quickly secreted about his person, and thanked Harrison for his kindness.[3] A young servant girl, a Mrs Crosby, even offered to help the king escape, but to no avail.

Charles was eventually taken to London, charged 'as a Tyrant, Traitor and Murderer', tried in Westminster Hall and executed on 30 January 1649. He was not the only Royalist to suffer. In Leeds, as elsewhere, those who had supported their monarch were known as 'delinquents' and found themselves persecuted by the appointed Parliamentarian sequestrators. The so-called delinquents paid a high price for their loyalty, the sequestrators taking possession of their assets and demanding payment for their restitution. John Harrison, in particular, was singled out and tormented by Martin Iles, Francis Allanson and William Marshall Snr. Although a somewhat faint-hearted Royalist, described by his enemies as 'a timorous man', Harrison was nevertheless fined £464 18s in 1654, not for his act of generosity to Charles but for supposedly supplying the Royalists with two horses when they occupied the town. He argued that he had acted under duress, but he was found guilty as 'an obstructor of the common good at Leedes … an enemy to godly ministers'.

Harrison was not alone. Robert Benson, a Briggate attorney, was heavily fined, saw his house vandalised and ended his days in Newgate Prison. Francis Jackson, a Wade Lane merchant, died in 1646 before any sequestration order could be issued on him but his son, Thomas, was not so fortunate. And there were others.

Some of the sequestrators in the town were corrupt. Iles was prepared to use his influence to soften the blow for anyone who was prepared to pay him. Others were more circumspect. William Marshall of Moor Allerton was careful to watch how the political wind was blowing, and when the time was right, in years to come, he supported the reviving Royalist cause. Marmaduke Hick, a Boar Lane salter and new council member, was shrewd enough in his behaviour to survive unscathed when the Royalists finally returned to power.[4] But in 1649 the monarchy was gone, the Commonwealth was firmly established and the period known as the Interregnum began.[5]

It was a time when a puritanical zeal swept the country. Drunkenness, swearing and gambling became illegal. The celebration of Christmas was condemned and 25 December became a fast day. Maypole dancing and festivals were outlawed. Any form of breaking the Sabbath, either by working or travelling,

was prohibited. Henery Cockill, a local farmer, was prosecuted at the Moot Hall in 1657 for travelling from Woodlsworth to Hunslet on a Sunday while John Batty was similarly prosecuted for 'doing worldly labour' on the 'Lord's day'; Ann Dobson was sentenced to the House of Correction at Wakefield for 'Fornication'; Thomas Wilcocke was fined for uttering 'one prophane curse in a feilde att Rothwell'.

Henry Robinson, the Royalist vicar, who had fled the town after Fairfax's victory in 1643, was replaced by Bramley-born Peter Saxton, newly returned from preaching in Massachusetts. Saxton, who had been educated at Cambridge, was a celebrated Hebrew scholar, but like many he deeply resented the neo-Catholic ceremonies of the Anglican Church and had left for America. On his return he was offered a valuable living in Kent but turned it down, preferring to return to Leeds in 1646 as the town's vicar. Saxton's bluff, coarse individualism allayed to his enthusiasm and sincerity appears to have been welcomed by his parishioners.

The community continued to be divided by political allegiance and religious sectarianism. It was a situation that existed not only in the townships of Leeds but also in the out-townships, where worshippers gathered in the local chapels at Headingley, Farnley, Chapel Allerton, Beeston, Armley and Bramley. The situation came to a head in 1651 when Peter Saxton died. Three candidates were in contention for the position of Vicar of Leeds: a Presbyterian, an Established Churchman sympathetic to the Royalist cause and William Styles, an Independent with more moderate Puritan views. Styles had been sacked from his living at Hessle and Hull for refusing to take the Engagement to the Commonwealth, the oath of loyalty to the new regime. Nevertheless it was he who was duly appointed to Leeds.

Times were hard. War with the Dutch and piracy both contributed to depressing trade, and the situation was compounded for the local wool textile industry by the continuing problem of faulty workmanship. Local merchants wanted further restrictions to be imposed on the clothiers to raise standards. Leeds clothiers, however, objected when clothiers in the rest of the West Riding were not so regulated, and they turned for help to Adam Baynes.

In 1653 Oliver Cromwell assumed the ancient title of Lord Protector, dissolved Parliament, and on 1 June 1654 he issued writs for a general election. It would be an election with a difference. Rotten and pocket boroughs were abolished and their seats were redistributed. Adam Baynes, from Knostrop, who had served as a captain in General Lambert's Parliamentary army, lobbied for Leeds to be awarded one of the redistributed seats. It was and Baynes, a dedicated republican and religious radical devoted to the Independents, was nominated to stand for the borough. His sympathies lay with the smaller clothiers. The larger merchants in the town were bitterly opposed to him, as they were to the smaller manufacturers. One of Baynes's supporters, John Walker, argued that Baynes 'is in a present capacity to doe us good'. The opposition nominated Francis Allanson as their candidate, claiming that Baynes was an 'atheist and schismatic' and that Allanson was of 'inconsiderable importance'.

Despite such allegations Baynes was victorious, but he had little chance to serve his constituents. The Protectorate's first Parliament was both argumentative and stubborn. Cromwell lost patience with it, and on 22 January 1655 dissolved it before it could pass a single act. In July 1656 a second election was announced and Baynes was duly elected, once again defeating Allanson. In December that year he was asked to present a petition to Cromwell of 700 signatures asking for a new charter that might remedy the grievances contained in the old one of 1626. The request was ultimately denied. Twelve months later the corporation itself made application for a new charter. That too failed. Then as the decade came to its end the influence of Baynes and other radicals began to wane. Cromwell died in 1658, and that same year the town lost its Parliamentary seat. The country had had enough of the Puritan Commonwealth. On Tuesday 29 May 1660 Charles II was received in London by enthusiastic crowds rejoicing that the monarchy had been re-established. It was Charles's thirtieth birthday.

But if there was universal rejoicing across the land, the new government faced considerable difficulties. As far as Leeds was concerned it needed to establish whether the members of the corporation created in 1646 held office legally, and to determine whether the old charter of 1626 was still valid. It was seventy-year-old Benjamin Wade, a merchant and dedicated Royalist, who came up with a solution. Well experienced in local government, he led a group of wealthy merchants, townsmen and country gentry to petition the king to remove the 'illiterate and ill-affected' republican individuals who had governed the town of late. The problem could be resolved, they argued, if a new charter providing for a mayor, aldermen and assistants were granted.[5] Inevitably the existing council members reacted, presenting a counter-petition and arguing that their opponents were trying to discredit them. They urged that the old 1626 charter should remain in force. The petitions were considered by the attorney-general, who took the view that council members had been illegally dismissed in 1646 and new councillors unlawfully appointed. The problem was that only one principal burgess and eight assistant burgesses of the old corporation were still alive. In the circumstances the attorney-general recommended a new charter of incorporation to be granted. On 2 November 1661 the king's seal was affixed to the document. The charter allowed for the leading townsman to be designated mayor and to be elected annually. Twelve aldermen and twenty-four assistants who made up the council were to be appointed for life – unless they were 'removed from their offices … for their evil behaviour or evil carriage'. A town clerk and recorder were also appointed for life. The council was allowed to regulate trade and to hold quarter sessions, conducted by the aldermen acting as magistrates.

The first mayor was Thomas Danby of Farnley.[6] The Danbys had held land in the area since the fifteenth century and Thomas was considered to be county gentry. His estates contained various collieries, but during the Civil War he had served as a captain in the Royalist Army. His coat of arms included three star-shaped silver mullets, and these were incorporated into the new Leeds coat of arms. He died in a tavern brawl in London in 1667.

The new council included Richard Armitage, a town merchant whose home on the Upper Headrow boasted a 'great orchard'; Daniel Foxcroft, a gentleman farmer from Weetwood, who owned one of the finest houses in the area; William Hutchinson, a Briggate salter, and one of the passionate Royalists who had supported Benjamin Wade's petition for the new charter; and the Parliamentarian William Marshall, whose political views had become decidedly monarchistic as the wind of change blew across the country.

Religious differences still divided the community. Some, like John Harrison, remained loyal to the Church of England and upheld Episcopalianism. However, a large number in the town, like Francis Allanson, were devoted to the Presbyterians whose church was governed by a minister and selected elders, and rejected government by bishops. Matters came to a head in 1661 when William Styles, the vicar, died. The Revd John Lake, a High Churchman, an opponent of Puritanism and a man who had fought in the Royalist army, was appointed. He was not popular: many in the town preferred the Parliamentarian and Presbyterian minister, the Revd Edward Bowles, who at one time had been chaplain to the Lord General Fairfax.

When Lake arrived at the church he found the way barred by a jeering crowd, and only the arrival of a troop of soldiers enabled the new incumbent to enter. Matters grew worse. In 1662 the Act of Uniformity of Public Prayers was passed, requiring schoolmasters and clergy to pledge a declaration of non-resistance to the king and to promise to conform to the liturgy of the Church of England or lose their livings. It had a devastating effect in Leeds. Christopher Ness, a lecturer at the parish church; Robert Todd and his curate, James Sale, at St John's; John Garnet, the master of the Grammar School along with its usher, Israel Hawksworth; and the curates at Hunslet and Holbeck all lost their livings.

The most famous casualty was Elkanah Wales of Pudsey. Although not particularly appreciated by many of his parishioners, he nevertheless preferred to remain in Pudsey rather than move to a more lucrative post, and large numbers travelled considerable distances to hear his sermons. When the Five Mile Act of 1665 forced him out of the township he moved to Leeds, where he remained a well-respected and moderate Puritan.

It is not surprising, then, that some Puritan, Presbyterian and republican sympathisers grumbled that the new reign was a galling irritation. Others did more than grumble. In August 1663 an uprising of disgruntled anti-monarchists in the North broke out, but it was a dismal failure. Not discouraged, a further plan was outlined for October. Conspirators gathered in Knaresborough and Harrogate and formulated a plan 'to re-establish a gospel ministry and magistracy; to restore the Long Parliament; to relieve themselves from the excise of all subsidies; to reform all orders of and degrees of men, especially lawyers and clergy'. Thus was born the Farnley Wood Plot. Intending to act on the night of 12 October, a small party of dissidents assembled in Westmorland and a larger one to the west of Leeds in Farnley Wood, led by an ex-republican officer and Morley schoolmaster, Captain Thomas Oates. At the appropriate moment Oates gave the order to act, drew his sword and dramatically flung his scabbard away.

The whole affair was an utter travesty. The authorities were well aware of what was afoot, to the point that the militia had been garrisoned in the town as a precaution. Some historians go so far as to allege that the whole conspiracy was engineered by *agent provocateurs*. In particular, accusations were levelled that Joshua Greathead, one of the conspirators, a local squire and cousin of Thomas Oates, had kept the authorities fully informed of every move the dissidents made. Was the plot a serious attempt by ruthless insurgents to overthrow the monarchy or simply an incompetent protest by a group of dissatisfied but misguided farmers? Whatever the truth, within forty-five minutes the attempt to restore the Long Parliament was over. Some accounts claim forty-four men were arrested; others argue that no more than thirty were involved in total.

Whatever the number, they were taken to York for trial. They knew what fate awaited them, and consequently some treated the court with a contempt that bordered on impudence. Peregrine Corney scoffed to the judge that he valued his life no more than his pocket handkerchief. The other uprisings across the North were also extinguished, but the conspirators in the North Riding, Westmorland and Northumberland were treated far more leniently than the men of the West Riding. Oates and between twenty-one and twenty-six of them – accounts vary – were found guilty and sentenced to death. Seven were Leeds men. On one single morning in York sixteen of the plotters were hanged, drawn and quartered: not for a century had anyone seen anything like it. Three men, however, were taken to Leeds for execution: Robert Atkins, John Errington and Henry Watson were to be made an example of on Chapeltown Moor. The day chosen was deliberate. Tuesday 19 January 1664 was market day, and thus a large crowd could be guaranteed to watch the brutal spectacle. After execution the victims' decapitated heads were displayed on Moot Hall in Briggate. For years they were exhibited there as a salutary warning to other potential rebels, but legend has it that one stormy night the heads were blown from their perches and at that very moment Sir John Armitage of Kirklees was fatally thrown from his horse. It was long felt that the real villains behind the uprising, Armitage and John Peoples of Dewsbury, had evaded detection.[7]

Despite the disruption caused at times by political and religious differences in the town, life still had to go on, and it was the duty of the new council to see that every effort was made to allow this. On 26 March 1662 it passed its first by-law, which forbade anyone to interrupt another member who was already speaking or suffer a fine for doing so. The borough was divided into six wards, and individuals in each ward were appointed to deal with the eternal problem of the poor – those made destitute by old age, illness or finding themselves impoverished and unemployed when trade slackened.

The council also felt it necessary to maintain a watchful eye over the way that trades in the town were conducted. Consequently six guilds were established to cater for eighteen occupations. Inevitably the clothworkers formed one guild; other specialist guilds accommodated cordwainers, tailors, building craftsmen and ironmongers, and smiths. The retailers guild included drapers, mercers, grocers and other traders. These guilds were controlled not by guild officers but by the mayor and corporation. It was they who settled guild disputes, regulated the entry of apprentices into any trade and checked anyone suspected of being unqualified. How effective quality control was in each trade is not certain.[8]

Market traders were also carefully controlled. For centuries the cloth market had been held on Leeds Bridge, with cloths displayed on the parapets, but as the population grew and the bridge became too congested the council decided, in 1684, to move it into Briggate itself. As with general goods both the quality and prices were monitored, and weights and measures were inspected regularly. At the market shoes, wicker baskets, wooden vessels, wanded (wickerwork) chairs and fruit and vegetables were sold. Fish was available from its own market higher up Briggate, and on the east side of Moot Hall was the butchers' shambles. At Harrison's new market cross poultry was sold. Higher up the street was the cornmarket. Available for shoppers was a Leeds speciality, the Brig Shot End. According to Ralph Thoresby, 'the clothier may, together with his Pot of Ale, have a Noggin of O'Porrage, and a Trencher of either Boil'd or Roast-Meat for twopence'. Sharp practice was not unknown, with forestalling one of the most serious crimes, particularly when there was a scarcity of a particular product. Merchants bought up entire stocks of specific goods and then held them back until prices had risen to dramatic heights. In an attempt to prevent this happening no sales could be made until the market bell was rung.

If the council was concerned with the mundane affairs of everyday life, Charles and his government took a major step towards creating a more tolerant society when in March 1672 the Declaration of Indulgence was announced. Dissenters and Roman Catholics rejoiced but many Anglicans were infuriated. The Declaration meant that Nonconformists could build their own places of worship; Quakers in the town no longer faced imprisonment; Catholics could worship freely in their own homes. The Presbyterians began building their meeting-house at Mill Hill that very year. It was the first such chapel built in the North.

But many, knowing Charles's leanings towards Rome, considered the Act was not intended as a sop to the Nonconformists but more likely a subtle strategy to open the door for a return of Catholicism. So great was the opposition that in 1673 Parliament forced the king to withdraw it.

Persecutions began all over again. In Leeds the Quakers were singled out. Their meetings were condemned and worshippers were imprisoned. Daniel Thackery of Holbeck was incarcerated in Wakefield's House of Correction 'for witnessing the Kingdom of God within'. On 18 November 1683 William Rooke, the mayor, confined fifty-two Quaker men and women in one single unheated room in the Moot Hall for four days before dispatching them to York Castle. As one group was marched through the streets, Ralph Thoresby watched and

Right Old Leeds Bridge seen here *c.*1870. The cloth market was held on it until 1684 and the bridge was widened on three occasions; 1730, 1760 and 1796. A new iron bridge replaced this one in 1873 at a cost £23,000.

Below Cloth dealers had transported cloth to Leeds market since the Middle Ages. George Walker, in his *Costumes of Yorkshire*, portrays some of them doing so in 1814.

remarked on these 'poor deluded Quakers'. The Religious Society of Friends, more commonly known as the Quakers, was founded by George Fox sometime in the 1650s and was known to be present in the Leeds area by 1651. A certain George Dewsbury and his wife, Ann, met Fox at Stanley near Wakefield that year, and it was shortly after their meeting that Dewsbury came to Leeds and preached there.[9]

If Parliament was dissatisfied with the Declaration of Indulgence, Charles himself grew more and more dissatisfied with the way the newly incorporated towns were beginning to flex their muscles – and his supporters urged him on. In Leeds no one was more active than the local attorney William Headley. A passionate Tory and a bitter critic of local Nonconformists, he stood by Charles in recommending his brother James to succeed him. One of the leading figures in the town, he led the campaign to get the charter of 1661 rescinded and replaced by a new one that limited the power of the council. On 24 December 1684 the new charter was sealed. Now the king had the right to dismiss the mayor, the council, the recorder, and the town clerk.

That year Gervase Neville was appointed mayor. His Royalist father had been a quartermaster general during the Civil War and Gervase was a devoted monarchist. It was a turbulent time in politics, with the nation divided over whether Charles, without a legitimate heir, could be succeeded by his brother James, a Roman Catholic. Thus the Exclusion Crisis developed. The council was anxious to prove its loyalty and sent Gervase, along with Alderman Hick, to Windsor to present the town's carefully worded and supportive address in reply to the king's declaration of his faith in the parliamentary system. It was, incidentally, during this crisis that two great political parties emerged that would dominate the politics of Britain and Leeds for the next 200 years: the Whigs and the Tories.

The following year Charles died and James did indeed succeed. For three turbulent years he reigned, his subjects bitterly resenting the fact that a Roman Catholic was once again sitting on the throne of England. In 1688 the Protestant William of Orange and his wife Mary were invited to England. William landed that November, but within a month rumours were rife that an invading army of Catholic Irish troops was intent on restoring James to the throne and ravaging the countryside. In Leeds on 17 December 7,000 troops gathered in the town to effect its defence should the need arise. Thoresby gives a graphic account of what happened next: 'Beeston is actually burnt, and only some escaped to bring the doleful tidings! The drums beat, the bells rang backward, the women shrieked, and some doleful consternation seized upon all persons ... [B]lessed be God! The terror disappeared, it being a false alarm, taken from some drunken people.'

On 14 February 1689 the people of Leeds celebrated the proclamation of William and Mary as king and queen. That same year the old 1661 charter was reinstated and James's Toleration Act of 1687 was modified, to the delight of the Nonconformists. Between 1689 and 1699 the Quakers felt they were able to lease a meeting-house on Boar Lane, build a new one on Water Lane and open others in the out-townships of Armley and Wortley.

What, then, was the town like at the end of the century? Impressive houses had been erected. By 1655 a new prison had been built in Kirkgate; a new grammar school had opened in Wortley (1677); Godfrey Lawson had added a library to Leeds Grammar School (1692), which could also be used by adults in the town; the medicinal spas at Camp Road, Gipton, Woodhouse Carr,

Burley Road and Meanwood were regularly visited; Holbeck Spa's sulphuric waters were extremely popular; and St Peter's Well on Quarry Hill was said to be good for treating rheumatism and rickets. Ralph Thoresby's diary shows us what life was like. He recalled the bitter winter of 1684 when the Great Frost Fair was held on the frozen river Aire. Tents and booths were erected on it, with ox-roasting and sports being enjoyed on the frozen surface. Thoresby himself walked on the iced-up waterway 'from the Mills below the Old Church, all up the main river'. He tells of horse races being held on Chapeltown Moor and of Edward 'Harefoot' Preston, a local butcher and a famous 'footman', whose races attracted huge bets. Thoresby also describes some of the bizarre events that took place in the town: 'November 1683 – Abroad at Alderman Sykes's; went to see a man (one Sam Fry of Dorsetshire) eat brimstone, lead, bees-wax, sealing wax, pitch, rosin, blazing hot … he walked on a red hot bar of iron.'

In 1698 Celia Fiennes travelled extensively through England. She recorded her experiences in detail and left behind a graphic description of Leeds:

> Leeds is a large town, severall streets cleane and well pitch'd and good houses all built of stone, some have good gardens and steps to their houses … this is esteemed the wealthiest town of its bigness in the country … its manufacture is the woollen cloth of Yorkshire … their ale is very strong – but for paying a groat for your ale you may have a slice of meate either hotte or cold according to the tyme of day you call or else butter and cheese gratis into the bargaine.[10]

Crime as ever captured the attention of the public. Following the murder of local colliery owner Leonard Scurr and his family in their Beeston home in 1678, an estimated crowd of 30,000 turned out on Holbeck Moor to see the killer hanged. Probably the most infamous case of the time, however, involved the local silversmith, Arthur Mangey, who in 1694 had been employed to provide a new ceremonial mace for the town at a cost of £60 11s 0d, which is still in use to this day. On 1 August 1696 Mangey was tried at York Assizes for forgery, then a treasonable offence that carried the death penalty. Mangey protested his innocence, was found guilty and executed. In 1825 when Middle Row, the row of buildings that ran up the middle of Briggate behind the Moot Hall, was demolished, Mangey's old workshop was discovered among them – and there the forger's secret room was found.[11]

But all was not doom and gloom. Improvements came, and none more so than that of George Sorocold. An hydraulic engineer from Derby, he was

Above left The mace made by Arthur Mangey in 1694 and the clippers he used for clipping coins. They were discovered when his workshop was demolished in 1825.

Above right The opening of the Aire and Calder Navigation made Leeds into an important port. The busy docks are seen here in the late nineteenth century. Note the parish church in the distance.

employed to provide a decent water supply to the town in 1694. Water was pumped by an engine near Leeds Bridge to a reservoir at the top of Briggate near St John's church and then flowed through a series of lead pipes to various houses in the town.[12] The other improvement that proved of inestimable value to the merchants of the town was the opening of the Aire and Calder Navigation. For years plans had been discussed to improve the varying levels of the river Aire and make it a reliable waterway, thereby allowing the carriage of goods to Hull and onward to markets overseas. It was not until the 1690s that sufficient interest was shown to make it a viable possibility, and at last in 1699 an Act of Parliament was passed for the 33-mile waterway to be built.[13]

Running from Leeds to Goole, it linked Wakefield to Castleford. Its opening in 1700 heralded a bright new future for the merchants, manufacturers and the general economy of the West Riding in general and Leeds in particular. The eighteenth century would see this blossom to fulfilment.

THE KING AND MRS CROSBY

On 9 February 1647 a Parliamentarian troop of soldiers arrived in Leeds escorting no less a person than Charles I, King of England. He was their prisoner, delivered to his enemies by the Scots. On arrival in the town he was taken to Thomas Metcalfe's home, Red Hall. So much is fact. As might be expected legends grew up around the royal visit. One of them related to Metcalfe's servant girl, a Mrs Crosby, whose husband was the local bailiff. She approached Charles and suggested either that he should disguise himself in a woman's clothes or that she would give him her clothes – the story varies. Then under cover of darkness she would smuggle him out of the rear door into the garden, down the short back alley of Lands Lane, and take him to the safety of a friend's house. From thence he could make his escape to France. The king declined. Nevertheless he was grateful for the offer, and gave Mrs Crosby his garter saying that should he or any of his relatives ever ascend the throne again she should present the garter and explain what had happened.

The years passed. Charles was executed, Cromwell reigned supreme and then in 1660 Charles's son, Charles II, returned in triumph to London. Mrs Crosby journeyed to the royal court and told her story. Charles listened intently, then asked what her husband did. She explained he was a bailiff in Leeds. The king announced, 'Then he shall be High Bailiff of Yorkshire.'

Crosby went on to build Crosby House in the town, but historians dispute where it was. John Mayhall placed it somewhere on the Upper Headrow, while Joseph Sprittles is more specific, according it the site where Lewis's department store was built. However, J. Heaton in his *Walks through Leeds* contends it was near the site of the old corn exchange at the top of Briggate. Richard Jackson in his *Guide to Leeds* claims the building became the Haunch of Venison Inn, then pours water on the whole story: 'What are we to think of the under-bailiff story? John Metcalfe was the under-bailiff, and had the opportunity of plundering a large fortune from his office. Crosby had the same opportunity. Is the whole story a fable?'

six

LEEDS AND THE AGE
OF ENLIGHTENMENT

The beginning of the eighteenth century saw Leeds on the threshold of a new age. Historians call it the Age of Enlightenment: new ideas swept the world and new technologies began to transform it. In England a new monarchy was establishing itself under Protestant William III, while in Leeds a one-time cloth merchant devoted his time to antiquarian studies and settled down to write the first ever history of the town. Ralph Thoresby's classic work, *Ducatus Leodiensis* published in 1715, gives the most detailed account of Leeds and its surrounding areas since Domesday Book had been compiled 700 years before.

Thoresby mentioned Gipton and its 'curious *cold spring*' well, and Potter Newton where more gentry lived than in any other local township. He wrote of the 'pure Air' of Chapel Allerton, or Chapel-Town as it was more commonly known. He reflected on Headingley, on its Shire Oak and old chapel. Weetwood at that time was a mixture of cultivated land and rocks, crags, trees and bushes. At Cookridge there was a 'House of publick Reception' called Halfpenny-House and Mr Kirke's famous wood laid out in a geometrical design. At Kirkstall were the abbey's celebrated ruins, but there were also mills for grinding corn and fulling cloth, similar to those at Armley, an indication of the importance of the wool textile industry in the area. It was a point he also brought home in his reference to Hunslet, which was 'chiefly inhabited by *Clothiers*'. Bramley meanwhile was famous for producing roofing slates. Wortley boasted 'a good Vein of *fine Clay*' for making tobacco pipes. Farnley had 400 acres of wood and 'plenty of good Stone and Coal'. The same could be said of Middleton. Beeston was famous for the manufacture of bone-lace and straw hats.

Of Leeds itself Thoresby described Briggate and its market with the 'best furnished *Flesh Shambles* in the North of England' and its twice, sometimes thrice, weekly fish market. 'Bur Lane' contained several gentlemen's houses; Kirkgate boasted a new prison; while the pillory and stocks were in front of the

Above left Ralph Thoresby's home on Kirkgate. Here he established his celebrated museum, which included medals, geological specimens, books and manuscripts.

Above right Ralph Thoresby (1658–1725). Antiquarian and topographer, he is best known as the Father of Leeds History. His *Ducatus Leodiensis*, published in 1715, was the first history of the town ever written.

new Moot Hall, which had been rebuilt between 1710 and 1711. Butchers' shops occupied its ground floor, with the council chamber and the meeting place for the local JPs above.[1]

William III had died in 1702, and when a new Moot Hall was built Alderman William Milner saw the opportunity to make a political statement, a demonstration of loyalty to his new monarch.[2]

It was, after all, a time when Jacobite threats to reinstate the Stuarts on the throne were very real. Thus Milner ordered a white marble statue of Queen Anne to be sculpted by Andrew Carpenter. It portrays her in her Parliament robes, wearing the crown and Order of the Garter, and carrying the orb and sceptre. It was a masterful piece of work, clearly demonstrating Carpenter's skill in handling marble. When it was unveiled in the niche in front of the building on 12 May 1713, Thoresby commented it was 'generally esteemed ... the best that was ever made' and chose to include an engraving of it in his *Ducatus Leodiensis*. When the Moot Hall was demolished it was moved to a new corn exchange built higher up Briggate, and today resides in the entrance of the City Art Gallery.

In 1714 Anne died and the town found itself divided. Those loyal to the heir apparent, the future King George I, were the Whigs; those who wanted a return to the Stuart dynasty were the Tories. The fear was that the Act of Settlement would be ignored, George's claim disregarded and the Stuart King James III proclaimed king. Neighbours and friends viewed each other with suspicion. The Revd Nathaniel Hough insisted that Leeds was 'deeply tinged with Jacobitism', and turned his ire on Ralph Thoresby as being 'a favourer of the

Moot Hall. The meeting place for the council. Originally built in Briggate in 1615–18, it was replaced between 1710 and 1711. The narrow street on the right was the Shambles, the one on the left the Back Shambles. Note the statue of Queen Anne, now in the Art Gallery. Moot Hall was demolished in 1825.

Pretender's cause'. But Thoresby had no such sympathies. His fear was that a 'dreaded invasion of the Pretender with an army of French and Irish' would take place. He need not have worried, and his fears of the return of a Catholic king turned out to be groundless: the Whig Duke of Shrewsbury ensured that George was speedily brought to England to claim the throne. Thoresby, who was in London when the king arrived, reflected on 'the most blessed sight of a Protestant King and Prince (whom I had a full view of) attended with the loud acclamations of the people'.

There were many in Leeds who did not share that view. The new mayor, Solomon Pollard, said that repeating the oath of allegiance to the new king was 'the bitterest pill' he had ever swallowed. Others decided to celebrate the birthday of James Stuart, the Old Pretender, and a Leeds mob drank his health. The *Flying Post* newspaper reported that Jacobites lit a bonfire in the streets of the town and rang the church bells. So unsettled were the times that William Cookson, a Leeds merchant from one of the most distinguished families in the town and its mayor in 1712, fell foul of the law. He went on a visit to Bath to take the waters, but was arrested in September 1715 on suspicion of helping to organise a West Country Jacobite uprising. He was imprisoned in Newgate, where he was held until the following April. Thoresby protested Cookson's innocence and claimed him to be 'most zealously affirmed to the Protestant succession', while Solomon Pollard, the Tory mayor, despite having swallowed his 'bitter pill', vigorously insisted that the Tories in Leeds were devoted servants of the Hanoverian king. But the Cookson affair well illustrated the volatile situation that existed in the country at the time.

However, by the time George II was crowned in October 1727 local political differences appeared to be over. The coronation was celebrated with illuminations, fireworks and the ringing of bells.[3] But in 1745 Charles Stuart, the Young Pretender, made his move to reclaim the throne. In Leeds two companies of volunteers were recruited to help combat the advance of 'Bonnie' Prince Charlie's army. Rumours were rife. John Wesley arrived in the town and warned of the rebel advance. Tales circulated that they would attack Wakefield and Leeds; that they were already in Otley. In fact the Young Pretender advanced through Lancashire. Nevertheless, in December Marshall George Wade arrived in Leeds with a combined army of Dutch, Swiss and English troops en route for Newcastle, to counteract the insurgents. The force, 13,000 strong, camped between Sheepscar and Woodhouse.[4] Meantime, in Edinburgh Leeds-born General Guest mounted a spirited defence of Edinburgh Castle against the rebels.

The threat of revolution passed, but in April 1747 sixty-eight Jacobite captives were held overnight in Leeds on their way from York to Liverpool and eventual transportation. However, other events rocked Leeds. As the Seven Years' War with France rumbled on the press gang arrived in the town seeking recruits for the Navy. In July 1759 the *Leeds Intelligencer* reported that 'thirty-five volunteers and pressed men' were boarded onto a vessel at Leeds Bridge from where they were to be ferried to Hull.

But the event that had the most disastrous impact on the nation during the first half of that century was the South Sea Bubble. This speculative venture saw a dramatic rise in the price of South Sea Company stock. In March 1720, as the company's stocks rose, the *Leeds Mercury* assured its readers, 'it must Redound to the Happiness of the Nation'. It reached its height in July, and then came disaster: the exact opposite occurred. The bubble burst and thousands, many in Leeds, were ruined. Thomas Hudson from the town was one such. The fortune he had inherited from his aunt disappeared overnight, and the remainder of his days were spent wandering around London as a barefoot lunatic. More fortunate was Rich, 5th Viscount Irwin of Temple Newsam. His irresponsible investments were only saved thanks to the intervention of Alderman William Milner, of Queen Anne statue fame.

Just how many of the population were affected is hard to say. Leeds had a population of both rich and poor. Many no doubt would have speculated. It was a diverse population made up of gentlemen, merchants, retailers, attorneys, doctors, clergy, craftsmen, apothecaries, schoolmasters, farmers and labourers, with some four-fifths of the townsfolk being engaged in the wool textile trade.

It was in about 1720 that Daniel Defoe visited the town as he compiled his graphic *Tour of the Whole Island of Great Britain*. He commented:

> Leeds is a large, wealthy and populous Town, it stands on the North Bank of the
> River Aire, or rather on both sides the river, for there is a large suburb on the South

Side of the River, and the whole is joined by a stately and prodigiously strong Stone Bridge ... [T]he High-Street, beginning from the Bridge and running North ... is a large, broad, fair and well-built Street ... The town of Leeds is very large, and ... there are an abundance of wealthy merchants in it.

He claimed its famous cloth market in Briggate was, 'a prodigy of its kind and not to be equalled in the world', and that between £10,000 and £20,000 of business was completed there in just over an hour.

In his poem *The Fleece* the mid-eighteenth-century poet John Dyer ruminated on the growing town; a town where 'trade and business guide the busy scene'. It was a town of rising scaffolding and 'growing edifices' as the reverberating sound of carpenters and stone-masons hard at work echoed through the air. It was a town of creaking corn-filled wagons, negotiating a way through 'slow pac'd streets', frequently obstructed by cattle being herded to market and competing with a multitude of carts and carriages. Making their way also were 'neat dress'd housewives ... Crown'd with full baskets'. New streets were being marked out 'in the neighb'ring fields' and new buildings, 'sacred domes of worship', soared heavenwards. The river, the very lifeline of Leeds, was filled with 'slow sailing barges'. His conclusion? 'Thus all is here in motion, all is life.'[5]

This was a romantic, idyllic view of 1757 Leeds – but historians know exactly what Leeds looked like in the 1720s thanks to surveyor and cartographer John Cossins, whose *A New and Exact Plan of the Town of Leedes* was published in

Samuel Buck's classic *East Prospect of Leedes in Yorkshire from Chavelier Hill*, drawn in 1720. Note St John's church on the right, the parish church by the busy river, a group of men beating fleeces and in the foreground Buck himself. The woods on the hills in the distant left are at Farnley.

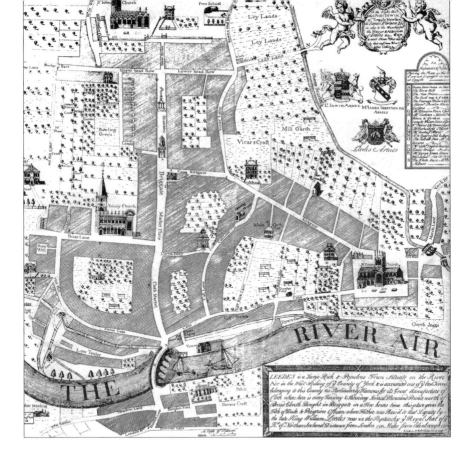

John Cossins' *A New and Exact Plan of the Town of Leedes*. It well demonstrates the vast open areas of central Leeds in 1726. Note the bowling green above Trinity church and top right the idyllic Ley Lands. This would become an insanitary area of squalid slum dwellings about 150 years later.

1726. The built-up areas were concentrated on Kirkgate, Vicar Lane, Briggate and south of Boar Lane. Very noticeable were the great open spaces in what eventually became the Park Row and Albion Street areas. Boats on the busy river Aire indicated its significance as a waterway, and the numerous tenter-grounds emphasised the importance of the wool textile industry. In cartouches around the plan Cossins featured illustrations of the impressive homes of various of Defoe's 'wealthy merchants' and prominent citizens.

William Milner and Thomas Kitchingman, another alderman and ex-mayor, typified that merchant class, both being actively engaged in wool textiles and coal-mining, the two industries that formed the basis of the Leeds economy. In 1710 that economy was seriously threatened when the wool merchants of Wakefield opened a covered cloth hall in the town. Merchants from the West Riding may well have enjoyed their Brig Shot End, but understandably they preferred to do business sheltered from the elements in Wakefield

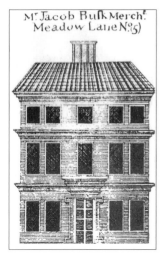

Above left Jacob Busk's house in Meadow Lane was featured by John Cossins as one of the cartouches he used to embellish his map of Leeds. The map was thought to have been drawn in 1725, until Professor Maurice Beresford showed that the house was not built until 1726.

Above right Originally a private house built in 1720, Richard Kemplay opened his writing academy here at the beginning of the nineteenth century. It today houses Nash's Fish Restaurant.

rather than be exposed to the cold and damp of Leeds open air market down by the river.

Leeds merchants were quick to respond. By April 1711 a white cloth hall, dealing in undyed cloth, had been opened in Kirkgate. Thoresby described it as 'a stately hall built on pillars on arches in the form of an exchange, with a quadrangular court within'. However, by 1756 it had outlived its usefulness. A new hall, an impressive three-storey building 70yds long and 10yds wide was opened in Meadow Lane. The old Kirkgate building was then used for a variety of purposes; for a time as the fashionable assembly rooms, as a Baptist church, as a hall for travelling players and as home for the first Lancasterian school in the town. It still stands in a dilapidated state awaiting restoration.

A growing town has developing needs, and in 1718 John Hirst, a journalist and printer, answered one long-felt want. On Tuesday 1 July he published the town's first newspaper. In was in fact more the size of a book or pamphlet. The *Leeds Mercury*, he promised, would be comprehensive and contain 'the freshest advices foreign and domestic together with accounts of trade'. In reality his 5,000-word paper was known as a 'scissors-and-paste news-sheet', with most of the news simply lifted from the London papers – although in 1723 he reported that 'From Tong, in Christmas last, Eggs were taken out of the Magpy Nest'!

Hirst died in 1732, and by 1735 the *Mercury* had a new owner, James Lister and by now the paper was more newspaper like in size. Lister ran the paper from its offices at New Street End, known as 'the cradle of Leeds journalism'. However, on 2 July 1754 Griffith Wright, the son of Griffin Wright, the clerk of St John's church, launched a rival newspaper, the *Leeds Intelligencer*. Lister found the new competition too strong. In June 1755 Wright was delighted to report that the *Mercury* 'had died after a tedious illness'. What is not clear is whether Wright took over the *Mercury* completely. He certainly bought wood blocks that Lister had used for printing and the rights to a cookery book Lister had published.[6]

Examining both the newspapers and the observations of John Lucas, a local schoolmaster, which he recorded in *The Memoranda Book of John Lucas 1712–1750*, a fascinating insight into life in Leeds at that time is revealed.[7] Sport was popular, horse racing particularly so. Ralph Thoresby mentions two men having a race on Chapeltown Moor as early as Monday 17 July 1682, but the first actual race meeting as such was held on the moor on Tuesday 25 July 1709. The prize was a plate worth £30. Races were also sometimes held at Temple Newsam, though Chapeltown was the favourite venue.

Cockfighting was keenly supported by all sections of society, with fights often taking place on Chapeltown Moor at the same time as the races. In 1725 a main of cocks was advertised – that is, a whole series of fights – with bets placed on individual battles being as high as 100*gns*. There were also cockfighting pits both in Leeds itself and in the local villages. The two most famous in the town were at the Talbot, and Rose and Crown inns in Briggate, while villages such as Middleton and Chapel Allerton boasted their own.

Football, too, was popular. Lucas recorded how in December 1715 the river Aire froze: 'I saw hundreds of men playing football upon the river,' he reported. It seems, also, that football hooliganism is no twentieth-century phenomenon. On 23 December 1718 some young men were playing football by moonlight on Boar Lane. The ball was kicked into a shop, and in the ensuing fight that followed Francis Brindholm, a glover, was killed.[7]

One other major need of the growing town was improved transport infrastructure: the roads around Leeds and district were appalling. As Thoresby said, some of the local highways were 'rougher than a ploughed field'. Attempting to transport raw materials to Leeds and carry finished goods away over potholed and badly drained roads was virtually impossible at times. It was not simply a local problem. Highways across the country had hardly been touched since Roman times. As early as 1662 the government recognised the problem and passed the first Act of Parliament to permit the building of turnpike roads. By 1706 nominated trusts in local areas were formed to build them: each trust invested in the construction of the road and then charged its users. In Leeds the trusts met at the Old King's Arms and the Royal Oak in Briggate to conduct their business. From 1740 a series of roads radiating out of the town were constructed. Leeds to Elland (1740); Leeds to Selby and Halifax, and Leeds to Bradford (1741); Leeds to Tadcaster and York (1751); Leeds to Harrogate, Boroughbridge and Ripon (1752); Leeds to Otley and Skipton (1755); Leeds to Wakefield, Barnsley and Sheffield (1758).[8]

Equally important was the need for an effective transport system. Leeds would ultimately become a major coaching centre but at the beginning of the eighteenth century it lagged far behind other Yorkshire towns. Barnsley, Sheffield, Doncaster, Wakefield and York had all developed regular coach services to London long before Leeds introduced one. No doubt attempting to drive coaches over the 'ploughed fields' Thoresby referred to was a factor in delaying the introduction of such provision. However, by 1754 a regular coach service had been introduced between Leeds and Scarborough. The coach left Thomas Spink's, a painter and undertaker in Kirkgate, every Wednesday. It returned from the Talbot Inn in Scarborough every Friday. On 19 May 1760 the first service from the town to London began. These 'flying machines on steel springs' left the Old King's Arms in Briggate at 4 a.m. every Monday and Friday morning. They went via Wakefield, Barnsley and Sheffield, stopped the first night at The Swan in Mansfield, the second night at the Red Lion in Northampton and on the third day reached the Swan with Two Necks in London. In reality it was often into the fourth day when the coach arrived.[9]

Another important need in any developing business community is easy access to credit. By 1738 Benjamin Worsdale of the Upper Headrow had instituted such a service, making loans available to local busi-

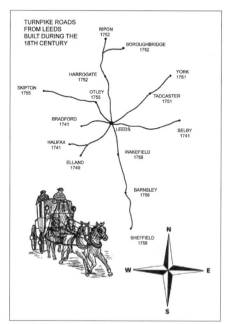

From 1740 a series of turnpike roads were built radiating from Leeds. They were a major stimulant to the burgeoning trade of the town.

nessmen. Then in 1758 the first real bank was opened in the town. John Lodge, an eminent London merchant, and John Arthington, a linen draper, opened the Lodge and Arthington Bank, a bank that would become more famous in the latter part of the century as Becketts Bank.

The town was developing, and the new roads certainly improved travel around Leeds. In principle the turnpike trusts seemed sound, but in practice they frequently fell far short of what was required. Trusts invariably failed to maintain the roads in a decent condition, and consequently travellers' resentment grew. In the Leeds area that resentment turned to violence, and the Leeds Fight, as it became known, broke out. In the summer of 1753 mobs from Yeadon and Otley destroyed several turnpikes; in Selby even the public bellman led the opposition. Then in June a Leeds mob attacked the toll bars at Halton Dial and on the Leeds to Bradford road. Troops from York were called in and four people were arrested. The prisoners were temporarily held in the Old King's Arms in Briggate, and a mob gathered outside the inn. That evening, being Saturday and market day, the street was crowded, and when the mob refused to disperse the militia opened fire. In the ensuing engagement several demonstrators and innocent bystanders were killed and about fifty wounded.[10]

This was not the only serious disturbance with fatalities that occurred in the early years of the century. In 1735 the escalating price of corn brought about violent protests across the country, and in Leeds a riot erupted. The authorities summoned the military, and only after eight or nine people were killed was order finally restored.

Crime was commonplace. Petty offenders were punished by spending time in the stocks or the pillory in front of Moot Hall. In January 1726 John Howson of Woodhouse was sentenced to stand in the pillory 'as a cheat, he having taken up goods at several shops in other person's names'. At Quarry Hill the ducking stool was still used for gossiping women and dishonest alewives, and public whippings were also carried out. Gambling was endemic throughout society and its results were felt, in particular, by the vulnerable wives and children of those involved. In 1754 the *Intelligencer* remarked on 'loose idle Fellows' playing 'Shake Cap' in Lands Lane; the gambler after revelling in ale-houses 'vents his ill humours on his Wife and poor Children'.

Petty crimes were tried at the General Quarter Sessions for the West Riding held from 1711 in the new Moot Hall. More serious crimes such as murder and forgery were sent to the assizes at York. A particularly common crime in the area related to cloths drying on the numerous tenter frames of the town, but in

March 1713 'an old man was set at the pillory for falsely accusing some person of tenter cutting'. Cloths on the frames were often vandalised or stolen, despite the punishment being possible transportation for seven years.

At this time some fifty crimes, such as fraud, forgery, receiving stolen goods and smuggling as well as murder, carried the death penalty, and the number increased as the century progressed. The theft of hops from Robert Hall and John Newsham's fields at Nosthorpe in 1736 was deemed a capital offence. Two local murder cases particularly caught the attention of the public. The first, in 1749, saw the only time when a lord of the manor of Leeds was executed for murder. Josiah Fearn had become a part owner of the manor in 1738. Having stabbed Thomas Grave four times, he pleaded self-defence at his trial in York. It was to no avail, and he was sentenced to death and perished on the scaffold in York. The parish church register claimed his 'Temper was extremely rigid to the Poor and his Dependents, that he was dreaded by All, but beloved by None'. The second case, in the same year, saw Thomas Mawson, an army drummer in Sir Robert Rich's Dragoons, accused of the murder of John Johnson, a servant of one of the officers. A quarrel broke out 'not with pistols, swords or staves, but with fists' and Johnson was killed. Mawson was sent to York and tried, but the jury found him not guilty. Mawson's arrival in the town was the first recorded visit of a black person to Leeds. There were other murders as well. That same year a woman's body was found in Lady Lane, probably murdered, while Mary Atkinson cut her own child's throat. She was 'acquitted at the Assizes as a lunatic'.[11]

Some crimes were no doubt the result of poverty, for poverty was endemic throughout the nation. Unemployment so often led to destitution, but most feared was the onset of old age and the grim prospect of hopelessness and penury. Long established in the town was the local workhouse on Lady Lane, set up, as Thoresby said, as 'a hospital for the aged poor'. By 1729 it was so badly in debt that it was forced to close, but the perennial problem of indigents necessitated its reopening in 1738. One positive step to help overcome such problems was the opening of a Blue Coat school for forty pauper children in 1707.

The morals of society left much to be desired. It was felt that one way to improve them was through religion, but religion itself was in a parlous state. Many of the clergy were unpopular, and the Church of England itself was seen by many to be divisive. No clearer example was seen than the newly opened Holy Trinity church. To accommodate the growing population in the town the building on Boar Lane was consecrated in August 1727, but it catered principally for the middle classes; the majority of its pews had to be rented. The

Church generally appeared to fail to understand the needs of a changing society, and many clergy neglected their duties. After a meeting of clergymen at the Angel Inn in Hunslet one cleric remarked, 'All clergymen and yet not one word of spiritual things among us.'

Rancorous disputes within the Church in Leeds did little to inspire confidence. In 1746 Joseph Cookson, the long-serving vicar, died. It took five years to appoint his successor as the trustees bitterly wrangled over two contenders, Samuel Kirshaw and James Scott. Only after appeals to the Court of Chancery and the House of Lords was Kirshaw finally appointed. But it was not simply in the borough itself that disputes broke out. In the out-townships, too, acrimonious squabbles disturbed the peace. In Hunslet in 1748 a similar argument occurred when two candidates were nominated for the vacant curacy in the township. Opinion was so divided that both men, William Pashley and Henry Crooke, were invited to preach trial sermons. But the crowd had already made up its mind. Pashley began speaking to an almost empty chapel, but a large mob burst in to show their displeasure and after five minutes he withdrew. Crooke was appointed.

In Holbeck in 1754 a new curate, the Revd Mr Fawcett, was appointed. The majority of the inhabitants of the township were furious. The *Leeds Intelligencer* relished the scandal and graphically reported on the 'furious, frantic rabble of Holbeckers' assaulting the new incumbent, and how fifty dragoons were required to escort him into the chapel. Fawcett's problems did not end there. That night hooligans broke into the building, destroyed the Book of Common Prayer and smeared human faeces on the seats. The *Intelligencer* loftily declared, 'Let them not assume the name of CHRISTIAN ... much less a Protestant!'[12]

There were Christians, however, who were passionately Protestant. They were the Nonconformists, those Dissenters who were critical of the ritual and teachings of the Church of England. The Independents, later known as Congregationalists, worshipped at their chapel in Call Lane. The Quakers gathered in their meeting house on Water Lane, while in Holbeck Benjamin Ingham, who had broken away from the Moravian Church, set up a small chapel for his followers the Inghamites. The Moravians, or the Renewed Unity of the Brethren, were a group that originated in Bohemia and believed in spiritual rebirth and individual conversion. In 1742 a group of Moravians settled at Fulneck at Pudsey, thanks to the help of Benjamin Ingham. It was the first such settlement in England. Their chapel was completed in 1748 and by 1753 a school had been opened to provide an education for the sons and daughters of the Church's ministers and missionaries.[13]

One man greatly influenced by the Moravians was an Anglican cleric, the Revd John Wesley. A charismatic preacher, he brought about momentous changes in the religious landscape of the country. With his brother Charles and a colleague, George Whitefield, Wesley sought to reinvigorate the Church of England and make it more meaningful and relevant to ordinary people. Travelling anything up to 5,000 miles a year, he spoke to vast crowds, always urging them to remain faithful to the Church of England. Doctrinal differences eventually saw Whitefield split from the Wesleys. Nevertheless, they saw their evangelical movement, known as Methodism, flourish. Local societies known as Connexions were set up, and in 1742 John Nelson, a Birtsall stonemason, established one at Armley. In 1743 Mary Shent, the wife of William Shent, a local barber and wigmaker, heard Nelson speak. So impressed was she with the new Methodist thinking that in April that year, when John Wesley visited Leeds, the great preacher was invited to speak to an interested group in Shent's shop, at the junction of Briggate and what was known later as Duncan Street. Wesley later remarked that he found in Leeds that 'no man cared for the things of God: but a spark has now fallen into this place also and it will kindle into a great flame'. It did indeed. Methodism became part of the religious landscape in Leeds and went from strength to strength, so that by the mid-nineteenth century it was the most dominant of all the churches in the town.

Wesley himself, however, did not find that his visits across the country were always appreciated. Many local clergy bitterly resented both him and his fellow Methodist preachers and refused to allow them to use their churches. Leeds parish church, however, always welcomed him, but the town's inhabitants did not. In September 1745 Wesley was 'pelted with dirt and stones', while in February 1746 he was struck several times when he was assaulted by a 'great mob'. It was not only his enemies who gave him trouble in Leeds. Methodists were prone to arguing among themselves, causing him to remark in 1758 that 'I have had more trouble with the town of Leeds than with all the societies in Yorkshire.'[14]

The year 1758 was important in Leeds. Apart from the town's first bank opening its doors, two other important events occurred. The Coloured Cloth Hall, specialising in selling dyed cloths, was opened roughly where City Square and Infirmary Street now stand. It was one of the largest buildings in the town, 127yds long and 60yds wide, and, because of the vital role the cloth markets had in the Leeds economy, one of its most important. Known often as the Mixed Cloth Hall, it was designed by John Moxon and cost £5,300. There were

The yard of the Coloured Cloth Hall. Political meetings held here could attract up to 20,000. Note the steps on the right where the speakers addressed the crowd. It was here that the infamous Battle of Standard was fought in 1832.

Inside the Coloured Cloth Hall: George Walker well caught the immense size of the place. It provided 1,700 stalls. Designed by John Moxon, the building opened in 1758.

1,700 stalls and a huge open quadrangular yard capable of holding 20,000. It became the scene of some of the most memorable events in the town's history.[15]

The other significant event was the building of Middleton Railway, the oldest railway in the world. It symbolised, perhaps better than anything else, that Leeds stood at the forefront of a movement that would bring sweeping changes to the nation. In the next half century England would be transformed as the leviathan of the Industrial Revolution grew from strength to strength.

THE OLDEST RAILWAY IN THE WORLD

For centuries miners realised that the easiest way to move heavy wagons of coal both in the pits themselves and above ground was to lay rails and run the wagons on them. But it was Middleton colliery owner Charles Brandling who hit on the novel idea of using such a wagonway to deliver coals any distance. To build such a railway required an Act of Parliament. His was the first Act passed for the building of a wagonway, and thus the Middleton Railway can legitimately claim to be the oldest railway in the world.

In 1758 Brandling and his agent, Richard Humble, realised that their business was at a serious disadvantage in relation to its competitors from Rothwell. They could use the river to transport goods to Leeds, whereas Brandling's route to the town was through narrow lanes, down a steep hill and over various bridlepaths. He arranged a meeting with the authorities in the town at the Three Legs Inn in order to get their blessing, and on 9 June 1758 Parliament passed an Act 'in order for the better supplying of the towns and neighbourhood of Leeds, in the county of York with coals'.

The route took it across Hunslet Moor and on to the coal staithe at Casson Close near Leeds Bridge. Horses pulled the wagons known as chauldrons. The rails were originally made of oak with renewable strips of beech on top, though later iron rails were introduced. On Wednesday 20 September 1758 the *Leeds Intelligencer* reported that the railway had begun operating: bells were rung, cannons were fired in celebration and 'a general Joy appear'd in every face'.

But the Middleton Railway was not finished with being a world record breaker.

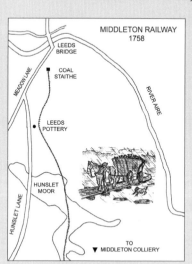

Middleton Railway opened in 1758 as a result of the first Railway Act of Parliament. It ran over Hunslet Moor and through the Leeds Pottery.

In 1812 the war with Napoleonic France had sent costs of fodder soaring, forcing Brandling's son, Charles John, and his agent, John Blenkinsop, to look for an alternative way of transporting the coal. They employed Matthew Murray to build a steam locomotive based on Richard Trevithick's design, to replace the horses. On 24 June 1812 the world's first commercially viable steam locomotive made a demonstration run across Hunslet Moor. The *Leeds Mercury* reported: 'Fifty horses will be dispensed with, and we cannot forbear to hail the invention as a vast public utility.' The two engines, *Salamanca* and *Prince Regent*, began operating in August 1812 and the railway continued running until the mid-twentieth century. Threatened with closure, the 1758 Middleton Railway Trust was established in order to preserve it, and today volunteers continue to run it as a passenger railway – the oldest railway in the world.

seven

LEEDS AND THE AGE
OF REVOLUTION

The last fifty years of the eighteenth century might well be called the Age of Revolution. Agriculture and industry were both transformed as new ideas and new technologies swept away centuries-old traditions. Political revolutions saw the fledgling United States throw off the yolk of colonialism to become a nation in its own right, while France was established as a beacon for radical political reform in Europe. Echoing these momentous changes were the social and cultural innovations that heralded the modern world. Leeds did not stand idly by, but played its part in that metamorphosis.

One such act that aided the transfiguration and had a lasting effect on the town was the establishment of the General Infirmary in 1767. Another occurred in 1769 when the exporters of Liverpool and the merchants in Bradford conceived an imaginative plan to build a canal from Liverpool to Leeds. Leeds, after all, was where the Aire & Calder Navigation began, and if such a new waterway were constructed the two great northern ports of Liverpool and Hull would be linked to each other. For the manufacturers of the West Riding it meant that the new canal would open up the markets of the Americas more easily. In 1770 an Act of Parliament was passed and the construction of the 127-mile waterway, the longest in Britain, began. The engineer John Longbotham supervised the building of the first 28 miles on the Lancashire side of the Pennines and the first 30 miles on the Yorkshire side. Most the work, however, was eventually supervised by John Hustler, a Bradford philanthropist and Quaker wool-stapler.[1]

The land to be traversed was at times difficult, and financial backing was not always forthcoming. At Foulridge a 1,630yds tunnel had to be dug, a project so difficult that the *Leeds Mercury* reported, when it opened in June 1776, that it had taken five years to build. The first stretch of the canal, between Bingley and Skipton, opened in 1773, and then in June 1777 the *Leeds Mercury* announced, 'On Wednesday last being his Majesty's birthday … Sir George Saville's Militia fired three excellent vollies [*sic*] and what added to the lustre of the day was the opening of the Leeds and Liverpool Canal.' It was in fact the section from Leeds to Skipton that had opened, and goods leaving Leeds on a Wednesday were scheduled to reach Skipton on a Saturday.

It was not until October 1816 that the final stretch was completed and Leeds and Liverpool linked. According to the *Mercury*, 'The work perhaps is the most stupendous ever undertaken in this country.'[2] That Saturday a convoy set off to celebrate the event, arriving in Liverpool the following Wednesday. Over the years canal barges would carry wool, wood, coal, iron ore and flax as well as food into the West Riding and transport finished products, including the textiles so vital to the local economy, westwards. The great industries developing in the town would come to rely heavily on the new waterway as the century progressed. Water transport was said to be 200 times more efficient than road transport.

When John Marshall, the flax spinner, decided to move his mill from Adel to Leeds he chose a site in Holbeck only yards from the new canal. Marshall had originally set up his flax mill at Adel in 1788, but as his business expanded he needed a larger workforce, which the sparsely populated area of North Leeds was unable to supply. Thus it was that in 1792 he moved to Holbeck, one of the most populous of the out-townships, and there set up business in Water Lane producing linen, canvas, hessian and raven-duck, a fine quality sail-cloth. The flax used was both grown locally and imported from the Baltic. He was one of the first people in the country to attempt to spin flax mechanically.

Politically he was a Whig, and became one of the mainstays of the party in Leeds during the early nineteenth century, being elected one of the MPs for Yorkshire in 1826. Marshall went into partnership with Thomas and Benjamin Benyon, but it was an unhappy relationship, and in 1804 he bought them out. He went from strength to strength, employing over 1,000 people and turning Leeds into the principal centre of the British flax industry.[3] Half Marshall's yarn was woven on his own handlooms; the rest was put out and were woven by weavers in the nearby townships and villages. Without doubt, much of his success was thanks to the machinery he used and the engineer he employed to create it.

Matthew Murray had arrived in Leeds having walked from Stockton-on-Tees. He found a position at Marshall's mill at Adel and there in 1791 he invented the wet process for spinning flax. He moved to Holbeck with Marshall and went on to produce machines for spinning and carding flax, until

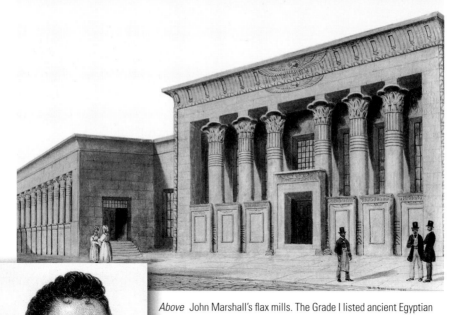

Above John Marshall's flax mills. The Grade I listed ancient Egyptian temple designs were built between 1838–43. The one on the immediate left is based on the temple of Hathor at Dendera, the central one on the temple of Horus at Edfu.

Left Matthew Murray (1765–1826) the celebrated engineer. His steam engines, built at the Round Foundry in Holbeck, attracted international acclaim. Among his most famous ones were *Salamanca* and *Prince Regent* which began work on Middleton Railway in 1812.

ultimately the Society of Arts recognised his genius and awarded him its gold medal. Murray's creativity demanded he expand his horizons, and so in 1795 he left Marshall's to set up his own engineering business with David Wood. Two years later they moved to the famous Round Foundry not far from Marshall's mills, and there it would be true to say the engineering industry of Leeds was born. Murray was rightly given the title the Father of Engineering in the town.

For Murray steam was the future, and in the early years of the next century he would come into his own. In 1812 his steam engines *Salamanca* and *Prince Regent* began operating on Middleton Railway; in 1813 he converted the captured French sailing ship *L'Actif* to steam power; and one of his engines powered a tugboat on the Mississippi river. He even centrally heated his Holbeck home with steam, and not surprisingly the locals called it Steam Hall. Despite his Birmingham rivals Boulton and Watt resorting to industrial espionage against him and doing their best to destroy his reputation and prevent his business expanding, Murray went from success to success. He was internationally recognised to the extent that the King of Sweden presented him with a gold snuff box and the Czar of Russia with a diamond ring. Had he not died in 1826, it is possible that he may well have played as great a part in the development of railways nationally as George Stephenson did.[4]

By the last decade of the eighteenth century steam was the power of the moment. In 1790 Richard Paley, a local property speculator and entrepreneur, introduced steam engines to drive the spinning machinery in his two cotton mills, and by the end of the eighteenth century 2,000 people were employed in the cotton industry in Leeds. It was a short-lived venture, however. Within ten years most of the cotton mills had closed, and the town concentrated on wool textiles and the flax industry.

Paley himself was principally a property speculator. Between 1787 and 1803 he built over 150 small working-class dwellings mainly in the Quarry Hill and Marsh Lane areas. He also had interests in iron-founding, potash manu-facture and soap-boiling, as well as his two cotton mills in the notorious Bank area of the town. His wide-ranging commitments led to his downfall, however. Going famously bankrupt in 1803, he was seen as a warning to future Leeds entrepreneurs, a warning that influenced the local housing market for the next twenty years.

But if Paley was a failure, Benjamin Gott was not. By the time he died in 1840 he was a multi-millionaire in today's terms and a highly respected member of the community, a passionate Anglican and Tory, and a man who was elected mayor in 1799. In 1780 he joined the firm of woollen merchants owned by Joseph Fountaine and John Wormald, and in 1785 was made a junior partner. Within six years both senior partners had died and Gott took over the running of the firm. In 1792 he developed a brilliant new concept, deciding to concen-trate all the processes of wool cloth manufacture under one roof – at a stroke revolutionising the wool textile industry. Gott built Park Mills on a 16-acre site close to both the river Aire and the newly built canal, at Bean Ing, to the west of the town. The mill was built round a huge quadrangle, with the scribbling and fulling mills on the south side, the mills that ground the dyestuffs to the front, three-storey spinning rooms to the west, and two-storey weaving shops on the east and west sides. Still remembered by older people was the 300ft long, four-storeyed front that ran along what became Wellington Street. Here the finishing processes were carried out. As indication of its enormity, the build-ings were insured for £18,000, while Edwin Lascelles paid out only £12,000 to insure his palatial Harewood House.

By 1797 Gott's workforce had reached over 1,200 and he was one of the largest employers in the country. Not all the people who worked in the complex were employed by him, as he let out part of the mills to five other manufacturers, who paid him a percentage for using his machinery; Gott then bought the cloth

Benjamin Gott's Armley House. Originally built as a villa in about 1781, Gott commissioned Robert Smirke to remodel the house in a Grecian style. The work was completed in 1822.

they produced. He added to his empire by acquiring Armley Mills (now the Industrial Museum) in 1800, and then Burley Mills. His superfine cloths were in great demand but Gott also made blankets and uniforms, a demand that was unending during the wars with Revolutionary France.[5]

There were other wool textile manufacturers in the town who, though not as successful as Gott, nevertheless contributed to the local industry and provided much-needed work. For example, James Walker employed over 100 people in his small factory in Wortley.

Other industries blossomed as well. Some, like coal-mining and quarrying, had long been pursued in the area, but in 1770 John and Joshua Green and Richard Humble established the Leeds Pottery. Their most popular line was creamware, with its pierced decoration, and when William Hartley joined them in 1781 his business acumen and design flair saw Hartley, Greens & Co., as the firm became known, gain an international reputation. Meanwhile in 1779 the Butler family took over Kirkstall Forge and laid the foundations of a company which would earn an international reputation.

As trade and industry prospered in the town the need for a reliable and effective banking system became apparent. The Lodge & Arthington Bank had been established in 1758 and was flourishing. Joined by Thomas Broadbent and then in 1770 by John Beckett, it was more popularly known as the Leeds Bank, until in 1777 a second bank was opened. This was known as Leeds New Bank; not surprisingly the original institution was redesignated the Old Bank, though later it was generally referred to as Beckett's Bank. Wickham, Field, Cleaver & Greenwood's, the New Bank, was operating from Briggate by 1798, but it eventually failed in 1827. In April 1792 a third bank began operations in the town. Fenton, Scott, Binns, Nicholson and Smith Bankers eventually foundered in 1812.[6]

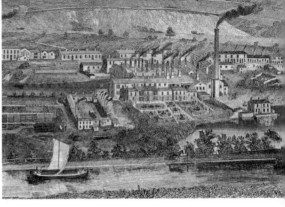

Kirkstall Forge. A forge certainly existed on the site *c.*1600 and during the seventeenth century came under the ownership of the Savile family. In 1779 the Butler family took it over and the works prospered. By the nineteenth century it was producing some of the finest axles in the world.

As the town grew and its business community expanded many came to rely on the banks to support their enterprises. The *Leeds Directory for the Year 1798* published by Griffith Wright, the owner of the *Leeds Intelligencer,* gives a graphic account of the variety of trades in the town by the end of the eighteenth century. Apart from professionals such as clergy, attorneys, surgeons, druggists and apothecaries, there are listed in Briggate alone a grocer, chandler, milliner, stuff merchant (dealer in wool textiles), whitesmith, gardener and seedsman, sadler, brazier (brass-worker), merchant, bookseller, printer, linen draper, shoemaker, glazier, tailor, flax-dresser, as well as several inn-keepers.

But wool textiles was always the main source of Leeds's wealth, and to this end a new White Cloth Hall was built between Kirkgate and the Calls. It opened on 17 October 1775. It was vast: quadrangular in design and costing £4,300, it was 99yds long, 70yds wide and contained 1,213 stalls.[7] Its immense open yard was used at times for public meetings, and on 4 December 1786 it witnessed a unique event in the history of the town. The famous Vincenzo Lunardi, the so-called 'Dare Devil Aeronaut', took off in a hydrogen balloon and flew as far as Thorp Arch. It was the first ever flight from Leeds.

Other famous people visited the town. The King of Denmark came to view the local textile industry in 1768, as did the Russian ambassador in September 1773. One less than welcome visitor was George Claus of Aix-la-Chapelle, who arrived in Leeds in January 1781. His sole objective was to enlist the help of a Hunslet clothier in order to steal the plans of a scribbling machine being operated at Armley. He was arrested, released on bail with sureties of £650, but disappeared before being brought to justice.[8]

In 1777 a new Assembly Rooms building was opened at the northern end of the White Cloth Hall. Elegantly furnished, it catered for the higher echelons of society, offering balls, card evenings and a variety of functions. Its admission charges – a guinea for one gentleman and two ladies – were prohibitive to the lower orders. The evening of Monday 9 June 1777 saw the building officially opened when Sir George Savile led Lady Effingham in a minuet. The

Leeds Mercury reflected that 'The appearance of Ladies and Gentlemen on the occasion was more brilliant than ever remembered.'[9] It was a sign of the times. Society in Leeds was beginning to fragment. In previous centuries the middling classes and labouring classes had lived adjacent to each other, but now they went their separate ways. The working classes remained in the old and more derelict parts of the east end of the town off Kirkgate and on the Bank; the middle classes moved into the newer developments to the west. Here the building of the Park Estate owned by the Wilson family typified the social changes. There a series of new sites were erected: Park Row (from 1770), South Parade (from 1776), East Parade (from 1779) and Park Place and Park Square (from 1788). Park Place was the most exclusive, offering unrestricted views southwards across open fields as far as the river.

The century was famed for revolutionary technological and political change but it also became known as the Age of Enlightenment. Science, Literature and the Arts caught the imagination of the middle classes. Unable to own the mag-

The White Cloth Hall between Kirkgate and the Calls. A huge building in its day, it opened in October 1775 for the sale of undyed cloths. From its yard balloon ascents were made in the early nineteenth century. The extension of the Leeds North-Eastern Railway between 1863 and 1869 severely truncated the site. The part of the building seen here still stands.

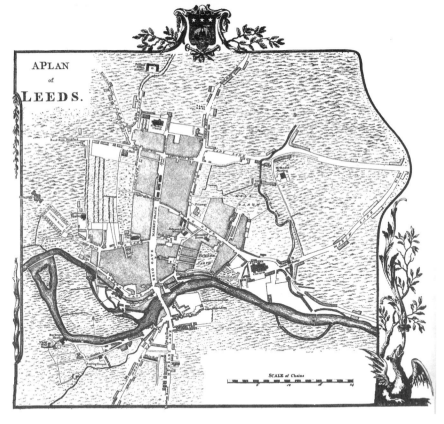

Thomas Jeffreys' *A Plan of Leeds in 1771* clearly shows the extent of undeveloped land there was about the town at the time.

nificent libraries that adorned Irwin's Temple Newsam or Lascelles's Harewood House, meetings were held in two Briggate inns, the Old and New King's Arms, to discuss the possibility of setting up a library in the town. On 1 November 1768 a group of 104 people gathered at Kirkgate-end at 'the sign of the Dial' in a room above Joseph Ogle's bookshop. There they founded the Leeds Library.

Ogle became its first librarian, while one the prime movers behind the scheme, Joseph Priestley the minister from Mill Hill chapel, became its first secretary. Ogle died in 1774 and his daughter, Mary, took over. Seven years later, in 1781, the library moved to new premises in Kirkgate into a building which later became the Rotation Office. Mary remained in office until 1813 but the library went on from strength to strength. In July 1808 it had moved to Commercial Street, where it still remains, the oldest surviving example in the British Isles of a 'proprietary subscription library' – a library created, owned and run by its members.[10]

To offer a further stimulation to intellectual activity between 1783 and 1786 a small philosophical society was formed in the town, and in 1793 the equally small Reasoning Society was set up to discuss literary and moral issues. Musical concerts featuring Handel, Vivaldi, Bach and Haydn were performed, with many being held in the new Music Hall in Albion Street. Opened in January 1794, it offered lectures and other events in addition to concerts, and was capable of seating 850 people, most of whom were of the middle class.

The wealthiest of the local families was undoubtedly the Ingrams, the owners of the rambling estate and impressive mansion of Temple Newsam, the 'Hampton Court of the North', some 4 miles to the east of Leeds. Elevated to the peerage as the Viscounts Irwin, the family exercised considerable influence in the town. They had also, by the end of the century, imposed several long-lasting changes to the great house and grounds, changes still to be seen today. In the 1760s Capability Brown was employed to redesign the 1,500 acres of parkland, woods and farmland at a cost of £2,000, while in 1788 the famous stone balustrade running round the house was replaced by an iron one. Then in 1796 Frances Shepherd, the Viscountess Irwin, had a major revamping of the south wing carried out. It is symptomatic of the life expectancy of the times that Henry the 7th Viscount was the first holder of the title to have reached fifty when he died in 1761.

The largest, most opulent and most impressive of the buildings in the town itself was Denison Hall. It was built in 1786 by John Wilkinson Denison, one of Leeds's wealthiest and most successful merchants. Designed by William Lindley of Doncaster, a pupil of John Carr, it was erected in just 101 days. Three storeys high with bow fronted windows and extensive grounds, it seemed a desirable residence. Denison, however, soon tired of it and left Leeds, but the property proved difficult to sell. It was said to be 'too large for a man of moderate fortune and too near the town to be relished by the country gentleman'. Today the 'grandest house in central Leeds', according to the blue plaque on its walls, has been converted into prestigious apartments.

Founded in 1768, the Leeds Library moved to Thomas Johnson's new Neo-Grecian building on Commercial Street in 1808. It is still there.

Denison Hall had been built to the west of the town, where the middle classes were establishing themselves away from the squalid squares and narrow insanitary yards that ran off Kirkgate and sprawled across The Bank, Quarry Hill and Marsh Lane; areas where the so-called 'operative classes' lived. Building speculators like Richard Paley erected cheap housing here; one-room cottages and two-roomed back-to-backs. After 1788 some groups clubbed together to form temporary building clubs and set about erecting back-to-backs on Union Street, George Street and Ebenezer Street.[11]

If the classes were beginning to live separately and enjoy different social pursuits, one place that brought the middle class and the poorer members of society together was the theatre. Troupes of players had regularly visited Leeds, performing at a variety of venues across the town, but in the eyes of many the theatre was an immoral place. In 1722 Ralph Thoresby bemoaned the fact that a company of players had arrived in Leeds and for six to eight weeks 'has seduced many'. But if some disapproved of the stage many others enjoyed the performances of the strolling players who arrived and entertained from an improvised platform at the Talbot Inn in Briggate and then in the concert room at the Rose and Crown Inn. By 1760 the White Swan offered a singing room; a venue that eventually would become the City Varieties, a theatre still in use today. On 17 December 1767 an additional venue opened its doors on Vicar Lane, and the New Concert Room also began offering performances. In 1771 Tate Wilkinson opened the Leeds Theatre, sometimes known as the Theatre Royal, on Hunslet Lane. Finally Leeds had its own true theatre. It was an event that led John Wesley to lament, 'I see you have a wicked play-house in Leeds.' The performers were Wilkinson's Yorkshire Circuit, who spent the winter performing in York, played Doncaster during race week and also visited Wakefield and Pontefract. In summer Leeds was their base. On 24 July 1771 the curtain rose for the first time when Wilkinson staged *A Word to the Wise*, a comedy by the Irish writer Hugh Kelly. Over the years the programmes he presented were varied, ranging from Shakespeare and Marlowe, operas and dramas, to outright comedies. Some performances were highly topical. In 1797, for example, the newly written opera *Bantry Bay* was performed to celebrate the failed French invasion of Ireland the previous year.

Among the great actors who performed there in the eighteenth century was the highly respected and accomplished John Philip Kemble, but undoubtedly the most famous actress to entertain Leeds audiences was Kemble's elder sister, Sarah Siddons. Considered by many the greatest tragedienne of the eighteenth century, she was heralded for her performance at Hunslet Lane in June 1789

when she played the heroine in *The Tragedy of Jane Shore*. A similar success followed in 1796, when she was cast in the title role of the tragedy *Isabella or the Fatal Marriage*.[12]

Wilkinson himself was no mean performer, but he was considered a better mimic than an actor. In 1795 he committed his theatrical memoirs to paper. It was an invaluable record of the theatre in Yorkshire but, as he commented, 'Had I but held my pen half as well as I have held my bottle, what a hand I should have wrote by this time'!

Another place the two classes could meet were at the races regularly held on Chapeltown Moor, at the equally popular foot races and at local cricket matches. In 1776 the bachelors of Leeds played the married men of the town for a stake of 5*gns* and won by six wickets. Cockfighting was still popular across the social divide, as was boxing. In Holbeck in January 1780 Lucas of Mabgate was engaged in a 'severe battle' with an Irish cropper for a prize of 2*gns* before battering him into submission.

For the most part, though, the wealthier members of Leeds society and the lower orders led significantly different lives. For the gentry, balls at the new Assembly Rooms and card and dancing assemblies were regularly enjoyed. The *Leeds Intelligencer* graphically caught the mood of the Yorkshire Archers ball held in 1790:

> The company consisted of 200 ladies and gentlemen of the first rank and fashion in the county. The Ladies appeared in white with, green ornaments, and afforded the greatest display of taste and elegance. The ball was opened at nine o'clock by a minuet danced by the Earl Fitzwilliam and the countess of Mexborough ... the effect of the festoons of coloured lamps was particularly pleasing. Dancing continued till three o'clock in the morning.

But whereas the higher orders of society frequented the more select inns and coffee houses, indulged in a game of billiards at Richard Taylor's coffee house, or played bowls on his greens at the bottom of Lands Lane, the lower ranks frequented the poorer inns and alehouses. Gambling was inevitable, and in 1757 led the magistrates to issue a warning to publicans:

> Publicans permitting Journeymen, Labourers, Servants, or Apprentices to play at Cards, Dice, Shuffleboards, Mississippi, or Billiard Tables, Skittles, Ninepins or any other Implements of Gaming in their Houses shall forfeit 40*s* for the first offence,

The Bull and Mouth Inn, Briggate. Originally known as the Old Red Bear, claims have been made that it was the town house of Lady Elizabeth Hastings. From 1800 it became one of the busiest coaching inns. It maintained thirty horses in its cellar stables.

for every subsequent offence £10, to be levied by distress & sale; a quarter to the Informer, the rest to the Poor.

The Leeds fairs, too, were a source of popular entertainment, but they frequently degenerated into a 'season for dissipation and debauchery'. The June fair was held for the sale of horses and November's for the sale of horned cattle. It was also at the latter fair that young men and women arrived in the town looking to be hired as servants, principally by farmers. Isaac Tyson, a local schoolmaster, viewed the carryings on and left behind a vivid description in verse of what he saw: 'Pretty Pollies, Jacks and Jennies, Swindlers cheating simple nannies ... Doxies dizzy, drunkards reeling ... Town bloods dem-ming, blustering puffing, Homespun Johnnies rudely cuffing'. He ends:

Pockets empty, bills unpaid, and
Rogues at dead of night afraid, and
Many a bargain – if you strike it –
This is Leeds Fair how d'ye like it?[13]

The fairs should not be confused with the annual local feasts – they were never known as fairs in Leeds – and which were held on the moors at Woodhouse, Armley, Holbeck and Hunslet. They always attracted vast crowds on a particular date each year. Armley was always – and still is – held on the first Saturday in September.

It was an age of sophistication and intellectual advancement; it was an age of harsh poverty and brutal criminality. Conscious of the need to improve the situation, a movement developed nationally. By 1787 William Wilberforce was one of its leading proponents. In Leeds, William Hey, one of the town's most respected citizens and its principal surgeon, was equally concerned about the laxity of morals in the town. Wilberforce wrote to him agreeing that something had to be done, and stressed that the cause 'is of the utmost consequence and worthy of the labours of a whole life'.[14] Hey then organised a society to combat immoral behaviour and 'the crime of drunkenness and its never failing concomitants, Sabbath breaking and lewdness'.

Inevitably drink contributed to the high crime rate that existed in the late eighteenth century. To combat the high crime rate punishments were severe: in 1774 Leeds magistrates ordered Elizabeth Winterburn to be stripped naked to her waist and 'privately whipt 'til her body be Bloody'. By the end of the century over 200 crimes could be punished by hanging, but many found guilty had their sentences commuted. Even so Thomas Stearman and John Lucas were convicted for burglary in Leeds and executed in 1792.

Despite such draconian punishments, crime was rampant to the point that the council applied to the government for an Improvement Act, which was granted in 1755. It was for 'Enlightening the Streets and Lanes, and Regulating the Pavements in the Town' in order to 'prevent many mischiefs which might happen as well from Fires, as Burglaries, Robberies and other Outrages and Disorders'. Among those outrages were thefts of cloth from the tenter frames, which still occurred on a regular basis. Prostitution, too, was an ever-present social problem. Vandalism, such as the deliberate destruction of 10yds of parapet of Leeds Bridge, and general theft, such as the stealing of hounds from the kennels of the Leeds Hunt, were commonplace. Isaac Tyson's poem identified the 'Swindlers cheating simple nannies', and the most infamous of such swindlers in eighteenth-century Leeds were the Clay Lads, confidence tricksters who specialised in crimes involving textiles. All were crimes frequently brought to the attention of the authorities.

Fortunately duelling was less so, and there are few reports of such events in the town. In 1775 two officers fought a duel at Kirkstall Abbey, though fortunately neither died. Nor indeed did anyone perish in the duel fought by two master breeches-makers near the bowling green in Lands Lane in 1803, which is hardly surprising – the seconds had only charged the pistols with powder!

By 1798 the responsibility of enforcing the law rested initially on the shoulders of the Chief Constable, John Fish, and his nine assistants. Each officer was responsible for a particular division of the town. The magistrates, sitting in rotation in their meeting place in Kirkgate – hence its name, the Rotation Office – issued warrants and examined people accused of offences with a view to committing them to trial. The building was also used for public meetings.

There were two broad approaches to improving the situation in society about which Hey and his fellow citizens were so concerned. One was education, which was seen as partly the answer. For the children of the middle classes adequate provision was made. Apart from the long-established Leeds Grammar School smaller grammar schools followed. The early lead had been given by Wortley in 1677, and during the eighteenth century Holbeck, Beeston, Chapeltown and Woodhouse followed suit. Private schools were also opened, among them Mr Castiglione's, which offered French and Italian classes, Jane Stock and Elizabeth Caulston's boarding school for young ladies near the vicarage and Mr Mills's writing school in Briggate. One of the most successful schools, Joseph Tathams' Quaker boarding school, opened in 1756, using the meeting house on Water Lane. For working-class children the Blue Coat School at the workhouse provided some with a rudimentary education, and by the end of the century girls were offered training in domestic service at the School of Industry in Beezon's Yard off Briggate. The Church of England also played its part by setting up the Parochial Sunday School Society in 1788, and by 1791 it claimed that 1,614 scholars were attending its seventeen schools. The Nonconformists, too, made provision, for they felt they had a vital role to play in the town.

But if the Established Church took some steps to alleviate social problems through its Sunday Schools, its ministers generally continued to fail to inspire its parishioners. St Paul's church was opened in Park Square in 1793 to cater for the inhabitants of the new development; the Albion chapel with its 'extremely commodious' interior was opened in 1796; and Zion chapel, opened in 1794, was taken over from the Countess of Huntingdon's Connexion and renamed St James's church. But it was left more to the Nonconformists and the passions of John Wesley and his followers to stimulate religious fervour in the town.

Several Nonconformist chapels already existed in Leeds when the Methodists opened the old chapel in Boggard Close in 1771. In 1779 the Baptists hired the old Assembly Rooms in Kirkgate, holding their baptisms in the river Aire itself. In 1780 they opened the Stone chapel, followed, in 1787, by Ebenezer chapel. That same year the Countess of Huntingdon's Connexion rented the newly built Bell chapel at Wortley. Then in 1794 the Roman Catholics in the town opened St Mary's chapel, appropriately on Lady Lane, the site of the medieval chantry chapel. It was the first Catholic church to be built in Leeds since the Reformation. Two years later a new Catholic chapel opened in Hunslet.

Of all the preachers in the town during the second half of the century, one man stood out not simply as a man of the cloth but as a scientist and political

philosopher. Joseph Priestley was a local man, born at Birstall. He was educated at Batley Grammar School and became a Presbyterian minister. In 1765 he happened to meet Benjamin Franklin while on a visit to London, and the American launched Priestley's interest in science. The following year he was appointed minister at Mill Hill chapel, and while there he influenced the congregation in a way that saw them becoming more in tune with Unitarianism, the belief that rejects the doctrine of the Trinity but accepts the unity of God.

In 1768 Priestley was active in establishing the Leeds Library and was appointed its first secretary. He lodged for a time on Meadow Lane, next to Jacques & Nells's Brewery. Fascinated by the gases created by the fermentation process in brewing, in 1772 he published a paper, *Impregnating Water with Fixed Air*, a work that in effect created the first carbonated drink. He left Leeds in 1773, and the following year published his discovery of oxygen, for which he is best remembered.

After he moved to Birmingham, Priestley's radical views saw a mob attack his home in 1791, and he eventually left the country for the United States. Those radical views, in which he supported the American and French Revolutions, were not restricted to the intellectuals of the day. Across society radical opinions were expressed, as poverty and political injustice galvanised groups to demand change.

Parliamentary reform was one area where people were to some extent united across the social divide. Leeds followed the national trend. The middle classes in the town, particularly Whig Party supporters, felt that a limited extension of the vote should be granted, whereas the Leeds working class and the Radicals wanted universal male suffrage. The Tory Party and the *Leeds Intelligencer* were bitterly opposed to any change, viewing with horror the bloody events of the French Revolution, which cast a pall of fear across the land. They feared that tinkering with the established constitution could lead to revolution in Britain.

In the 1790s the Radicals formed corresponding societies across the country, enabling their members to communicate with each other. The authorities considered them seditious. When the Bramley Corresponding Society contacted the famous London Corresponding Society, the *Intelligencer* railed that the magistrates in the town should act.

Aggravating the political tensions in society was the eternal problem of poverty. In 1797 the Strangers' Benevolent Society in Leeds reported on the condition of many in the town. 'Cellars, Garrets and such like Places, exhibit … abodes of human Misery, the wretched Inhabitants are frequently found either exerting the last Efforts of Nature to support themselves … or languishing under

Mill Hill chapel, initially Presbyterian, became Unitarian under the influence of Joseph Priestley. The original building seen here was modernised in the eighteenth century and was finally replaced in 1847.

Chapels proliferated across Leeds. This Wesleyan Methodist church built in 1797 became known as Farnley Hill Methodist chapel in 1932. It is a listed building.

Salem chapel. This Grade II listed building was opened in 1792 by the Independents, later Congregationalists. In 1839 its congregation was 1,200 but by then most of the worshippers lived north of the river and they moved to a new chapel on East Parade in 1841. The building was then taken over by the Independents from Bethel chapel, George Street.

the most powerful Influence of complicated Disease.' The corporation struggled to cope with the needs of a growing population as the township reached 30,000 souls and the out-townships a further 23,000. Exacerbating these problems were poor harvests, which sent the price of food soaring. The winter of 1794–95 was particularly severe, and the magistrates, fearing the worst, met at the Rotation Office to discuss what steps could be taken to help the needy, but also to 'prevent them tumultuously assembling'. As the problem continued, to the end of the century, a soup kitchen was opened and benefit clubs such as the Hunslet Humane Society and the Strangers' Benevolent Society were formed. Wealthy manufacturers like Benjamin Gott, John Marshall, firms like Fenton's and Murray and Wood's, and wealthy landowners, like Earl Cowper and Earl Cardigan, all made charitable contributions.

But as the price of corn soared some dealers, like Sowden at Leeds Mill and Sarah Stephenson, another local miller, were investigated for inflating the price of corn. Dealers were so unpopular that they had to be given protection. Miners at Middleton struck. Rioters in Beeston and Holbeck attacked Johnson's mill. The Home Secretary, the Duke of Portland, was so concerned that he wrote to the Leeds mayor for a detailed report on the violence.

The reputation of the town was not helped when the *Evening Mail* claimed that Grey, one of the mutineers at the Nore, had come from Leeds, that 'hot bed of sedition'. Seditious papers and pamphlets were circulated in the town, and the radical writings of Tom Paine were to be found in the homes of many Leeds cloth-dressers.[15] Adding to this were the demands that the war with Revolutionary France made on the nation and the effects it had on the town. As trade was disrupted unemployment added to local woes.

There were, however, moments of celebration. In May 1795 some 60,000 spectators turned up to see the Leeds Volunteers and other corps from West Riding engage in manoeuvres on Chapeltown Moor.[16] In 1797 feeling was so jubilant that Fleet Street was renamed Duncan Street following Admiral Duncan's naval victory at Camperdown. The following year, when news of Nelson's triumph at Aboukir Bay reached Leeds, a great illumination as held.

A new century dawned. Britain stood at a watershed as the old agricultural economy gave way to the emerging industrial one, and the rural way of life was replaced by an urban one. It was to be a century of dramatic social upheaval. But how would Leeds react to the turbulent years that lay ahead?

Kirkstall Abbey had a small infirmary built sometime after 1152 and a small Benedictine hospital was opened in Beeston *c.* 1233. By *c.*1500 a hospital was operating in Kirkgate, but as the population of the town expanded during the eighteenth century the need for a new purpose-built building was becoming more and more apparent. In June 1767 a meeting was called at the New Inn to consider provision 'for the Relief of the Sick and Hurt Poor within this Parish,' but rather than catering simply for the people of Leeds and the out-townships it was decided it would be a general infirmary. It was to be a charity, and the sixteen men gathered at that meeting initially offered £352 10s 6d to start the project. By October temporary premises had been found in a property in Kirkgate owned by Andrew Wilson. The Infirmary was to be maintained by public subscriptions; collections from local churches were donated; many people made annual subscriptions; and even fines for non-attendance at drill sessions of the Leeds Volunteers were added to the coffers.

One of the leading supporters of the move was William Hey, a local surgeon who would go on to achieve a national reputation in surgery and who, in 1773, became the hospital's senior surgeon. For forty-five years he served the Infirmary and was active politically in the town, being elected mayor twice, in 1787 and 1802, and publishing extensive medical works. He was elected FRS in 1775 on the recommendation on his friend Joseph Priestley. And all this was achieved despite the fact that he had been blinded in one eye as a four-year-old and was so crippled that from his early forties he was forced to walk with a crutch.

In March a new purpose-built hospital designed by John Carr was opened in 1771 on what became, appropriately, Infirmary Street. It offered just twenty-seven beds. To the *Intelligencer* it was 'dedicated to Christian charity', while to John Howard, the penal reformer, it was 'one of the best [hospitals] in the kingdom'. Extensions to the building followed and soon 108 patients were being catered for. By the 1860s, however, the building had grown old, and it was felt that a new one was required to meet the needs of the modern world. On 19 May 1868 Sir George Gilbert Scott's new building was opened on Great George Street.

Through the twentieth century the hospital grew both in size and stature, and today the General Infirmary at Leeds ranks among the leading hospitals in Europe, providing many general acute hospital services and a specialist regional centre for a number of complex conditions.

The Old Infirmary was founded in 1767 but moved to a new building on Infirmary Street in March 1771. It remained here until 1868. For a time it was used as the Reference Library and Central Library.

eight

A TOWN DIVIDED

I t is easy for historians today to view the dawn of the nineteenth century as a time that heralded great opportunities for the country. Throughout the century industries would develop, education would be brought to the masses, major breakthroughs would occur in medicine and Britain would eventually boast an empire on which the sun never set. But during the opening years of the new century what caught the attention of the men and women of Leeds going about their daily business? They talked of the war with Napoleonic France and the price of food. They talked of the mundane reports that appeared in the columns of the *Leeds Mercury* and the *Leeds Intelligencer*. There were sad events recorded: in July 1800, for example, the body of a young servant girl, Sarah Furnish, was hauled from the river by the steps of the great bridge. She was found to have been pregnant. There were scandals revealed: in May 1804 a man sold his wife for 5*gns* at the market cross in Briggate, according to the *Mercury*, to a 'man acquainted with her merits'. Reports in 1802 appeared on dangerous driving in the town and a suggestion made for building a railway – horse-drawn – from Leeds to Selby; complaints were reported in 1805 of vandals smashing windows in Park Row, of the state of the roads in the town and how Leeds needed a new Town Hall, a new library, a new prison and a public baths.[1]

By now the *Leeds Mercury* had a new owner. Edward Baines had bought the paper, and on 7 March 1801 the first edition he edited came out. In the next half century he would make that Leeds newspaper the voice of the Whigs and Nonconformists, and turn it into the most influential provincial newspaper in the country. He reported in November 1801 how a virulent fever epidemic was sweeping through the town and described the horrific scenes he saw: a family of thirteen with nine of its members felled; six adults sharing two forlorn beds covered only in rags, with the dead and dying lying together. Leeds General Infirmary did not cater for people suffering from infectious diseases, so Baines

The first edition of the *Leeds Mercury* published by Edward Baines in March 1801. The high price of 6*d* was due to the government tax. Note the stamp on the top right. The *Mercury* would become the most influential provincial paper in the first half of the nineteenth century.

supported the proposal to establish a House of Recovery in the town. The situation was dire. 'Numbers of the poor, have been obliged to dispose of their cloaths to buy food', he reported.[2]

There was, however, a short period of relief for the troubled townsfolk. In October 1802 a peace treaty with France was announced. The Leeds Volunteers were stood down and Leeds celebrated. A magnificent illumination literally lit up the town, sheep were roasted whole and the mutton was washed down with 'copious libations of brown stout'. But the Peace of Amiens was not to last. In May 1803 the British Government declared war on France. A meeting was held in the Rotation Office and it was decided to re-form the Leeds Volunteers. Just twenty men turned up, and the *Mercury* thundered that 'Leeds is within an ace of being eternally disgraced by its apathy.' It need not have worried. The following week 1,000 men pledged their support. They were formed into two battalions of infantry under Colonel Lloyd and two troops of Gentlemen Volunteer Cavalry under Captain Rhodes. Their uniforms and equipment were paid for by the people of the town; their arms by the government. The Quakers, being pacifists, donated £1,400 to Leeds Infirmary instead.[3] High on Seacroft Moor a beacon was erected to warn the town should France invade. In the event it did not. In August 1805 Napoleon moved his Army of England from the coast to embark on his conquests of eastern Europe, and in October Nelson ensured that Britain ruled the waves with his famous victory at Trafalgar. The nation was grateful, and the people of Leeds showed that gratitude in November when they attended Maillardet's exhibition of automata at the Music Hall in Albion Street. The evening's proceeds went to support the widows and orphans of those who had fallen in the battle.

If the threat of invasion came to an end, the year 1805 saw a conflict begin in the town that would drag on for years. A young Griffith Wright Jnr, grandson of the founder of the *Leeds Intelligencer*, succeeded his father Thomas as editor. Thomas had turned the *Intelligencer* into the most powerful Tory voice in Yorkshire; now his son, an equally passionate Tory and Anglican, would wage war on the Whig and Nonconformist Baines and his *Mercury*. Both resorted to personal invective and bitter accusations as week after week they fired their deeply entrenched and vitriolic partisan editorial salvos at each other. On the subject of the war they were as far apart as they could possibly be. Once the threat of invasion had disappeared Baines spoke for those in the town suffering immeasurably as a result of the conflict. The restrictions on exports that were created by the war with France, and later the war with the United States, devastated local trade. Unemployment was rampant, and thus as early as 1807 a petition for peace was signed by 28,628 Leeds people with the *Mercury*'s full backing. The *Intelligencer*, ever suspicious of Napoleon, took the opposite view. 'Our only hope of safety … is in war', it warned.

There were a few moments of diversion for the anxious townsfolk. One was the celebrated murder case involving the infamous 'Yorkshire Witch' Mary Bateman. This Leeds confidence trickster, who told fortunes to gullible young women and eventually resorted to poisoning her victims, was hanged at York in 1809. Such was her influence that 2,000 Leeds folk paid 3*d* each to gaze on her corpse in the surgeon's room at the Infirmary, and when William Hey dissected her body in public he raised £80 14*s* 0*d* for the hospital.[4] Another memorable event occurred in October 1812 when Madame Tussaud brought 'her unrivalled collection of Grand European Figures to Briggate' – admission 1*s*, children half price.

A small number of children were fortunate enough to be catered for in the schools that

Mary Bateman (1768–1809) the celebrated Yorkshire Witch. Leeds confidence trickster and poisoner, she was hanged at York in 1809. Note the miraculous egg in her hand. For a charge she would get her hen to lay an egg with 'Christ is coming' written on it.

had opened in the previous century, but in 1811 a major step forward was made. In January a Lancasterian school was established in Leeds for boys, and later another for girls. These were non-denominational schools, and some criticism was voiced from the Nonconformists when the Church of England opened a mixed National School near Kirkgate.

But the opening of new schools, Mary Bateman and Madame Tussaud, however, were but momentary diversions. Unemployment and poverty were constant threats, exacerbated by the advent of new machinery which could at a stroke replace dozens of factory hands. Not surprisingly the threatened workmen took action. In 1811 Luddism raised its head in Nottingham, and by spring 1812 it was raging through the West Riding. The first outbreak of violence in Leeds occurred in January 1812, when demonstrators tried to set fire to Oates, Wood and Smithson's mill. In April a contingent from the town went to join the ill-fated Luddite attack on Rawfolds mill, but on hearing gunfire, discretion rather than valour ensued, and the Leeds group withdrew before reaching their destination.[5] Further disturbances took place in the town: Dickenson, Carr and Shann's mill on Water Lane saw £500-worth of cloth destroyed; Shackleton's corn mill in Holbeck was attacked; while in August a major demonstration erupted outside the King's Mill, and a woman styling herself Lady Ludd led a corn riot in Briggate. Charles Brown, the mayor, wrote that the 'lower class

Commercial Street seen in the early years of the twentieth century. The street was developed from c.1806. Note the Salvation Army Insurance Company offices on the left and the Irish Linen Company on the right. The street is now a pedestrianised precinct.

of people' were 'v. agitated at present'.[6] To contain the situation the West Kent Militia and the Scots and Queen's Greys were garrisoned on Park Lane; even so, Benjamin Gott employed armed guards to protect his home at Armley.[7]

In 1815, for a brief moment, the nation could breathe a sigh of relief. The wars with France and the United States were finally over, but the demobilisation of between 300,000 and 400,000 men, a series of bad harvests and the impact of new machinery once again created massive problems of unemployment and suffering across the nation. Thomas Nicholson of Roundhay offered a temporary solution locally. Developing his new estate, he employed ex-servicemen to dig out a lake. Appropriately enough the result of their labours is still called Waterloo Lake.

For a long-term solution, though, many felt the answer lay in a reform of Parliament. What nonsense, it was argued, that places like Old Sarum, now no more than a field and an earthwork, still returned two MPs, while the towns of Leeds, Manchester and Birmingham had none. Through the following years mass meetings were held in the town. In 1819 as many as 10,000 gathered on Hunslet Moor demanding change. The middle classes and the Radicals were divided over whether such reform should give every man the vote or whether it should be restricted to the middle class. One thing that united many people of all classes, however, was the fact that every rate-payer had to contribute to paying for the parish church, whether they were Anglicans or not. Naturally Nonconformists, Roman Catholics and even some Anglicans, like those at Wortley who had to pay for the upkeep of their own chapel in the township, resented this payment. But at least all rate-payers had the right to attend the vestry meetings and have their say there. Here decisions regarding the church building were made, and among other responsibilities the vestry was responsible for the running of the workhouse. The Whigs and Nonconformists realised that though the council was dominated by the Tories and Anglicans they could strive to gain control in the vestry. Thus began a protracted battle in the town that dragged on for years, with the Whigs finally triumphant.[8]

But politics was only part of what was going on in Leeds. In the twenty years that followed the end of the war major changes took place in the town that cut across the political divide. Middleton Railway began operating its steam engines in 1812. In 1816 the Leeds and Liverpool Canal finally opened. On 14 February 1818 the Leeds Skyrack and Morley Savings Bank began to provide 'for the safe Custody and Increase of Small Savings Belonging to the Labouring and Industrious'.

George Walkers' picture of the Middleton Railway engine working in 1812 is the earliest known painting of a working steam locomotive. Compare it with the famous 1829 print where the artist has distorted the height of the chimney and added an additional one!

The following year the Leeds Philosophical and Literary Society was founded. Di Vernon wrote to the *Mercury* urging the new organisation to admit women. It rejected her plea. That same year, as threats of civil disturbances over parliamentary reform hung over the country, the government saw fit to establish a permanent military presence in the town and opened a cavalry barracks on what is now Barrack Road.

The 1820s was an active period in the town. A public baths opened on Wellington Street in 1820 and in 1824, with support from members of the Philosophical and Literary Society, a Mechanics' Institute was formed to provide educational opportunities for the working classes. In 1826 John Marshall proposed that a university should also be established in the town, but his suggestion fell on deaf ears.

Meantime, while Gott and Marshall, the great manufacturers, saw their businesses boom, others also made their mark in the town. Joshua Tetley launched his famous brewery company in 1822 when he bought Sykes's brewery, but in his first month of trading he failed to receive a single order. It was in Leeds in 1824 that Joseph Aspdin invented Portland cement, and in 1826 that Charles Turner Thackrah opened a private school of anatomy in South Parade. It was a forerunner of the Leeds Medical School, which would open on 6 June 1831.

For a time the town prospered, and changed its face. The Moot Hall, which had stood in Briggate for 200 years, was finally swept away, creating a broad and impressive thoroughfare. New buildings opened: the Courthouse (1813), the Bazaar and Shambles (1823–25), South Market (1823–24), Central Market

(1824–27), the Corn Exchange (1826–29), Commercial Buildings (1826–29) and the Free Market (1826–27).[9] Three more hospitals opened in the town in the same period: the Leeds Eye and Ear Hospital in 1821 and the Lying-In Hospital and the Public Dispensary, both in 1824.

The hall of the Leeds Philosophical and Literary Society. Founded in 1819 the society opened its hall on Park Row in 1821. It became the City Museum in 1921. In 1941 it suffered severe bomb damage during an air raid. The museum was closed in 1965 and the building demolished.

Another desperately needed institution also opened. For some time letters had appeared in the local press expressing concern about prostitution in the town, and in 1821 the Leeds Guardian Society was founded. It opened its 'commodious' asylum in St James's Street in July 1822 to help those 'desirous of abandoning their present abject and wretched condition'. There was no doubt that the opening of the barracks in the town in 1819 exacerbated the problem, as did the Leeds Races, held from 1824 to 1832 at Haigh Park. Over the race period there was an estimated annual influx into the town of some 100,000 people. Many were genuine spectators, but a fair percentage were prostitutes, pickpockets and gamblers. The races opened on 23 June 1824 with the first race, worth 100 sovereigns, witnessed by between 20,000 and 30,000. It was claimed that in some years between 30,000 and 40,000 watched the most valuable race for the Gold Tureen.

There were other diversions. Balloon ascents by aeronauts became a national pursuit in the 1820s, and thus in 1823 a committee was formed to invite an aeronaut to Leeds and demonstrate a flight from the town. On Thursday 4 September 1823 Charles Green took off from the yard of the White Cloth Hall at about 6.30 p.m. He flew over Garforth, Sherburn, passed north of Selby and finally landed at South Cliff near Market Weighton an hour and ten minutes later. The next day W.W. Sadler flew from the same destination and landed near Gainsborough. On 9 June 1825 Charles Green was back in Leeds to make his third flight from the town. He flew from the Coloured Cloth Hall Yard, this time taking with him a Miss Stocks as his passenger. It was the first time a woman had flown from the town. They landed near Askam Richard.[10]

If aeronauts showed the people of Leeds the way to the future, other pursuits in the town were relics of a barbaric past. Men paid 2*s* in Meadow Lane to watch Billy, a local dog, kill 100 rats in twelve minutes. At Beeston and in West Leeds they gathered to watch bull-baiting. However, by the early 1820s the last bull-baiting in the West Riding had taken place at Lower Wortley, known more pejoratively as Sodom because of the criminal activities and blood sports that went on there. But things were becoming more civilised. In October 1823 a Leeds man was prosecuted for beating a horse, the first such prosecution in the town – a result of the new law regarding cruelty to animals.

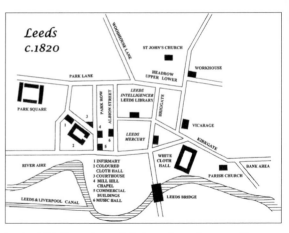

Leeds c.1820. Note what a relatively small area the town still covered. Even today central Leeds is very concentrated. Many of the places shown are still to be seen including Park Square, the Leeds Library, the White Cloth Hall and St John's church. Mill Hill chapel and the parish church were rebuilt on the same site.

By 1825 other issues were attracting the attention of the people of Leeds. In December the country was plunged into one of the worst banking crises it has ever faced, when irresponsible speculation in South America led to a number of bank failures. An urgent meeting was called at the Courthouse in Leeds at noon on Monday 12 December to form a committee devoted to diffusing panic in the town and expressing confidence in Leeds bank notes. That evening the Courthouse was packed again, this time the audience meeting to express its opposition to slavery and to call for its abolition in the British colonies.[11]

All these events were carefully recorded in the pages of the town's newspapers. The *Leeds Mercury* and the *Leeds Intelligencer* held sway for the first nineteen years of the century. True, the *Leeds Correspondent* appeared in 1814, but that was a bi-annual publication devoted to literary, mathematical and philosophical issues. On 1 January 1819 competition finally arrived when William Headley and George Mudie launched the *Leeds Independent and York County Advertiser*. Mudie soon left, and the newspaper was eventually absorbed into the *Intelligencer*. Two other short-lived ventures appeared. The *Leeds Gazette*, launched in 1820 and again by Mudie, proved another failure for him, and closed in 1822. The *Leeds Patriot* was also not destined to live long. Launched in 1824, it ceased publication in 1832. The following year a paper to challenge the *Mercury* and *Intelligencer* did appear. The *Leeds Times*, a

Central Market opened on Duncan Street in 1827. An impressive building, it was described as 'one of the principal ornaments of the town'. It burnt down in 1895.

Commercial Buildings were opened in 1829 and were the spiritual home of the Whig Party. When the council decided to widen Boar Lane in 1871 the building was demolished and the Royal Exchange Buildings built on the site.

A panoramic view late 1820s at the junction of Park Row on the right and Infirmary Street and the Coloured Cloth Hall. Behind that is the old Infirmary. Prominent right centre is the Courthouse and on the far right the Philosophical Hall.

The old Corn Exchange was at the junction of the Upper and Lower Headrows and Briggate. It opened in 1829 and was used until 1868. Note the statue of Queen Anne removed from the old Moot Hall when it was demolished in 1825.

radical journal, lasted until 1901 and boasted among its editors Samuel Smiles of *Self Help* fame. But until 1833 the *Intelligencer* and the *Mercury* dominated the market.

No issue divided the papers and the town more than that of rights for Roman Catholics. In 1828 the restrictions on Nonconformists were removed, and that year a campaign was launched to do the same for Catholics. Anti-Catholic Brunswick clubs were established across the country to oppose any such change in the law. Leeds was no exception, and anti-Catholic letters from such people as Richard Oastler and the Revd Patrick Brontë appeared in the *Intelligencer*, with one from 'Philanthropos' arguing that 'The Pope remains in Rome ... but the way is rapidly preparing for the transition of his throne to the British capital.' The *Mercury* thundered that the Brunswickers were 'lighting up the flame of religious hostility'; the *Intelligencer* accused the *Mercury* of 'wantonly inciting ... popular violence'. And violence did eventually break out in the town. On Friday 28 November 1828 a crowd of some 16,000 gathered in the yard of the Coloured Cloth Hall to support the Catholic claims. Another smaller crowd gathered outside the *Intelligencer*'s offices, and at 10 a.m. the demonstrators marched to the yard, bearing placards proclaiming 'Vote Against Popery'. John Marshall, now one of the MPs for Yorkshire, tried to chair the meeting and urged that there should be no violence. Both sets of supporters ignored him. Missiles were thrown, some people were injured and the meeting broke up in disorder.[12] Nevertheless the following year the law was changed, and in 1838 James Holdforth became the mayor of Leeds – the first Roman Catholic mayor in England since the Reformation.

In May 1832 a far greater threat than the pope setting up his throne in the English capital occurred when a major cholera epidemic swept the country and struck the town. Caused by contaminated food and polluted water, it was rampant in the poorer areas. The first to die in Leeds was Dock, the two-year-old son of an Irish family that lived in the appalling slum of Blue Bell Fold in the notorious Bank area. The disease reached its peak on 16 August, on which day twenty-one people succumbed. By November 702 had perished in the town. A cholera hospital was set up in St Peter's Square, but the inhabitants forced its removal to Saxton Lane. Robert Baker, the town's medical officer, highlighted the fact that it was in the poorer areas where the majority of cases occurred, and spent his life campaigning to improve conditions in Leeds. He recorded how massive overcrowding occurred in the filthy, ill-ventilated and squalid yards and folds of the town. In one instance he quoted the infamous Boot and

Shoe Yard off Kirkgate, which had thirty-four houses and contained 340 inhabitants. He went on to say that during the outbreak 'the commissioners removed in the days of the cholera, seventy-five cartloads of manure which had been untouched for years'.[13]

Yet even as this sickness raged across the nation – it was estimated 21,500 died in England and Wales – political fever gripped the country. The juggernaut of parliamentary reform had eventually reached its objective, with the Reform Bill finally passed. In December 1832 Leeds, which had been granted two Parliamentary seats, was all set to elect its MPs. The vote was given mainly to middle-class male voters who lived in the parish of Leeds, so those in Seacroft, Osmondthorpe and Coldcotes were excluded, not being part of the parish. The town was bitterly divided. Many Tories did not want reform, while Radicals and the working class were angry that only the middle class had been given the vote. To complicate matters further, Leeds-born Richard Oastler introduced into the election his campaign for a Ten Hour Bill to restrict the hours that children worked in the mills. As polling day drew near violence broke out in the town. Whig supporters, known as Orangeists, attacked Tories. Equally violent Tories, nicknamed Blue Bludgeon Men, retaliated against the Whigs. Nominations were to be made in the yard of the Coloured Cloth Hall. John Marshall Jnr, the

When the Reform Bill was rejected in 1832, Leeds campaigners met in the yard of the Coloured Cloth Hall to protest. Queen Adelaide was opposed to reform, hence the placard 'No petticoat government', the speech bubble 'Three groans for the Queen', and the female effigy on the stick.

flax manufacturer's son, and Thomas Babington Macaulay, the historian, were to stand for the Whigs, and Matthew Thomas Sadler, who sympathised with Oastler's views on factory reform, for the Tories.

On nomination day the Whigs gathered piecemeal in the yard. The Tories chose a more dramatic entrance: with flags flying, they marched four abreast from Briggate. One banner in particular attracted the most attention. Over 200ft long and containing 4,000 signatures, it showed a snowstorm and half-naked child workers dragging themselves wearily to Marshall's Water Lane mill. When the marchers arrived at their destination the offensive banner led to a riot. Tiles were hurled from the roof of the building and broken pieces of banner staffs were used for weapons as the Whigs sought to remove the standard and the Tories determined to keep it flying. Only when the mayor sent special constables in to separate the warring factions was peace restored and the Battle of the Standard finally terminated.

Votes were cast at a variety of polling stations. In Leeds itself the courthouse on Park Row, the Coloured Cloth Hall and the Grammar School were used. In Bramley, Headingley and Hunslet schools were employed, and at Chapel Allerton an empty house, while voters from Armley, Wortley and Farnley made their way to the Star public house on Tong Road. After two days' polling the two Whig candidates, Marshall and Macaulay, were triumphant.[14]

In 1835 the Municipal Reform Bill changed the structure of councils, allowing for the formation of the first proper police force in the town. It meant that Leeds was no longer a closed corporation. The Liberals – for by now the two parties were becoming known as the Liberal and Conservative parties – were swept to power, and held office in the town for the next half century. But that same year, in the general election, the parties shared the two Leeds seats. Sir John Beckett, the local banker, was successful for the Conservatives. Not only did he top the poll, but he was the first Conservative to win a seat for any of the newly enfranchised boroughs.

In 1837 another Conservative supporter arrived in the town: the new Vicar of Leeds. Dr Walter Farquhar Hook was horrified on his arrival to find out that many of the town's inhabitants showed little interest in religion, and those who did tended to be Nonconformists and in particular Methodists. Hook set out to change all that. A man of unbounded energy and imagination, he declared he would enable 'every poor man to have a pastor and every poor child a school'. In the coming years he saw twenty-seven church schools opened, and his Vicarage Act of 1844 enabled new parishes to be created and

new churches built in them. His own parish came to be looked on as a model parish, and his fame spread internationally.

Undoubtedly Hook's most popular contribution to Leeds was a new parish church. Shortly after he arrived it became obvious to him that the old, rambling building on Kirkgate was totally inadequate. Thus it was that Robert Chantrell was employed to design a new one. Chantrell, a local architect who had offices on Park Row, had already built Christ church in Meadow Lane (1825) and St Matthew's church in Holbeck (1829). An appeal was launched to raise £26,000 for the new building. The design followed that of the old medieval church, and although it gave the pulpit a prominent position it

Dr Walter Farquhar Hook (1793–1875), Vicar of Leeds 1837–59. Under his inspirational guidance the Anglican Church in the town received a tremendous stimulant. It was Hook who was responsible for building the new parish church.

also made the altar highly visible. Economy, however, was essential. The pew ends, apparently beautifully carved wood, are in fact iron frames enclosing panels of pine wood. The sculpted 'stone' arcading of the choir and the nave is moulded plaster. The vaulting over the crossing is wood and plaster, not stone. The overall effect is memorable, though, and the building deserves its Grade I listed status. Consecrated on 2 September 1841, it was the largest new church to be built in England since the opening of Christopher Wren's St Paul's cathedral. The church went on to gain a reputation for musical excellence under the influence of Hook and Dr Samuel Sebastian Wesley, who was the organist from 1842 to 1849.

One new church in Leeds, however, caused Hook concern. St Saviour's opened in Ellerby Road in 1845, built by Dr Edward Bouverie Pusey, one of the leading members of the Oxford Movement – which argued that it was perfectly possible for a Protestant to follow many of the practices of Roman Catholicism. The majority of Leeds Anglicans and Nonconformists were horrified by St Saviour's. They pointed out that many of the clergy there lived in a community similar to a monastery, and felt justified in their criticisms when some of the priests defected to Rome.[15]

St Saviour's was not the only church to cause concern and division in the town. Brunswick Methodist chapel opened on Brunswick Street in 1825. It was a huge building, catering for as many as 2,500 worshippers, and was said to be 'one of the largest and most magnificent ecclesiastical buildings in the empire'. But in 1827, when some of the members of this 'cathedral of Methodism' wanted to install an organ, another group argued that this smacked of popish symbolism and middle-class pride. When the organ was installed they decided to leave. Other Methodists in local chapels, disaffected over doctrinal differences, also decided to break away from their chapels, and together they formed what eventually became the Wesleyan Protestant Methodists. It is hard in the twenty-first century to imagine the bitter divisions religion could cause in the town. Even in death they were present.

The church of St Peter-at-Leeds, the parish church, was consecrated on 2 September 1841. The inspiration of Dr Hook, Robert Chantrell's building was the largest new church built in England since Christopher Wren's St Paul's Cathedral. It is a Grade I listed building and became a minster on 2 September 2012.

The problem of full local graveyards had long occupied the authorities. In 1833 the Leeds General Cemetery Co. opened a non-denominational private cemetery at Woodhouse, and in 1842 the Leeds Burial Act was passed – so that a municipal cemetery could be built in the town, the first such to be established in England. The site chosen was on Beckett Street and it opened in August 1845. The authorities recognised that religious differences existed and two identical chapels were built: one for the Anglicans and one for the Nonconformists.[16]

Nevertheless, the differing religious groups in Leeds were united by a proper observance of the Sabbath. In the 1820s the churchwardens took it upon themselves to see that there was 'a proper degree of decorum in the streets on the Sabbath'. By the 1840s Sabbatarianism had taken hold across the country.

In Leeds, Robert Perring, the editor of the *Intelligencer*, decided to launch another newspaper, the *Leeds Wednesday Journal*. He recognised that all the town's papers were published on a Saturday, including his own, which meant that in many cases they would be read on a Sunday – which he considered was 'not a day for political discussion or amusement'. The Leeds public in general did not agree. He launched the *Journal* in January 1841, and closed it in February that same year.

Some people in the town took a dim view of restrictions that were imposed by passionate Sabbatarians.

In 1840 the Leeds Zoological and Botanical Gardens was opened in the Burley area. Laid out with shrubberies and trees, and boasting an ornamental

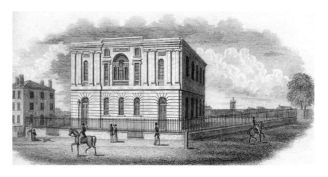

'The cathedral of Methodism'. Brunswick chapel opened in 1825 catering for 2,500 worshippers. 'One of the largest and most magnificent ecclesiastical buildings in the empire', it became notorious for the famous Organ Dispute of 1827.

fountain and ponds, a variety of activities were held there. Exotic animals, like bears in the famous bear pit, still to be seen on Cardigan Road, were shown, balloon ascents were made, and band concerts and firework displays were held. The big issue was whether the gardens should open on a Sunday. Sabbatarians in the town were adamant that Sunday was not a day for pleasure activities, but the radical *Leeds Times* and its editor Samuel Smiles thought differently. They argued that Sunday was the only day that the working classes in the town could get to see the gardens; it was 'part of the great question of civil and religious liberty'. The arguments dragged on until a compromise was finally reached, and the gardens remained open on Sundays from 4 p.m. to sunset.

The moral guardians of society were also appalled at the extent of gambling in the town. In January 1844 George Roberts, who owned a beerhouse at Quarry Hill, was prosecuted for allowing dominoes to be played there. They were also extremely concerned when Joshua Hobson opened the Leeds Casino and Concert Hall (1845). Although no more than a ramshackle wooden building in Lands Lane, it was one of the first music halls in England. The middle classes considered that what went on there was both 'humiliating and appalling'.

Prostitution, too, was still a major problem. One report on the situation in Leeds in 1832 claimed that 'Vast numbers of girls who have wrought in factories are driven to prostitution when they are deprived of employment … [they] have absolutely no alternative but that of prostitution when trade is low and times are bad.' Kirkgate and the Bank were the areas where it was most rife, but the *Leeds Times* identified the Ship Inn as a notorious brothel. To ease the problem the Probationary Penitentiary was opened in 1839 to cater for females 'desirous of returning to the paths of rectitude'.

A report published in January 1840 in the *Leeds Mercury* stated that there were 175 brothels in the town, and went on to claim that there were 700 women employed in them, earning on average £1 10*s* a week. Most were between fourteen and twenty years of age, though some were recruited as young as ten or eleven; it was estimated that a third were encouraged to act so by their mothers. Approximately 14,000 men used the brothels in Leeds each week.[17] The fact that eight out of every ten women involved were diseased led to the Leeds Lock Hospital being opened in 1842.

The Bear Pit on Cardigan Road. The only remains of the Leeds Zoological and Botanical Gardens which opened in 1840.

The other social issue that caused major concern was excessive drinking. A meeting at the Courthouse on 9 September 1830 formed the Leeds Temperance Society, its general aim to combat 'intemperance and its attendant evils' among the working class and to improve its morals and manners. Its principal objective was 'the entire suppressing of the use of distilled spirits, except where recommended medically and to check the immoderate use of all other kinds of liquor'. Among the strongest supporters of the movement in the town were the Baptists and the Methodists. To augment the work of the society, Dr Richard Frederick Lees and three other members launched the *Leeds Temperance Herald* in January 1837, but it failed to gain the public's support and closed within a year.

Ten years later another initiative, still active nationally, was launched in the town. The Band of Hope was formed near Leeds Bridge in 1847 when Ann Jane Carlile, a seventy-two-year-old Irish Presbyterian, met the Revd Jabez Tunnicliffe, a local Baptist minister. Tunnicliffe had recently witnessed the death of an alcoholic who had urged him to warn children of the dangers of strong drink. Together Carlile and Tunnicliffe set up the movement. Weekly meetings were held, with Tunnicliffe writing popular songs in order to help spread his message in schools. In 1855 the UK Band of Hope was established in London, and today, known as Hope UK, it concerns itself with young people suffering from drug- and alcohol-related problems.

If social problems occupied the minds of many Leeds people so too did ongoing political ones. The working classes and Radicals across the country still felt that their voices were not being heard and demanded further parliamentary reform. To achieve it the Chartist movement was born in 1836, taking its name from the People's Charter drawn up in 1838. It demanded universal manhood suffrage, vote by ballot, no property qualification for MPs, payment of MPs, equal constituencies and annual parliaments. In August 1837 at a meeting on Woodhouse Moor the Leeds Working Men's Association was formed, in anticipation of the launch of the charter. Its plan was to gain control of public meetings in the town and then use them for propaganda purposes.

Leeds was to play a crucial part in the Chartist movement. Feargus O'Connor, its leader and a demagogic, charismatic individual, established the movement's national newspaper, the *Northern Star*, in the town in 1837, and by 1839 it boasted a national circulation of 50,000. The movement was divided between those who favoured using violence, the physical force Chartists, and those who were more moderate in their approach, the moral force Chartists. Leeds generally was known for its moderation. However, in 1842 violence flared up on its streets during August's Plug Riots. Across the North of England Chartist protesters attacked mills and factories, in particular smashing the plugs from boilers and thus bringing production to a halt.

Demonstrators attacked mills and factories in Armley, Wortley and Farnley, and then sought reinforcements in Pudsey. From there they marched to Marshall's mill in Holbeck, but were unable to locate the boiler's plug. The police, armed with cutlasses and heavy batons and supported by special constables and a military contingent which included the 17th Lancers under Prince George, met them. The Riot Act was read, and peace was finally restored.

The moderate Chartists in the town continued their campaign more peacefully, and played a significant part in the next few years in the vestry, on the board of highway surveyors and for a time on the Improvement Commission. In 1848 a massive petition of 5,706,000 signatures was drawn up nationally, and meetings were held on Woodhouse Moor, Vicar's Croft and Wellington Street to support it. However, the petition was discredited and after that the movement waned.[18]

One of Marshall's mills that the rioters had attacked was unique. Based on the ancient Egyptian temple of Horus at Edfu, it contains papyrus and lotus capitals and a winged solar disk. Not surprisingly it is known as Temple Mill. Designed by Joseph Bonomi Jnr – not his brother Ignatius as frequently claimed – it was built between 1838 and 1843. Adjacent to it is a single-storey weaving shed based on the temple of Hathor at Dendera, illuminated by sixty-five glass domes. Marshall had grass sown on the roof and a flock of sheep grazed there quite contentedly. This weaving shed was the largest single room

A typical Leeds textile mill. Stonebridge Mill in West Leeds was opened *c.*1800 as a fulling, scribbling and carding mill powered by steam. This was probably one of the mills targeted during the Plug Riot of 1842.

in the world, and was capable of holding between 6,500 and 7,000 people. The factory chimney was shaped like a huge Egyptian obelisk. Marshall was an enlightened employer for his day. His building offered both baths and shops for his workers and air conditioning through ducts beneath the floor. Although he was bitterly criticised for employing children in his factory, in 1823 Marshall introduced a school for his child workers and even made some provision for infants. Two years later he opened a night school, offering classes to his workers from fourteen to thirty years of age. The building is today Grade I listed.

Several boarding schools in the town, schools for workers' children and the opening of a retreat at Armley for *'the Reception and Cure of Persons affected by Disorders of the Mind'* were indications of the changes that were occurring in society. None was greater than the railway revolution. This transformed Britain during the 1830s and '40s, when railway mania swept the country. Goods and people could now be transported faster and farther than was conceivable before. Between 1844 and 1846 a total of 6,220 miles of track was laid across the country – over half the mileage of today's railway system. The town's press was full of the proposals: in October 1845 the *Leeds Mercury* had to issue three special supplements to carry details of them all. The first railway from the town, the Leeds and Selby line, opened in 1834; then followed one to Derby, thus

linking Leeds to London (1840), to Manchester (1841), to Bradford (1846) and to Thirsk (1848).

A further benefit indirectly brought by the railways was the introduction of Railway Time. Up to 1846 Leeds was six minutes and four seconds behind London. On 10 January 1846 the *Leeds Times* announced that 'the clocks in Leeds will until further notice be set to Greenwich time ... to accommodate railway travelling'.

If the 1840s was a period of dramatic technological expansion, it was also a period of grim human suffering. The years became known as the Hungry Forties, and an estimated 1 million paupers died from want of employment in Britain. In the first three months of 1842 it is claimed that 16,000 individuals were being catered for in the Leeds workhouse, with a further 10,000 others in receipt of outdoor help. One example of that suffering was Peter Brabson, an eighty-seven-year-old Irish vagrant, who was found dead in Kirkgate. He had starved to death.

The Poor Law Amendment Act of 1834 hoped to solve the problem of poverty by making workhouses austere and forbidding places. Implementing the

Castleton Lodge. This retreat at Armley was opened for 'the Reception and Cure of Persons affected by Disorders of the Mind'. Note in this mid-nineteenth-century engraving the rural nature of the surroundings.

James Sigston's Academy in 1826. One of several boarding schools in the town, this academy was sited in Queen's Square.

Poor Law was the single largest item of expenditure in the town, and by the 1840s it was obvious a new workhouse was needed – but ratepayers in the town refused to enforce the Act and build one. It was finally agreed to implement part of the legislation, and in 1842 a Board of Guardians was formed. However, instead of building a new workhouse they built the Moral and Industrial Training School for pauper children, which opened in 1848 and eventually formed part of what became St James's Hospital.

As poverty was the cause of much crime, the authorities were forced to deal with its consequences. Leeds had a small prison in the Courthouse for holding local drunks or criminals temporarily, but those convicted served their time at Wakefield House of Correction. However, disputes arose between Wakefield and Leeds over whether an economic rate was being paid, and in 1837 the council decided to draw up plans to erect a jail in Leeds itself. Arguments over the cost dragged the issue out until 1842. Perkin and Backhouse were employed to design the building, which was placed on an elevated position in West Leeds on the borders of Armley and New Wortley. Its central tower, built in the same style as Windsor Castle, dominated the skyline. It was opened in 1847, catering for 334 men, women and children prisoners. For petty criminals in the 1840s the stocks were still used.

But it was in Ireland that the worst suffering of all occurred in these years, as the great Potato Famine of the 1840s swept across the country. Ironically the *Leeds Intelligencer* reported in August 1845 that 'The potato crop in the north of Ireland will this year be the most abundant ever known.' But in fact 1845 heralded the worst potato famine ever experienced in Europe: Leeds lost 20 per cent of its crop, Scotland was seriously affected, and Ireland, totally dependent on the potato, was devastated. Historians claim that a million died of starvation there, though the real number will never be known. In January 1847 a meeting was called at the Courthouse in Leeds to see what help could be given to both Ireland

A common punishment for minor misdemeanours was confining people to the stocks. This unfortunate is suffering the fate in Hunslet. The stocks in Leeds itself were before Moot Hall. The name Stocks Hill at Bramley, Armley and Holbeck indicate these townships also had stocks whilst those at Tong still exist.

and Scotland. Meanwhile 1½ million Irish people emigrated, many coming to Leeds; by 1851 there were 10,333 Irish living in the town. They settled in the poorer areas of Leeds, and it was here in 1847 that typhus, the 'gaol fever', struck. It ravaged the Bank and similar insanitary districts of the town, so that in June, at the height of the epidemic, the House of Recovery and the temporary fever hospital were so full that additional premises had to be found. There were

Alphonse Douseau's work, painted c.1840, clearly shows the serious problem of pollution at the time. Note the tracks of Middleton Railway in the foreground, the kilns of Leeds Pottery on the left and Bower's glassworks in Hunslet on the right.

relatively few deaths among the middle class, but the working-class areas suffered enormously, with five Catholic priests and a curate from the parish church all perishing as they continued to minister to their flocks.[19] From 1848 to 1849 cholera returned. Once again it was the poorer areas that were scourged. Leeds itself saw 1,674 people die; in the out-townships a further 300 perished.

But it was also in the 1840s that a new dawn arrived in the town. In 1842 John Barran, the son of a London gunmaker, sailed from London to Hull, then travelled to Leeds by rail. After a time he set up as a tailor in his own shop at No. 30 Bridge End South. By 30 September 1848 the *Leeds Mercury* announced the 'Removal of Business and the opening of the Emporium of Fashion' at No. 1 Briggate. From Saturday 7 October John Barran would offer 'an immense assortment of ready-made clothing'. Little did Barran or his potential customers realise that they were witnessing history in the making. Not only had ready-made clothing, a new industry, arrived in the town, but it would eventually replace the wool textile industry to become the bedrock of the Leeds economy – and give the town an international reputation for the next century.

THE FACTORY KING

Richard Oastler was born in St Peter's Square, Leeds, in 1789. In 1820 he took over from his father as steward of Fixby Hall near Huddersfield, but it is as the leading factory reformer of the nineteenth century that he acquired the name of the Factory King. In September 1830 John Wood, a Bradford worsted manufacturer, described to Oastler the horrendous conditions to which children in the local mills of the West Riding were subjected. Oastler was horrified. He sat down and penned what would become one of the most famous letters in nineteenth-century social history. In it he graphically outlined the appalling situation, comparing the conditions children worked in as similar to those of Negro slaves; indeed his letter was headed 'Slavery in Yorkshire'. He finished by reminding his readers 'That the nation is now determined that Negroes shall be free. Let them, however, not forget that Britons have common rights.' Edward Baines, the editor of the *Mercury*, was happy to publish the letter in full, as long as Oastler put his name to it. Further letters from him appeared. Then in 1831 he submitted another letter, which Edward Baines Jnr edited. Oastler was furious and took it to the *Leeds Intelligencer*. The event created a bitter rift between Oastler and the Baineses. It never healed.

Oastler's proposal was to limit the hours children could work in factories and mills, and thus the Ten Hour Movement was born. The government set up a Royal Commission to investigate the situation, and its reports show the extent of the problem. Elizabeth Bentley began work at six years of age in a Leeds flax mill and was employed from 6 a.m. to 9 p.m. Ann Coulson, working in a mill at Stanningley, was so badly beaten by an overlooker that her back was turned 'nearly to a jelly'. Charles Burns began work at eight years of age in another Leeds flax mill. He told the committee that when he was working he was denied the right to go and relieve himself. He was 'forced to let it go' where he was.

The Ten Hour campaign became part of the 1832 election, and Radicals and workers campaigned long and hard for a change in the law. The Factory Act of 1833 brought some limited changes, but it was only after continued campaigning that the Ten Hour Bill was finally passed in 1847. Oastler, however, had made many enemies. He was accused of embezzlement at Fixby Hall and imprisoned from 1840 until 1844. However, when he died in January 1861 he was given one of the largest funerals the town had ever seen, before being buried at St Stephen's church in Kirkstall. Even the *Mercury* had to admit that he died 'without an enemy' and that 'the factory operative's condition is now vastly superior to what it was in 1830'.

Richard Oastler (1789–1861), the Factory King. Oastler, born in Leeds, led the campaign for the Ten Hour Bill in an attempt to improve working conditions for children.

nine

CIVIC PRIDE

On Tuesday 7 September 1858 the *Leeds Mercury* was euphoric. For the first time since Charles I's ill-fated visit to the town a reigning British monarch was in Leeds: Queen Victoria had come to open the new Town Hall. Excitedly, the paper declared, 'The Borough of Leeds ... this old and busy seat of industry becomes in a sense the seat of Empire.' In 1851 the council had voted to make a bold public statement about the success of 'this old and busy seat of industry', and determined to build a Town Hall as a mark of civic pride, which, in the words of Dr John Deakin Heaton, the project's most passionate advocate, would compare favourably with 'the best Town Halls of the Continent'. A competition was held for its design, and twenty-nine-year-old Cuthbert Brodrick, despite his mother advising him he that he was too young, was the successful architect. Its erection was not without problems. Samuel Atack, the builder, went bankrupt, and costs soared from the estimated £41,835 to £122,000. The foundation stone was laid in 1853, but it was not until that memorable Tuesday five years later that Queen Victoria, in a mauve silk dress and bonnet trimmed with green flowers, accompanied by Prince Albert and her daughters, the Princesses Helena and Alice, opened the building. The *Mercury* estimated that between 400,000 and 600,000 people crowded the streets. Shops were shut and mills stood idle. At the workhouse generous helpings of roast beef and plum pudding were offered in celebration, while Mr Yewdall, the Water Lane chemist, offered 'Leeds Royal Bouquet', a 'new and lasting PERFUME' to commemorate the occasion.

Queen Victoria herself left behind a graphic account in her diary of her visit:

6 September
We reached Leeds where there were great crowds at the station ... The Mayor (a perfect picture of a fine old man with flowing beard) ... Mr Fairbairn by name ...

Cuthbert Brodrick's drawing of the new Town Hall. Queen Victoria opened the building in 1858. Note that William Day Keyworth Jr's four Portland stone lions are not to be seen. They were not unveiled until 1867.

looked quite like a Titian Duge [*sic*]. We drove in procession through the beautifully decorated & densely crowded streets, all admirably arranged. It was only a short drive to Woodsley Hall, the Mayor's pretty home, standing on an eminence overlooking the town, which he has entirely given up to us. His wife (his 2nd) is much younger than him and very ladylike.

7 September

Rather a dull rainy morning ... We made the entire tour of the town, which took more than an hour, & nothing could have been more enthusiastic than the reception we met with, or better than the way the people behaved. Beautiful decorations with endless wreaths & festoons of flowers across the streets, along the houses no end of flags ... The Town Hall is really a magnificent building of very fine proportions ... Got meet [*sic*] there & entered the principal Hall, where (as usual) we ascended a throne. Prayers were read by the Bishop of Ripon ... there followed the Address to me ... after which I knighted the Mayor, which was greatly applauded ... The Hall was then declared open by the Ld Derby & the Hallelujah Chorus was sung ... We left the town & drove in a similar manner to the station (another one).[1]

Brodrick went on to produce other memorable buildings in the town. His Oriental Baths (1866) in Cookridge Street were widely acclaimed, but his two greatest works were the Mechanics' Institute (1868), which became the present museum, and the Corn Exchange (1862).[2]

Building was not restricted to fine civic structures. As the population soared from 172,720 in 1851 to 428,969 in 1901 the need for new housing escalated. That provision reflected the marked social divisions in Leeds as the middle classes moved to the less polluted and more salubrious areas north of the town. Between 1851 and 1861 Burley and Headingley saw a 50 per cent increase in population, mainly of the 'mercantile community of Leeds', while through the latter years of the century Potternewton, Roundhay and Adel saw a series of expensive villas being erected for the wealthy and successful. Meanwhile back-to-back houses mushroomed across the working-class areas of the expanding town. Concern was raised about many of the slum dwellings that still blighted the landscape in these parts. Despite efforts by individuals like James Hole, who argued that housing conditions were 'intimately connected with other social issues', some of the streets made infamous during the cholera epidemic of 1832 were still inhabited in 1914. There were, however, 57,029 new houses built in Leeds between 1886 and 1914; two-thirds of them were back-to-backs. Indeed, by 1890 it was claimed that 70 per cent of Leeds houses were back-to-back dwellings. In effect they were half a house. The front door opened straight onto the street, and the back wall of the house was the back wall of the house behind it. The lavatory and midden were down the street and shared by several houses. Some were known as one-up-and-one-downs: these had a cellar, a living room and kitchen combined, a bedroom and possibly an attic. The majority, however, had two cellars, one for coal and one for general purposes. On the ground floor were the living room and a separate kitchen or scullery. Above them were two bedrooms and, often, an attic. Houses had one cold water tap. Water was either heated on the fire or in a set-pot. This was a copper boiler encased in bricks, usually in the kitchen. The water was heated and the smoke was emitted from a small set-pot chimney, usually not on the hip of the roof with the other chimneys but positioned near the gutter.

Many of these houses were jerry built, and it was only after an outbreak of typhus in 1890 that the council agreed to two major slum clearance schemes.[3] Ever conscious of its dedication to the principles of free trade, the Liberal council was loath to impose regulations on builders, and only three times did it enforce compulsory purchase orders on unsatisfactory dwellings. Fearful of 'municipal socialism', it was slow to act; but gradually it began to recognise that municipal ownership of public utilities was becoming a necessity.

First came water. In 1842 only 10 per cent of Leeds houses had mains water. It was provided by private suppliers until the council took over the

Tadcaster Street in West Leeds built c.1890 and seen here in the early 1960s just before demolition. It is typical of the back-to-back houses of Leeds. Note the lavatory yard down the street, the washing hanging across the street and the set-pot chimney on the gutter. The house sporting a lighter door was hit by an incendiary bomb in 1941.

supply in 1852. This was a positive move: by the 1860s the number with mains water had risen to 95 per cent. Then in 1867 the Leeds Waterworks Act enabled the building of three new reservoirs at Linley Wood (1875), Swinsty (1877) and Fewston (1879), with an extension made to Eccup Reservoir in 1883. A similar dramatic improvement was noted regarding sewage. In 1856 a total of only 1,005 houses possessed water closets; by 1889 the number had dramatically increased to 27,990. Gas and electricity supplies eventually also fell under the council's aegis. Gas had been available from a private company from 1818, and from 1835 a second company supposedly offered competition. In reality they operated a cartel, not only fixing prices but making considerable profits into the bargain. The option to take over the companies was appealing, and on 1 September 1870 the corporation did so – at a cost of £763,245. Electricity was not as straightforward. The council set up the Electric Lighting Committee in 1883 to conduct experiments in supplying power, and eventually the committee recommended that the corporation itself should provide power both to the public at large and in particular to light its own offices. However, the council decided against such action, and in April 1891 the private Yorkshire House-to-House Electricity Company was established on Whitehall Road. The *Mercury* bemoaned this, pointing out that eventually the council would need to take over the responsibility. Its prophecy was correct, and in 1895 the council reversed its decision at a cost to ratepayers of £63,011.

Public transport, too, was an area where the council hesitated. James Sykes had begun operating a coach service in 1818 from West Leeds to the Talbot Inn in Briggate, and in June 1838 John Wood began his omnibus service from Headingley to Leeds. By the 1860s such services were operating to Hunslet, Kirkstall, Chapeltown, Whitkirk, Meanwood, Roundhay and Wortley. Horse-drawn trams had begun running in London and Liverpool by 1870, and Leeds was quick to follow. A private company, the Leeds Tramway Company, was given council approval to establish tram routes from the town centre to Far Headingley, Chapeltown, Hunslet, Kirkstall and Marsh Lane. On Saturday 16 September 1871 the first route, Boar Lane to Headingley, opened. By the end of the century over 27 million passenger journeys took place annually over the 58 route miles of track that by then covered most of the town.

On Tuesday 17 June 1880 steam trams began operating to Wortley. Eleven years later, on Thursday 29 October 1891, the first electric tramway to use an overhead wire system anywhere in Europe began to run in Leeds, operating between Sheepscar and Roundhay. The company showed no desire to renew its lease, however, and thus on 2 February 1894 the council took over the tramway system.[4]

If the council was hesitant about some public provision, it was very active in the provision of public parks, the 'lungs of Leeds' as they were known. In 1855 Woodhouse Moor was purchased; then between 1870 and 1897 eleven parks across the town came into public ownership. By the end of the century Leeds was second only to Liverpool in providing open public spaces. Of all these, the jewel in the crown was undoubtedly Roundhay Park, purchased in1871. Ironically John Barran, who was instrumental in Roundhay's purchase for £127,000, was maligned for wasting public money and caricatured as the buyer of a white elephant. In reality it would become one of the town's finest assets.

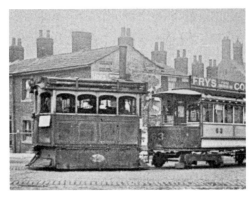

Steam tram passing Five Lane Ends on the Wortley route. Such trams began operating on this route on Tuesday 17 June 1880.

If the council was far sighted in purchasing Roundhay Park, it was simply fortunate in gaining its other great acquisition of the nineteenth century. In 1873 Sir George Gilbert Scott was employed to submit a plan to renovate the ruins of Kirkstall Abbey and convert it into a training college for clergy, but the idea was finally rejected and the Brudenell family, who owned the abbey, decided to put it on the market in 1888. The council could not meet the reserve price, but Colonel John Thomas North, the Nitrate King, bought it for £10,000. The following year he gave it to Leeds, and in 1895 it was opened to the public.

Private baths had been provided in the town from 1820, with the Cookridge Street Oriental Baths (1866) being the most famous of several that subsequently opened. However, on 1 January 1886 the council decided to build a recreation ground at Oldfield Lane in Wortley. It was to include a swimming pool. Once that decision was taken other public baths followed: Kirkstall Road and Union Street (1895), Holbeck and Hunslet (1898) and Meanwood Road (1899). A major advance in public health occurred in 1868 when Sir George Gilbert Scott's new Leeds Infirmary replaced its now outdated predecessor.

Provision of public amenities was important to an increasing population, but there were those in the town who were wary of too much public expenditure. Archibald Witham Scarr, a local market trader, was one such individual. Known as 'the Mayor of the Masses', he entered politics and led a revolt against council expenditure – even objecting to Leeds's petitioning to become a city. His main criticisms were of the purchase of the town's gas supplies, the building of several reservoirs, the attempt to acquire Roundhay Park and, in particular, the School Board's decision to buy expensive plots and build costly schools on them. Others, however, were adamant that if the nation was to progress far greater attention must be given to education. In 1867 concern was voiced in the West Riding about the need for 'increasing the efficiency of scientific education', and following a report published by the Yorkshire Board of Education the Yorkshire College of Science opened on 26 October 1874 in Cookridge Street. It widened its range of subjects to become the Yorkshire College in 1876, moved to the Woodhouse Lane area in 1877, amalgamated with the Medical School in 1884 and in 1887 linked up with Manchester's Owens College and the Liverpool College to form Victoria University. In April 1904 it became the University of Leeds, a university in its own right.

Gladstone's government was well aware that a better educated and more literate population was also required to meet the needs of a developing country. In Leeds middle-class children were reasonably well catered for. The old

Grammar School was still educating boys, and in 1870 the Leeds Church Middle Class School opened, followed, in 1875, by the Leeds Girls' High School. But of 48,787 school-age children in the town only 27,329 were attending either Church or dames' schools, and of these one in three were often absent. According to a Parliamentary Commission, Leeds was 'the darkest and most benighted town in the kingdom from an educational point of view'.[5]

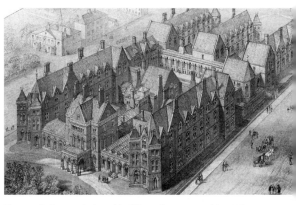

The new infirmary, designed by Gilbert Scott, opened in 1868. The entrance faces onto Great George Street. Today the site has expanded until it stretches from central Leeds as far as the University of Leeds.

From the 1840s a great national argument had rumbled on as to whether the government or volunteer organisations should provide education. Edward Baines Jnr, like his father editor of the *Leeds Mercury* and Liberal MP for the town, led the voluntaryists. But in 1870 the decision was made. William Forster drafted a bill and Gladstone's Liberal government passed it, making education compulsory and permitting local councils to set up school boards to provide it. On Monday 28 November that year ratepayers in Leeds were asked to vote for the establishment of a school board for the town. It was the first time that women in Leeds were allowed to vote, and they did so, according to the *Mercury*, with an 'air of satisfaction on their faces'. Plans were drawn up, and in 1872 thirteen schools opened in temporary premises. Bewerley Street Board School, the first purpose-built board school in the town, followed in August 1873. The School Board then controversially opened the Central Higher Grade School in 1885, which moved to a brand new building on Woodhouse Lane in 1889. The arguments levelled by opponents were that the board was only permitted to provide elementary education, was misusing the funds available and compounding the problem by choosing an expensive prime location. However, the dispute passed over, and the council itself took over direct responsibility for education in Leeds in 1902 when the Education Committee was formed.[6]

From 1873 the School Board determined to aid adult education by opening four evening schools and seven science and art classes in the town. To encourage more cultural participation a public art gallery was opened on 3 October 1888, funded by a public subscription raised to celebrate Queen Victoria's

Golden Jubilee. The council continued its policy of stimulating further adult learning by deciding to provide public libraries. In 1870 the first opened, and the townships chosen were quite deliberate: Hunslet and Holbeck. That was 'where the masses lived', insisted the mayor, John Barran.[7]

In the 1840s it was Barran who had launched the ready-made clothing industry in the town. This would not only overtake wool textile manufacture, it would come to dominate the Leeds economy. Aided by Herman Friend, an immigrant Jew, he developed the concept of mass production, turning his company into one of the most successful in the country. Clothing manufacture expanded rapidly, to a great extent relying on new Jewish immigrant labour. Various small firms were established in the town, while by 1914 there were 100 clothing manufacturers there. By 1911 some 25 per cent of the female workers in the city were employed in the clothing industry.[8]

Fortunately Leeds was never solely dependent on any single industry for its economic growth. While the wool textile industry fell into decline – Gott's famous firm ceased production in 1870 – and the flax industry, after reaching its peak in about 1850, lost out to overseas competitors, other industries flourished. Coal-mining by 1877 was still dominant, with 102 collieries still operating in the Leeds area. Engineering spawned by Matthew Murray in the late eighteenth century flourished, with various firms rising to pre-eminence. Smith's of Rodley (1820) produced internationally renowned cranes. The Airedale Foundry (1839) made engines that hauled goods over the Andes. Greenwood and Batley (1856) supplied the arsenals of Britain, Germany, Japan and China. Manning, Wardle and Co. (1858) manufactured engines that were in demand from Africa to Australia. Hudswell Clarke and Co. (1860) supplied 'Tom Puddings' or tub boats for the Aire & Calder Navigation. Fowler's Steam Plough Works (1860) produced equipment that was in demand internationally, as were the locomotives from the Hunslet Engine Co. (1864). By the end of the century Samson Fox's Leeds Forge Co. (1874) produced boilers that were used by almost all major shipping lines. J. and H. McClaren (1876) produced irrigation equipment that was exported all over the world; while the Leeds Steel Works (1882–83) gained a reputation for the production of tramlines.

In 1873 R.W. Crabtree and Sons made its first web-fed perfecting rotary machine, giving a major boost to printing, another important industry in Leeds. Two of the largest printing firms in the town were Petty's (1865), which would go on to open branches in London, Reading, Belfast, Melbourne and Cape

Above Central Higher Grade School's new building, designed by Birchall and Kelly, opened in 1889 on Woodhouse Lane. It became the City High School in 1972.

Left George Corson's Municipal Buildings opened in 1884. Known as the Municipal Palace it housed the Art Gallery, Central Library, Reference Library and from 1934–66 Leeds City police headquarters. The building beyond is the School Board's offices. The building on the immediate right was demolished to make way for the Garden of Rest.

Town, and Alf Cooke's (1866), which was awarded the royal warrant as colour printer to the queen in 1895.

The leather industry also played a vital part in the Leeds economy. It developed particularly in the Kirkstall, Bramley, and Meanwood areas while, at Buslingthorpe, Wilson Walker and Co. established the largest tannery in England. A by-product of the industry was the manufacture of boots and shoes. By 1890 there were ninety firms manufacturing 100,000 pairs a week in Leeds, with the largest producers being Stead & Simpson and Joseph Conyer and Son. Several fireclay companies also operated, providing chimney pots and glazed sanitary ware. The most famous was Burmantofts Pottery (1842). It was, however, from 1879 when James Holdroyd took over the business that it achieved lasting fame. His Burmantofts Faience, salt-glazed bricks and decorative tiles and pottery, became internationally famous.

An efficient transport system was essential for the success of local industries. The growing railway networks and the development of the port of Leeds played a vital part in the town's economic expansion.

The Port of Leeds *c.* 1911. Arthur Netherwood's painting well captures the bustling activity of the busy port of Leeds. Throughout the nineteenth and early twentieth century vessels regularly sailed from here to Newcastle and London.

To smooth the passage of manufacturing and commerce various banks opened in the town in the second half of the century, with eight originating in Leeds. Becketts Bank, established in the eighteenth century, continued to flourish, but in 1859 the Yorkshire Penny Bank began trading. It was one of the most popular financial institutions in the town, perhaps best remembered for opening its famous School Bank: in 1891 the Leeds School Board, in an attempt to encourage thrift, urged it to open a bank in every school.

The retail trade was another major industry. Leeds had for centuries been the focal point for shopping, not only for the town's inhabitants but for the population of the West Riding generally. Briggate and Boar Lane were the main shopping centres. Marshall & Snelgrove, the London-based retailers, opened a store at the junction of Park Row and Bond Street in 1869, but what was probably the town's first full-scale department store opened in May 1888 on Boar Lane. The Grand Pygmalion boasted that it was 'The Largest Retail Drapery and Complete Furnishing Establishment in England', selling the 'Richest and Rarest Drapery Goods'. It was, however, Charles Thornton who was to develop a shopping concept for which Leeds would become famous. In 1878 he opened Thornton's Arcade, and the clever use of space that arcades offered saw several other developers follow him. After the Queen's Arcade (1889) came the Grand Arcade (1898) and, erected the same year, the Victoria Arcade, built to celebrate the Diamond Jubilee.

Two traders little known at the time launched businesses that outlived them. Edward Lewis is long forgotten, but the shop he opened in Marsh Lane in 1882 was a landmark. It was the first fish and chip shop in Leeds, and Leeds went on to be described as the 'capital of fish and chips'! Meanwhile in 1884 Michael Marks opened a stall in Leeds market. His Penny Bazaar proclaimed, 'Don't ask the price – it's a penny!' In 1894 he famously went into partnership with Tom Spencer, the cashier in Isaac Dewhirst's warehouse on Harper Street near the market, and Marks & Spencer was born.

Traders kept their shops and stalls open until late each day, though by 1858 early closing on Wednesdays had been introduced and shops shut at 7 p.m. In 1866 the Leeds Industrial Co-operative Society, one of the largest employers in the town, introduced a half day a week holiday for its staff. The Co-op, as it was more commonly known, grew out of the Holbeck Anti-Corn Mill Association. This had been formed in 1847 initially with the object of erecting a mill to provide unadulterated flour. In 1854 it extended its scope and became the Leeds Co-operative Flour and Provision Society. By the 1860s it was the largest Co-op in the country, and opened its head offices in Albion Street in 1884. It provided a vast array of goods, including meat, milk, groceries, clothing, fuel, footwear and additional services. By 1896 it boasted 33,000 members, catered for in seventy local stores. According to the *Yorkshire Factory Times*, 'the Leeds Industrial Co-operative Society [was] the largest on earth'.

Provision of leisure also became an important industry as the century developed, as people found themselves with more money in their pockets and more time to spend it. Nine new theatres opened in the town in the latter years of the century. The most popular were the Hippodrome (1874) in King Charles's Croft; the Theatre Royal (1876) built in just seven months, and the magnificent Grand Theatre and Opera House (1878). The oldest existing theatre in Leeds started life as the White Swan Singing Room in the 1760s, but in 1894 changed its name to the City Varieties. In 1897 a young Charlie Chaplin performed there with the Eight Lancashire Lads, and a year later Lily Langtry was the star. It is claimed by some that the Prince of Wales, the future

Briggate in the 1860s. Note Trinity church beyond.

A typical Leeds Industrial Co-operative Society store. By the 1890s there were seventy across the town. This Lower Wortley store had four departments. Left to right they were butchers, boots and shoes, grocery and provisions and drapery. The store seen here was decorated for the coronation of Edward VII in 1902.

Edward VII, made clandestine visits to see her when she was on stage. The theatre, like the Grand, is still in use today. The Coliseum (1885), which opened in Cookridge Street, was also used for great meetings, and by the end of the century it occasionally showed films; it was renamed the Gaumont cinema in 1938. The last of the town centre theatres to open was the Empire (1898), which attracted music-hall performers such as Vesta Tilley and George Robey.[9]

There were still, however, those in the town who thought the theatre was an immoral place. When Wilson Barrett became manager of the Grand Theatre at its opening, the Vicar of Leeds, Dr Gott, expressed his concern. Barrett assured him he would produce plays that 'would not bring a blush to the youngest girl in the theatre'. Years later, when Barrett left the Grand and Gott had become the Bishop of Truro, the cleric presented him with a Worcester vase. Inscribed on it were the words, 'From the Bishop of Truro to Wilson Barrett in grateful acknowledgement for a promise well kept.'

More socially acceptable cultural activities saw several societies formed. The Leeds Photographic Society (1852) was founded a year before the Royal Photographic Society, while the Leeds Astronomical Society (1859) was the earliest such amateur society in the United Kingdom. Others followed: the Leeds Naturalists' Club (1870), the Leeds Fine Arts Society (1874) and the

Thoresby Society (1889), which was devoted to preserving the history of Leeds. Other societies campaigned for improving the town. The Leeds Society for Promoting Public Improvements (1851) campaigned against pollution, as did the Leeds Smoke Abatement Society (1890), which claimed that in any one day half a ton of soot fell on the town.

Sport also began to occupy people's leisure time. Football, generally the rugby code, was played on Woodhouse Moor from 1864, though at Hunslet in 1877 one of the first Association Football clubs in the town was formed. In 1889 what was said to be the finest sporting arena in the world was opened at Headingley. It catered for Association Football, originally Rugby Union but later Rugby League, athletics, tennis, cycling and, of course, cricket. Ironically, in September 1890 the Australian cricket team played there, beat the North of England by 160 runs and thus played at Headingley before the Yorkshire county side ever did! As the century progressed tennis, bowls, cricket, football and rugby grew in popularity, as did cycling. In 1882 a purpose-built cycle track was opened in Hunslet, while in 1890 several hundred people took part in the Leeds Cycling Club's lantern parade. The club had been founded in 1876.

That same year a skating rink was opened by the council at Roundhay. Golf, too, was becoming a popular middle-class pursuit, with two clubs opening: Headingley (1892) and the Leeds Golf Club (1896), though this is often referred to as Cobble Hall.

One unique sporting event that attracted several thousands took place on Cardigan Fields on 6 November 1878. Leeds St John's played Bradford Zingari at rugby, and for the first time in the town a game was played under floodlights. The result was never in doubt. The teams had agreed that whatever the score the game would be considered a draw![10]

Cardigan Fields off Kirkstall Road was a popular venue, where cricket, rugby, lacrosse and knur and spell were played, but not just sporting events were held there. Whitsuntide galas, the Leeds Flower Show and the Royal Agricultural Show all took place there at some time or other. One of the most popular events occurred in June 1891, when Colonel William Frederick Cody's Wild West Show and Congress of Rough Riders arrived. For a fortnight Buffalo Bill's famous show, with its cowboys and Indians performing daring deeds, entertained the people of Leeds, stimulating a considerable amount of coverage in the Leeds press. But the fields were also featured in less enthusiastic press coverage in November 1886 when it reported on a mob of hooligans attacking a group of Greek gypsies encamped there.[11]

Thomas Cook established his cycle business in 1882. In 1898 he opened a large showroom in Park Row. He stocked over 300 machines and, it boasted the largest riding school in the North. Note the number of women under tuition.

Mistrust of ethnic minorities ever lurked beneath the surface of the town. Two major waves of immigrants occurred, affecting the demography of Leeds and leading to tensions and difficulties. The vast numbers escaping the appalling Great Famine of the 1840s saw the Irish population in Leeds rise dramatically. They settled in the poorest areas of the town, where crime and prostitution were rife, and the majority of the indigenous population viewed the newcomers with suspicion. It was an attitude enhanced by crime statistics which showed that 14 per cent of cases coming before Leeds Quarter Sessions and a third of all assaults on the local police and breaches of the peace from 1851 to 1861 were committed by Irish individuals. It was a great embarrassment to the English Roman Catholics in the town, who were increasing in number. Indeed in 1878 the Roman Catholic Diocese of Beverley was divided into two and the new dioceses of Middlesbrough and Leeds were created. Consequently St Anne's church became a cathedral that year.

The second wave of immigration occurred in the 1880s. Escaping the anti-Semitic pogroms of Eastern Europe, hundreds of Jewish immigrants arrived in Leeds. In 1841 only fifty-six Jews were recorded in the town; by 1881 the number had reached 2,937 and ten years later 7,856. They were not welcomed. Many settled in the Leylands, an area of run-down properties with an unsavoury reputation. A large number were labourers but some were skilled tailors, and by 1891 it was estimated that 72 per cent of the tailoring workforce in Leeds was Jewish. By 1893 there were ninety-eight Jewish tailoring workshops in the town, with many being notorious sweat shops where workers were appallingly exploited. By the 1890s anti-Semitism was prevalent throughout Leeds, with many factories and workshops displaying the notice 'No Jews Need Apply'. The council, however, took a more enlightened view. When it realised the day for the 1880 general election was fixed for a Friday, the Jewish Sabbath, it changed the date to Thursday so that Jewish voters could take part. Throughout the next century both Irish and Jewish communities would make a significant and valuable contribution to the development of the town. [12]

That 1880 election was a memorable one. It was the election that saw William Ewart Gladstone, the Liberals' GOM or Grand Old Man – the Tories referred to him as God's Only Mistake – elected as one of the Leeds MPs. Gladstone, who had also stood for Midlothian, opted to represent the Scottish constituency, and his son, Herbert, was returned unopposed for Leeds. The Conservatives deemed it pointless to incur the expense of a second election when the Liberal majority had been 11,000. It was also the last general election where the whole of Leeds voted together for its Members of Parliament. In 1885 the town was divided into constituencies. From 1832 until 1867 Leeds returned two Members of Parliament. That year the number was increased to three. In 1867 the Second Reform Bill increased the number of Leeds voters by 30,000, most of whom voted Liberal. Then from 1884 the town was served by five members, representing Leeds Central, Leeds East, Leeds North, Leeds South and Leeds West.

Although the Conservatives struggled hard to achieve power during local elections in the town – from 1835 until 1895 the Liberals controlled the council – in every Parliamentary election from 1857 at least one Leeds MP was a Conservative. If the Conservatives did not fare well in local elections at least

Park Row. On the left is P.C. Hardwick's Bank of England opened in 1864. Right centre is St Anne's Cathedral. It was built in 1838 but demolished c.1904 to cater for the widening of Cookridge Street.

the council election of 1890 was significant. It saw a young thirty-one-year-old accountant stand for the Conservatives in North Ward. He was successful, and Charles Henry Wilson would go on to dominate Leeds politics for the next forty years.

The Liberals, however, were dominant in Leeds, long aided by the fact that as the franchise was extended to more and more of the working class they tended to vote for the party. Notwithstanding, John Shackleton Mathers, a shrewd Liberal agent, anticipated the damage the emerging Labour movement could have on his party, and for a time was able to forestall its progress. But by the late 1880s the Liberals were disastrously split over Home Rule, and while the Conservatives gained power Labour gained in strength.

Tom Maguire, a photographer's assistant, and John Lincoln Mahon, an engineer, were instrumental in setting up in Leeds first the Socialist Democratic Federation, in 1884, and then, when the SDF split, the Socialist League. In November 1892 seven Labour clubs in the town decided to create an Independent Labour Party, and the following year joined the national one when it was established in Bradford. A number of ILP candidates unsuccessfully contested various wards in council elections in the town before 1900, but it was not until 1903 that a Labour councillor was finally elected.[13]

The other great political movement which emerged in the latter half of the century was that for women's suffrage. A woman calling herself Laone had written to the *Leeds Times* in March 1841 arguing that 'It cannot be asserted that women are indifferent to political existence … there are many women in England who think,' but little appears to have been done about her letter. Then in 1868 a petition was sent from the town in support of women's suffrage. Two years later, in 1870, women ratepayers voted in Leeds for the establishment of a School Board, and the following year a Leeds branch of the Society for Women's Suffrage was created. Within a year it was attracting over 100 women to its meetings. By 1889 the Leeds Suffrage Society was active in the town; among its keenest activists were Emily and Isabella Ford of Adel and Leonora Cohen. The Leeds suffragists, like suffragists generally, sought to achieve their ends by peaceful means. It was not until the creation of the Women's Social and Political Union in 1903 and its adoption of a more militant stand that the name 'suffragettes' was used to distinguish the two groups.[14]

Militancy in various forms scarred the face of the town on several occasions. The most bizarre occasion was in the Dripping Riot of 1865, but it was claimed that the worst street violence seen in nineteenth-century Britain occurred in

1890 during the Leeds gas workers' strike. Called to draw attention to the need to improve workers' conditions, the large gasworks on Meadow Lane and those at New Wortley were targeted. Despite factories and mills being forced to close and streets being left unlit, Leeds people generally supported the strikers. Serious violence erupted, and the police and the military were forced to take action. In the end the workers won a significant victory.

Numerous other Leeds strikes were recorded. In 1888 the Jewish Tailors' Union strike was said to be the 'first Jewish strike by the first Jewish trade union in the modern world'. A year later building labourers went on strike and won an increase to the hourly rate of 1½d, while in October that year the boys of Holy Rosary School on Barrack Street also went on strike; and other schools followed.

Crime was still a major concern for the authorities. The Chief Constable's report for 1867 claimed that there were 479 known thieves in the town, 293 prostitutes and 500 suspicious characters, and that on any one night there were 972 tramps and vagabonds on the streets. Children involved in crime were also a problem, and thus in 1857 the Leeds Reformatory School for sixty-five boys was opened at Adel. Murder, carrying as it did the death penalty, had a macabre fascination for the public. During the last fifty years of the century twenty-five men were executed at Armley, though only the first two, Joseph Myers and James Sargisson, were executed in public in 1864.

Graphic reports of the executions appeared in the Leeds press – which dramatically expanded in the second half of the century. Among forty new publications that appeared were the *Leeds Express* (1855), first a weekly newspaper and then a daily, a monthly magazine the *Leeds Herald* (1859), a satirical magazine the *Yorkshire Busy Bee* (1881) and for sporting enthusiasts the *Sporting Pink and Yorkshire Mid-day Tissue* (1890), known locally as the *Tisha*. Some catered for specific groups, like the *Leeds Catholic Herald* (1898), and others for local areas, like the *Hunslet and Holbeck News* (1887). Four papers, however, dominated the market. The old *Leeds Mercury* became a daily paper in 1861, followed by its arch-rival, the *Leeds Intelligencer*, in 1866, when it re-launched itself as the *Yorkshire Post*. The *Leeds Daily News* (1872) was, by 1891, able to claim it had the largest circulation outside London.

But what kind of reports did the people of Leeds read? Henry Irving and Ellen Terry were performing at the Grand Theatre in September 1881. Oscar Wilde was lecturing at the Albert Hall, in the Mechanics' Institute, in December 1884. The bellringers at the parish church rang 1,891 changes to celebrate the new year in February, and in April the price of flour in Leeds soared by 8s 6d a sack in just two months. A fatal prize fight at Temple Newsam in September 1892 saw the victor arrested for manslaughter, while at Headingley in July 1899 the first ever test played there between England and Australia ended in a draw. It was rained off.

Naturally, the weather as ever was contentious. In December 1894 a violent gale swept the country: factory chimneys were blown down at Pudsey, Rothwell and Morley, a child was killed at Woodhouse Carr and an old man killed in Holbeck, while properties across the town were damaged and the roof of the NER goods sheds on Gelderd Road simply disappeared.

Meantime, in 1884 Henry Ingland wrote to the *Yorkshire Weekly Post* to explain why Leeds people are often referred to as Loiners. He wrote in the vernacular, and gives an excellent example of the way the vast majority of the people of the town spoke at that time:

> Hevvin tane a gurt intrust in the vernackular of aar taan, I hav allus been towt that t'reason why we arr calld Leedz Loiners is becoss thear is so monny Loins in Leedz, Nearly all t'owd Streets are name'd Loins or wun soart or anuther, and I beleev is the oanly real caase of uz bean called Leedz Loiners.

One report was remembered well after all the rest were long forgotten. On 1 September 1890 the *Yorkshire Post* launched a sister paper, the *Yorkshire Evening Post*. It appeared on the streets just in time to report on the town's worst tragedy during the nineteenth century. 'Terrible Fatality in Leeds', its headline proclaimed. On the evening of 1 January 1891 Wortley church had held its annual bazaar. As part of the festivities a troupe of young girls was to perform a dance, dressed as snowflakes and carried paper lanterns with lighted candles inside. One girl's cotton wool dress caught fire, and in the panic that followed the fire spread. In all, eleven of the children were burnt to death. The youngest to die was nine years old, the oldest fourteen. Queen Victoria sent her condolences. The national press was scathing in its criticism, and the local press was equally furious that such a situation should have been allowed to happen. There had been a 'lamentable lack of caution' according to the *Armley and Wortley News*. The *Leeds Evening Express*, reflecting on the inflammable dresses and candle lanterns, considered the whole affair 'reckless and stupid'. According to the *Yorkshire Post* it was a 'fearful risk that these children … were permitted to run'. The *Yorkshire Evening Post* remarked on the 'palpable lack of forethought and caution which led to the sad affair'. And there were those who

claimed that it was an act of Divine Retribution for allowing wicked 'theatricals' to be part of the entertainment.[15]

Religion continued to dominate much of daily life, a fact demonstrated by the fact that twenty-nine new churches were opened between 1850 and 1900. The great American evangelists Sankey and Moody drew thousands to their revival meetings in the Coliseum during May and June 1883, despite the fact that the building was not completed and required a temporary roof. From 1876 the Salvation Army was also active, helping to deal with the numerous social problems that beset the town.

To combat these problems the Unmarried Mothers' Benevolent Institution was set up in 1860, and the eternal problem of drink was addressed by the opening of British Workmen public houses – pubs that did not sell alcoholic drinks. The first in Leeds opened on Fountain Street, off West Street in 1869, while the Albion at Upper Wortley bore a sign over the door: 'A public house without the drink, Where men can sit, talk, read and think, Then safely home return.' James Hole, the social reformer, was adamant that any of the public houses, beerhouses, singing rooms and casinos in the town have 'a larger nightly attendance than the evening classes of all its seventeen Mechanics' Institutes put together.'

But there was also much to celebrate in those years. One major event was little appreciated at the time. Leeds, according to many historians, saw the birth of the motion picture industry. In October 1888 Louis le Prince filmed moving pictures in a garden at Roundhay, and then filmed traffic crossing Leeds Bridge. If le Prince had not mysteriously disappeared on a trip to Paris in 1890 he may well have played as great a part in the development of cinematography as the Lumière brothers or Thomas Edison. Other events, however, were more widely celebrated. Some were joyous occasions – such as the first great Leeds music festivals held in the new Town Hall in 1858. Others were sad. On the evening of Monday 1 May 1865 hundreds gathered again in the Town Hall, shocked at the news of the assassination of President Abraham Lincoln. In solemn silence they heard the proposal 'That the inhabitants of Leeds in public meeting assembled would emphatically express the feelings of horror and intense regret with which they have heard of the atrocious acts by which the United States of America have been suddenly deprived of their President'. A happier occasion was seen on Friday 18 May 1900, when thousands packed Briggate to celebrate the relief of Mafeking during the Boer War. It was a war in which two Leeds men won the Victoria Cross, Sergeant Alfred Atkinson and

The unassuming building on the right, seen *c.*1970 is of some historical importance. Here in 1847 Jabez Tunnicliffe founded the Band of Hope and in October 1888, from the second floor window, Louis le Prince filmed some of the first ever moving pictures.

Crowds in Albion Street celebrating the relief of Mafeking during the Boer War in May 1900. The building left mid-centre with the awning is the offices of the *Yorkshire Post* and *Yorkshire Evening Post*.

Private Charles Ward of Hunslet – who was one of the last, if not the last, to receive the award from the hands of the queen herself.

But some would argue that the greatest event in the town's history occurred on Monday 6 February 1893, when the mayor received a telegram from Herbert Gladstone, the Under Secretary of State at the Home Office: 'Have much pleasure in informing you that Her Majesty has assented to the petition of the Council that Leeds should become a city.' In 1897 the mayor became a lord mayor.

On 31 December 1900 the citizens celebrated again. Not only was the old year ending, it was the last day of the nineteenth century.[16] That evening watch night services were held at, among other places, the chapels at Belgrave Congregationalists, Mill Hill, and Victoria Road, Headingley. The same Monday evening the Grand Theatre was featuring its pantomime *The Sleeping Beauty* while the Theatre Royal competed with *Aladdin*. The Coliseum, however, proffered a glimpse of things to come, announcing that it was offering a 'special new programme of entirely new pictures and music' from the American Biograph Company.

The *Leeds Mercury*, after looking back on the achievements of the last century, looked prophetically to the future and reflected, with more accuracy than it can ever have dreamed, 'The new century will bring with it wonders far surpassing anything the wisest among us can foresee or imagine.'[17]

There have been many strange events in the history of Leeds. People were no doubt puzzled in 1767 at the Leeds man who, for a bet, ate twenty-seven 1*d* pies, drank what was described as 'a dozen of ale' and went on to lose the wager. They must have been bewildered by William Baxter, a local businessman from Hunslet, who launched an international campaign that rejected the need for doctors and claimed the body could cure itself if a patient drank his own urine. In February 1880 the townsfolk were shocked at the report that baby-farming was being carried out in Leeds. But no event was quite as bizarre as the infamous Dripping Riot of 1865.

Eliza Stafford had been appointed cook by Mrs Chorley, wife of the surgeon and local magistrate Henry Chorley, who lived in Park Square. At the end of January 1865 Eliza either gave or sold about 2lb of dripping to a dressmaker. Chorley was a benevolent and well-respected man and popular with the poor of the town, yet Eliza's action incensed him. She claimed it was a natural perk of the job; he claimed it was but one of several instances of thieving from his house, and the theft of the dripping was the last straw. Eliza was prosecuted and sentenced to serve a month in Armley Jail.

Some in the town took exception to the harshness of the sentence and began haunting the neighbourhood of Chorley's house. Graffiti was scrawled on walls, abusive letters were sent to his home, large placards were displayed declaring support for Eliza and doggerel ballads were sung:

> Now all you cooks and servant girls wot's very fond of 'tipping'
> Don't take your master's scraps of fat and boil 'em down for dripping:
> For if you do bear this in mind, the magistrates won't fail
> To try you in a private court and send you off to gaol.

Sensing trouble, the authorities elected to discharge Eliza at 7 a.m. on Wednesday 22 February instead of 9 a.m. as scheduled. She was spirited away to the station, where she boarded a train for Scarborough and the home of her daughter. When the crowd realised they had been denied the right to demonstrate at her release, they marched to Chorley's home – despite snowfalls. There, in the snow-covered square, they made their feelings clear, and missiles were thrown. The police turned out in strength, supported by officers from Bradford and two troops of cavalry from York. In the ensuing confrontation George Hudson, a potter, was killed, the Chief Constable, William Bell, fell and broke his arm, and another officer received a serious head wound. Four men were arrested, but the magistrates, sensing the injustice that had precipitated the event, took a lenient line. A public collection was carried out and Eliza contemplated opening a beerhouse with the proceeds – appropriately enough, she intended calling it the Dripping Pan.[18]

ten

MOMENTOUS CENTURY

'This century, like the last, is likely to witness momentous changes.' So wrote *The Times* on 1 January 1901. The first of those changes came just before 6.30 p.m on Tuesday 22 January 1901 as the Bishop of Winchester and the Revd Clement Smith quietly read special prayers in the royal bedchamber at Osborne House and Victoria's grieving family stood by. A few moments later the queen was dead. At 7 p.m. exactly the news reached Leeds. The great bells in the parish church and the Town Hall sonorously boomed their sombre tidings across the city and a special edition of the *Yorkshire Evening Post* was rushed onto the streets.

The next morning the world considered the news. 'A dreaded blow has fallen and a world-wide Empire mourns', *The Times* reflected, while the *Daily Mail* solemnly announced 'Her Majesty Passes Away in Peace Surrounded by Her Children and Grandchildren.' Over 3,000 miles away the *New York Times* ruminated on 'The greatest event in the memory of this generation'. In Leeds blinds were drawn and flags were flown at half mast. The lord mayor, Alderman Lawson, presiding at the police court, 'expressed on behalf of the magistrates their sense of the loss the nation had sustained'. Theatres and music halls in the town were closed. Various public functions were postponed, including the dinner of the governors of the Yorkshire College.[1] Just before noon on Friday 25 January the lord mayor, town clerk, chief constable, councillors and magistrates assembled at the top of the Town Hall steps. At the bottom a detachment of the Royal Field Artillery and the local Volunteers stood to attention as a crowd of 50,000 looked on. The mayor read the proclamation of Edward VII, called three cheers for the king and the National Anthem was sung.

They called the years that followed the Edwardian Summer, sometimes even extending it up to 1914, thus including the four years after Edward's death.

Lord Mayor, Frederick Willliam Lawson, reads out the proclamation of Edward VII from the steps of the Town Hall on Friday 25 January 1901. The fountain on the right was demolished in 1902. Note at the bottom of the steps a detachment of the Royal Field Artillery and the local Volunteers.

For some it was an idealised romantic period, a time for pleasurable pursuits. The members of the Thoresby Society enjoyed their trips out – for example, to Blackstone Edge in 1901. Society weddings were held, although one in December 1902 had a significant difference: for the first time in Leeds the bride arrived at the church in a motor car.

Visits to Roundhay Park and Kirkstall Abbey were popular, visits to the Grand Theatre to enjoy the performances of the Leeds Operatic Society equally so – although the society ran a risk in May 1907 when it deliberately ignored the Lord Chamberlain's diktat not to perform the *Mikado* while a Japanese royal prince was in the country.

But Leeds, like Britain, was also a bitterly divided society. Of every 1,000 babies born in the north of the city 89 died. In the south-east for every 1,000 born it was claimed that 152 perished. The years from 1901 to 1914 may well have seemed like the final days of a glorious golden summer, but in the decades that followed loomed the spectre of two of the bloodiest wars ever fought, social discord that divided the country and mass unemployment that brought untold suffering. Nevertheless, there were those in the city courageous enough and determined enough to grapple with the difficulties that lay ahead, and to transform the city and the lives of its people.

One major transformation occurred when Colonel Walter Thomas Harding, a local industrialist, saw his dream of a new and impressive entrance to the city realised. Proposals had been made in 1893 to transform the area in front of the station. One proposal was to name the new development after John Smeaton, the famous local engineer, but not surprisingly the council unanimously opted to call it City Square – as Leeds was being made a city that year. The initial plan had tramway waiting rooms and public lavatories greeting new arrivals to Leeds, but Harding had a much more dramatic and aesthetic concept in mind, and commissioned William Bakewell to design a square filled with statuary. The statues of four men who had made major contributions to the city were chosen: Dr Walter Farquhar Hook, Joseph Priestley, John Harrison and James Watt. Dominating the centre was to be an equestrian bronze figure, Edward, the Black Prince, by Sir Thomas Brock. A circular balustrade was to run round the square, surmounted with eight electric torch-bearing nymphs sculpted by Alfred Drury. Four were called Morn, standing proud and erect; the others, called Even, rested their weary heads on their shoulders. On Wednesday 16 September 1903 thousands gathered to see the square officially opened, and the freedom of the city was then conferred on Colonel Harding.[2]

But if the new City Square was a welcome cosmetic transformation, a far more serious one faced the authorities. Nothing in Leeds was more pressing when Edward came to the throne than the issue of public health. In 1904 the Leeds Children's Relief Fund was established to feed needy children, and the Education Committee began to issue a mixture of cod liver oil and malt. An improvement to diet generally was essential. In 1906 the city analyst revealed that 25 per cent of all food in the town was adulterated. Demerara sugar, he claimed, was often a mixture of dyed sugar and sand; tinned peas had copper added to give them colouring; coffee contained up to 30 per cent chicory; and at least 21 per cent of milk was diluted. To overcome the last problem the Leeds Pure Milk Supply Movement was set up that year. Its office was in Kirkgate, and from there unadulterated milk was available – sourced from a farm at Potternewton, and guaranteed to be sold within twenty-four hours of milking. From 1912 the Education Committee provided free dinners for children in need and from 1929 made available a third of a pint of milk a day for 5d a week. Medical inspections of children in Leeds schools commenced in 1910 and dental inspections in 1916.[3]

It was recognised that only by giving practical support to working-class parents could any real improvements to public health be made. Consequently

City Square opened in 1903 and is seen here in the early years of the century. On the left is the GPO building and on the right Mill Hill chapel. Dominating the square is Sir Thomas Brock's bronze statue of the Black Prince.

the Babies' Welcome Association was established in July 1907 to cater, as *The Times* reported, for the 'welfare of nursing mothers and suckling infants'. In October 1909 the first Leeds centre opened on Ellerby Lane. The council took over responsibility for the service in 1916, and by 1926 eighteen such centres were operating across the city, giving advice and training to mothers – particularly stressing the need for the prevention of disease. By the mid-1920s it was reckoned that 50 per cent of Leeds children were being catered for at Babies' Welcomes. So successful was the movement that when a new branch was opened at Armley on 9 August 1928 the Princess Royal came to perform the ceremony.[4]

The various Labour organisations in the city, including the Independent Labour Party, trade unions and the Co-operative movement, also campaigned for social change, and in February 1900 the Labour movement was unified nationally with the establishment of the Labour Representation Committee. Subsequently a Leeds branch was formed. In 1903 the Leeds LRC won its first seat on the council, when it captured New Wortley ward. That same year the Leeds party sent Isabella Ford as a delegate to the national conference in

Newcastle. She was the only woman delegate among 250 men. That year had a further significance for the new party. The Liberals and the LRC agreed that in certain constituencies they would not put up candidates in competition with each other, so they could concentrate on beating the Conservatives. In the general election of 1906 Herbert Gladstone, the Liberal, was victorious in Leeds West, having been given a free hand, while in Leeds East James O'Grady similarly won the seat for the LRC, which in February that year became known as the Labour Party. It was Labour's first Parliamentary seat in the city. O'Grady, a passionate Irish Nationalist, would hold the seat until 1918 and then represent Leeds South-East until 1924. That year he was knighted, and went on to be Governor of Tasmania (1924–30) and Governor of the Falkland Islands (1931–34).[5]

In October 1911 the Labour Party set up its own newspaper, the *Leeds and District Weekly Citizen*. It was a good-quality paper voicing the concerns of the working class and invariably supporting strikers during their disputes. Its support never faltered during the Municipal Workers' Strike of 1913. Sometimes called the Syndicalists' Strike, this broke out when workers claimed that despite increases in the cost of living no pay rise had been forthcoming for some years. An interim settlement temporarily ended a strike in June 1913, but on 11 December an estimated 3,000 council employees struck again. Power supplies were disrupted and brought chaos to the city; streets were plunged into darkness, trams brought to a halt, factories and mills were forced to work short-time, and tons of stagnant refuse lay uncollected. Charles Wilson, leader of the council, led a determined response and set up a committee of Conservatives and Liberals to handle the dispute. The *Citizen* called them the 'five intolerant Pharoes [sic]'; the *Yorkshire Post* responded that the strikers were 'anarchical' and 'hotheads'. Non-union labour was brought in, strikers fought with mounted police and bombs were planted at the electric power station at Crown Point and at Harewood Barracks – though no-one was hurt. By January 1914 the strike had been broken, but the council realised there was a desperate need to modernise itself.

The other great political movement of that Edwardian Summer was for women's suffrage. Leading activists in the Leeds Suffrage Society were still Emily and Isabella Ford and Leonora Cohen. The militant Women's Social and Political Union held meetings on Woodhouse Moor and Hunslet Moor, which attracted crowds of 100,000, while in 1906 Christabel Pankhurst addressed a gathering in the Queen's Theatre.

In 1907 Herbert Gladstone, the local MP, was faced with demonstrators at Bramley and Wortley, and even the Prime Minister was not immune. When Morley-born H.H. Asquith visited Leeds in October 1908 suffragettes besieged him at the Coliseum in Cookridge Street. Five protesters were arrested and incarcerated in Armley Jail, but suffragettes flew kites over the prison to show solidarity with their imprisoned colleagues.[6]

Three men in particular dominated Leeds politics during this period: Charles Wilson, the Conservative leader who led the council for virtually the first twenty years of the new century, James Kitson, Liberal politician and ironmaster, and William Lawies Jackson, Conservative politician and tanner.

The year 1906 saw Herbert Gladstone elected for Leeds West, suffargettes active in Leeds, football hooliganism at Elland Road break out and in December a snow storm brought the city to a halt. This is Thornhill Road so affected.

Kitson, employed first at the family's Monkbridge Iron and Steel Co. and then at their Airedale Foundry in Hunslet, became a highly successful businessman, and a dedicated Liberal politician who played a significant part both locally and nationally. It was he who was mayor in 1897 when the position became that of lord mayor, and, as a great local benefactor, he supported both the hospitals in the city and the Art Gallery. He was MP for Colne Valley (1892–1902), was knighted in 1886 and was ennobled as Lord Airedale in 1907. Like his Conservative opposite number, William Lawies Jackson, he was a passionate supporter of free trade.

Jackson took over his family's near-bankrupt tanning business in Leeds and turned it into one of the largest and most successful in the country. He became Conservative MP for Leeds in 1880 and then, when the town was divided into constituencies, sat for Leeds North in 1885. He famously chaired the Jameson Raid enquiry (1896–97), and it was under his leadership that the Conservatives gained control of the council in 1895. He was recognised as a God-fearing Conservative imperialist, and was ennobled as Baron Allerton in 1902.

But across the whole of Leeds society not all was political conflict and social struggle. People still enjoyed their leisure time. Huge crowds gathered

A Leeds soup kitchen set up for children during a miners' lock out. This was one of the many industrial disputes that took place between 1910–14.

at Elland Road to see Leeds City AFC – though in April 1906 many were appalled when Leeds played Manchester United and some bad refereeing decisions saw violence break out. Football hooliganism was not the only problem the club faced. In October 1919 the club was accused of making illegal payments to players and was expelled from the Football League. Leeds United AFC was then formed in May 1920. Rugby League had three well-supported teams, with crowds packing Barley Mow to watch Bramley RLFC, Parkside to watch Hunslet RLFC and Headingley to cheer on Leeds RLFC. The city also had two top-class Rugby Union sides: Headingley RUFC (1877), which played at Kirkstall, and Roundhay RUFC (1924). Headingley stadium, of course, also saw some of the great cricket matches involving both England and Yorkshire.

Meanwhile, in 1908 crowds flocked to see King Edward VII and Queen Alexandra drive round City Square on their way to open an extension at the university. Others, seeking a new experience in 1911, went for a ride on the strange-looking trolley bus that began running from the city centre to Farnley – it was the first such service in Britain. Even so trams remained the mainstay of public transport in Leeds.

The Education Committee first opened a pupil teacher college and then, in 1907 a new training college which moved to Backett Park in 1912.

Theatres like the Hippodrome, Theatre Royal and the Empire still played to packed houses, but it is significant that between 1900 and 1914 no new

The crowd waits the royal arrival of Edward VII and Queen Alexandra on Tuesday 7 July 1908. Ostensibly their visit was to open a new wing at the university. Note the statues of Queen Victoria unveiled in 1905 and moved to Woodhouse Moor in 1937.

Open-topped tram *c.*1901 passing through Victoria Square. Note on the immediate left a lion by the Town Hall and the Municipal Buildings. The fountain was demolished in 1902 and beyond it is the Leeds Permanent Benefit Building which would be removed to make way for the Garden of Rest.

Thoresby High School. The Leeds Pupil Teacher College on Great George Street opened in 1901. With the opening of the City of Leeds Training College the girls from the Central Higher Grade School were moved into the building to form a separate school in 1910.

theatres were built. Fashions were changing: in that same period fifty-seven cinemas were opened across the city. Two of them, the Cottage Road (1912) and the Hyde Park (1914), are still open.

But harsh reality swept away the fantasy world of films. On 28 June 1914 a Serbian student shot dead the Archduke Ferdinand of Austria. He was the first casualty of a war that would sweep the world. The *Leeds Weekly Citizen* prophesied it would be 'a war of dimensions unprecedented'. It was. Britain declared war on Germany on 4 August, and by September over 5,000 men had volunteered in the city. Three battalions were formed: the Leeds Pals, the Leeds Rifles and the Leeds Bantams. The *Yorkshire Post* reported that Leeds 'had the appearance of a town in military occupation'. While the men marched off to the front, women took over their role at home, acting as conductresses on the trams and working in the vital munitions industry. At Barnbow, between Cross Gates and Garforth, the most important shell factory in the United Kingdom was established. Women and girls made up 93 per cent of the workforce. It was a dangerous job, and on the night of 5 December 1916 an explosion ripped through Room 42, killing thirty-five women and seriously injuring others.

The 'war of dimensions unprecedented' that the *Citizen* had foretold became a reality in Leeds on 17 September 1914, when the first convoy of eighty wounded British troops arrived in the city. Hospitals were established to cater for the wounded; the City of Leeds Training College, which had opened in 1907 and moved to its new site at Beckett Park in 1912, was commandeered, as was Temple Newsam House. A hospital was opened at Chapel Allerton, and the Leeds Union Infirmary at the workhouse became the East Leeds War Hospital, later St James's University Hospital. Such unimaginable slaughter at the front had never been experienced before, and that carnage was felt in Leeds with a vengeance on 1 July 1916. It was the city's greatest disaster. On a fine sunny morning along a 20 mile stretch of the river Somme in France, the British army was given the order to advance. It was their worst military disaster: some 57,470 men perished on that day alone. The Leeds Pals were ordered to attack German machine-gun posts near the village of Serre – and of the 900 Pals no more than 150 were alive at sunset; every officer was dead. People reflected that it was as if every street in the city had lost someone.[7]

Not everyone agreed with the war. Sixteen conscientious objectors were imprisoned in Richmond Castle, and transported to France in 1916. When they refused to fight, the Richmond Sixteen, as they became known, were sentenced to death. Eight of the men came from Leeds. The sentences were commuted, however. They were not the only objectors. Objections to the war and to the old social order generally were raised across the world. In Russia the Czar was overthrown, and in 1917 a special meeting was arranged in Leeds. The Leeds Convention, or Socialist Convention as it is also called, was to meet on Sunday 3 June 1917. It was to show support for the Russian revolution, to campaign to end the war, to demand a charter of liberties and to argue for the setting up of 'town, urban and rural district' councils of worker and soldier delegates. Representatives came from the Labour Party, trades unions, the Independent Labour Party, the British Socialist Party, women's organisations, adult schools, Co-operative societies and peace societies. Delegates included some of the most famous political figures of the time: Ramsay MacDonald, Philip Snowden, Herbert Morrison, Ernest Bevin, Bertrand Russell and Sylvia Pankhurst. The two Leeds delegates were D.B. Foster and Bertha Quinn. The council was furious, refused permission for the Albert Hall in the Mechanics' Institute to be used and urged hoteliers not to accept bookings from the delegates. The police banned public meetings that weekend. The *Yorkshire Evening Post* insisted that 'There is plenty of evidence that the overwhelming mass of the people of Leeds object to the name of the city being associated with the Convention,' while the *Daily Express* sneered, 'Anarchy in Petrograd, chaos in the Russian armies and silly talk at Leeds.'[8] Nevertheless the 3,500 delegates managed to hold their meeting, using the Coliseum in Cookridge Street.

But that very weekend, on the nights of 3 and 4 June, the authorities found themselves distracted from the revolutionary goings on in Cookridge Street. Less than a mile away in the Leylands, a predominantly Jewish area of insanitary, mean back-to-backs, an anti-Semitic riot burst out. Youths egged on by miners and older men rampaged through the area, and inevitably Jewish youths retaliated. In all 1,000 young men were involved, but press reports were adamant that only Jewish properties had been singled out and destroyed. Eventually a strong police presence diffused the situation.[9]

The war dragged on for another year. Twelve Leeds men or men with strong Leeds connections were awarded the Victoria Cross, while a Leeds army chaplain received the Military Cross: Geoffrey Studdert Kennedy, however, is best remembered by his nickname, 'Woodbine Willie'. Another Leeds man also played his tragic part in the conflict. On Monday 11 November 1918 Private George Edward Ellison, a Leeds coal-miner serving with the 5th Royal Irish Lancers, was on duty near the Belgian town of Mons. At 9.30 a.m. a shot rang out, and the forty-year-old Leeds man fell dead. He was the last British soldier to die in the

First World War, and did so just ninety minutes before the ceasefire commenced. He was the last of 9,640 men from Leeds who perished in the conflict.

But if the world thought its tribulations were over it was sadly mistaken. A pandemic of influenza, Spanish Flu as it was known, was sweeping from continent to continent, killing between 20 million and 40 million people worldwide. It first struck England in June and July 1918. The attack appeared to be relatively mild, and on 5 November *The Times* was delighted to announce that 'The decline of the "influenza" epidemic continues, and it is evident the worst has been experienced.' It should have paid more attention to the concluding part of that same report, where it stated: 'There were 202 deaths from "influenza" in Leeds last week as compared with 101 in the preceding week and 41 the week before.'

Leeds had known influenza epidemics before. In 1837 large numbers in the town died, including the Vicar of Leeds. In 1847 and 1889–90 the virulence returned, but it was in 1918–19 that the city suffered worst of all. Pressure on doctors was enormous: one made 104 calls in a single day. Undertakers could not cope. Soldiers were drafted in as grave-diggers. Staff at the city's hospitals were decimated. Theatres and cinemas had restricted opening times. Elementary schools were closed. By December 1,132 people in the city had died. For a moment the outbreak waned temporarily, but in February 1919 it returned, and by the end of March a further 623 had perished.[10]

Dr J. Johnston Jervis had only been in his post as Medical Officer of Health for a couple of years when the epidemic struck the city, but he handled the situation well. Afterwards, with a team of gifted subordinates, he set about transforming the general health of Leeds people. The majority of people lived in back-to-backs and he identified one cause of ill health as poor housing, and claimed that 30,000 properties in the city needed demolishing.

Another was poor nutrition, though his argument that fish and chips contained 'all the necessary vitamins to build the body tissue of the human body' would not find favour with some nutritionists today. His campaigns for better nursery provision and against pollution without doubt enhanced the lives of thousands in the city, and it was under his guidance that St James's Hospital became one of the great hospitals in Britain.

If Jervis made his mark in public health it was an Anglican priest, the Revd Charles Jenkinson, the Vicar of St John and St Barnabas, combined parishes in Holbeck, who made the greatest contribution regarding housing. By 1926 the Conservative council had begun to build council estates at Hawksworth,

During the 1920s and 1930s extensive private housing developments took place across the city. Blue Hill Lane was one such development on a seventeenth-century highway.

Wyther Park, Meanwood, Cross Gates, Middleton and on York Road. Some 7,000 houses had been built by 1930, but Dr Jervis complained that the new tenants were 'not the class that stands most in need of improved conditions'.

It was, however, Charles Jenkinson who, appalled at the ineffective housing programme in the city, highlighted its shortcomings in a pamphlet *Sentimentality or Commonsense*, and drew attention to the problem. When Labour gained control of the council in 1933 Jenkinson was the obvious choice to become the Housing Committee's chairman. He drew up a plan – the 'Red Ruin', his opponents called it – to demolish 30,000 slum houses. It was far too ambitious, but by 1939 some 14,000 properties had been cleared away – by which time twenty-four housing estates had been launched. Jenkinson's most imaginative scheme, however, was the building of Quarry Hill Flats. These accommodated 3,000 people, and became internationally famous.[11]

In 1930 the Revd Don Robins became Vicar of St George's in the city centre. He saw the need for practical help for those who had fallen through the net of society, and turned the crypt of the church into an asylum where food, shelter and various forms of help were made available to those in need. St George's Crypt is still in operation to this day. Others also made strenuous efforts to improve the quality of life for the poorer sections of society. The Leeds Poor Children's Holiday Camp Association was founded in 1904 by Mrs Helen Currer Briggs, the lady mayoress, and Miss M.E. Richardson, to give poor children a holiday by the sea. In 1914 it opened its Silverdale camp near Morecambe Bay, and by 1922 was providing 10,000 of the city's children with a healthy break. That same year, in order to raise funds for the holiday camp,

Children's Day was instituted. This unique annual event saw the local community unite with the Education Committee, local newspapers and numerous businesses. On the appointed Saturday a vast cavalcade paraded through the streets of the city with the Queen of Children's Day, a girl selected from local schools, riding in style with the lord mayor. Their destination was Roundhay Park, where crowds in excess of 60,000 were waiting to greet them and to see demonstrations of maypole dancing, gymnastics and the finals of the schools' athletics championships.

More practically, the Boots for the Bairns charity was established in 1921. The Education Committee and the *Yorkshire Evening Post* agreed to act to prevent feckless parents from selling or pawning their children's boots and shoes. The organisation gave away boots with three small holes punctured at the top – pawnbrokers having guaranteed to refuse to accept such footwear as pledges. The scheme was a great success: between 1921 and 1930 it collected £60,500, and was able to provide 80,500 pairs of boots, 78,500 pairs of stockings and 184 other articles of clothing. The scheme showed just how hard the 1920s and '30s were for some families in the city. But Leeds was fortunate when economic crises struck because it had such a wide industrial base, thereby faring better than those towns dependent on a single industry.

In Leeds, of course, the major industry was ready-made clothing, and statistics for 1926 show that 30,837 people were employed in it. The next two most popular industries were the distributive trades (with 18,170 employees) and engineering (15,085 employees). In 1914 there were about 100 tailoring firms in the city, with unquestionably the three largest being Montague Burtons, Joseph Hepworths and Prices Tailors Ltd, which traded under the name of Fifty Shilling Tailors. It is said that between 1930 and 1960 these three firms produced half of all the suits worn by British men. The largest of these firms was Burtons. Montague Burton, a Lithuanian Jewish refugee, came to England in 1900, and in 1913 set up a bespoke tailor's shop in Leeds. During the war he made uniforms, and between 1920 and 1921 he opened a factory on Hudson Road. His firm went on to become the most popular clothing company in Europe, with 16,000 employees. The secret of his success was to make good quality suits at a price working-class people could afford, and which could be bought at any of his 595 shops. The company had a reputation for the care it provided for its workers.[12]

Not all firms were so thoughtful, and life continued to be a struggle for many Leeds people. Most, however, found an escape from their humdrum existence at the cinema, which continued to grow in popularity. From 1914 at least forty-two were opened. Some were deliberately designed to offer a luxurious environment where the public could escape the grim realities of a world scarred by pollution, and where economic gloom and, later, emerging German militarism threatened everyday life. Huge exotically furnished cinemas offered a gateway to the fantasy world of Hollywood. Such were the Majestic (1922) in City Square and the Paramount (1932) on the Headrow, later named the Odeon (1940), while in the suburbs similar grand schemes were developed with the Regal (1936) at Cross Gates, the Clock (1938) on Roundhay Road and the Clifton (1939) at Bramley.

Motoring grew in popularity, particularly among the middle classes, who by now were inhabiting the private housing that had proliferated at Roundhay, West Park, Adel, Moortown and Cross Gates. Such was the growth in traffic that a local Safety First Council was set up, and in March 1928 the first set of traffic lights in the city was installed at the junction of Park Row and Bond Street. Public transport flourished, with an extensive tramway system supplemented by petrol bus services from 1905. Local entrepreneurs like Sammy Ledgard and Robert Barr, through his Wallace Arnold Co., offered private bus and coach provision. From April 1935 Leeds Bradford Airport at Yeadon began operations.

Sport continued to offer a weekly escape from the mundane events of everyday life, with municipal parks across the city offering tennis courts, bowling greens, and cricket and football pitches. Golf also grew in popularity, though this was principally a middle-class activity. Golf clubs at Horsforth and South Leeds (1906), Alwoodley (1907), Moortown (1909), Sand Moor (1921) and Moor Allerton (1923) were all opened. That same year, thanks to the efforts of *Yorkshire Evening Post* journalist A.G. Bert Baker, the Leeds Municipal Golfers' Club was born, and two municipal golf clubs opened: Roundhay and Temple Newsam. In 1933 two more followed, at Gotts Park and Middleton.

At weekends many young men and women enjoyed ballroom dancing. Dances were held at church socials, while in winter the pools at Bramley and Armley Baths were covered over in order to convert them into temporary dance halls. The city centre ballrooms, such as the Majestic, Scala, the Mecca Locarno and the Empress Ballroom on Great George Street, better known as Mark Altman's, all attracted large crowds.

Most people smoked: Players, Capstan and Craven A were favourite brands, with the most popular cheap brand in Leeds being Woodbines, which could

be bought in packets of five. Pubs were ever busy, with Tetley and Melbourne, the local breweries, providing most of the beer. So popular were public houses that on one ½ mile stretch of Wellington Road there were eight pubs and three working men's clubs. Women were generally not allowed in the tap rooms. There were those concerned about the problems that drinking created. To counteract the drinking culture temperance organisations like the Rechabites flourished in the city, and the Nonconformists were also active. Church-going was still popular, although it was slowly beginning to decline from its height of the nineteenth century. Different denominations still viewed each other with suspicion at times.

One event united the city, however. Between 8 July and 17 July 1926 Leeds celebrated the tercentenary of receiving its charter in 1626. A replica of Moot Hall was erected in City Square, shops were decorated and special events were held. In Roundhay Park a children's tercentenary pageant was arranged and Sir Edward Brotherton, the Leeds benefactor, gave each of the 70,000 school-children in the city a bank book containing a shilling deposit. But 1926 also saw the nation bitterly divided. A dispute in the coal industry spread, and on 4 May the TUC called for a general strike to begin. In preparation the trade unionists in Leeds had already set up the Leeds Council for Action. The government and the council were equally prepared. Captain Hacking from the Home Office was sent to act as commissioner to the city, while Sir Charles Wilson and the council formed the Leeds Volunteer Services Committee. At least 10,000 volunteers came forward, though in reality only 2,000 were used. When the city's transport service was brought to a halt sixty police officers were called in to give protection to those transport workers who reported for duty, and at least 150 trams continued in service. That in turn precipitated a violent response from strikers, and rioting broke out in Duncan Street, Vicar Lane and outside the tram depot in Swinegate. On 12 May, however, the strikers accepted defeat, though the miners continued their action until November. The *Yorkshire Post* reported that as far as Leeds was concerned the picketing was 'by and large peaceful'.[13]

Two years before the strike the council had determined to embark upon an ambitious scheme to give the city an imposing thoroughfare. The width of the Headrow was to be doubled by sweeping away the buildings on the north side of the road, and the new buildings erected were to conform to a design by Sir Reginald Bloomfield. In 1929 the road was renamed Kingsway, but the people of Leeds were not happy: it seemed that they had had an Upper Headrow and a

Junction of Briggate and the Headrow. Opened in 1933 the new road was to be have been renamed Kingsway. Note the uniform style of Sir Reginald Bloomfield's architecture on the north side of the highway. Lewis's department store opened initially in 1932 and fully in 1938. Note also the policeman on point duty.

Lower Headrow in the city forever. The council relented, and the thoroughfare became the Headrows – though it was not long before the final 's' was dispensed with and it became simply the Headrow.[14] Another ambitious project, commenced in the 1920s, was the ring road, whose initial building used unemployed labour. Mass unemployment began to accelerate during the 1930s, until 17 per cent in the city were out of work, or 'laikin', as common parlance had it.

Unemployment relief schemes in Leeds helped to ease the burden by employing 34,000 on various schemes. New buildings arose; in 1932 the Duke of Kent opened both the baths at Armley and Leeds Modern and Lawnswood High Schools.

However, a much more grandiose scheme was contemplated, and this also ended in a Royal visit. No scheme was more imaginative and long lasting than the building of the Civic Hall. By 1930 it had become apparent that the growing city council was desperate for more room for its office staff. The departments of the town clerk, city treasurer, city engineer, the baths superintendent and the waterworks and sewerage engineer all needed extra accommodation. Using the Unemployment Grants Committee and employing a workforce 90 per cent of which came from the unemployment register, work began on the £360,000 project. On 23 August 1933 the Portland Stone building was opened by King George V and Queen Mary to a great show of loyal enthusiasm. The *Evening Post*'s headlines said it all: 'Record Crowds Assemble In Leeds To Greet The King – Every Vantage Point In The City Occupied – A

Leeds Modern and Lawnswood High Schools were opened by the Duke of Kent in 1932. Boys attended the Modern school on the right and the girls, Lawnswood on the left. The swimming bath separated the two identical buildings.

City Of Gaiety – Festoons And Streamers Deck The Streets.'[15]

Yet beneath that show of unity and joy an ugly element of anti-Semitism lurked in parts of the Leeds population. Following the riot in the Leylands in 1917 there were still places in the city that rejected Jews. Moor Allerton Golf Club was founded in 1923 simply because some clubs in the city operated a restricted membership policy. The 101 dance club advertised for 'English clientele only'. Some tearooms refused Jewish customers, while some firms, particularly in engineering and building, refused Jewish workers. This was not simply a Leeds phenomenon. Anti-Semitism was rampant across Europe, as Fascism grew more and more popular. In Leeds the Fascists established a club in Albion Street in 1926, and in 1933 Adolf Hitler rose to power in Germany on a programme based on hatred of the Jews. Within months a Jewish Refugee Committee had been established in England, and a branch was set up in Leeds under the supervision of David Makovski. It arranged for the admission of refugees to Britain and for their care, training, employment and, if necessary, their re-migration. By 1939 over 700 German Jews, fleeing persecution in their homeland, found help from the Leeds committee.

In Spain Fascists led by Franco revolted against the left-wing government. In the bloody civil war that followed twenty volunteers from Leeds went to join the struggle on behalf of the Socialist republicans, while Communists collected funds outside Kirkgate Market to aid their struggle. Meanwhile refugee children from Spain were brought for safety to Leeds and housed in a home at Hill Top, Armley. The greatest fear of Fascist aggression, however, came from a militarily resurgent Germany.

On 30 June 1936 people on the streets of Leeds looked up in astonishment to see one of the wonders of the age drifting slowly over the city's rooftops, and marvelled at the magnificent German airship, the *Hindenburg*, heading westwards on its way to America. But Vyvyan Adams, Unionist MP for Leeds West, did not marvel: he furiously demanded in the House of Commons why the airship had been allowed to fly over the city twice within a matter of weeks. Many held the view that its object was to photograph key installations in the Leeds area.[16]

But that same year, as Hitler flexed his muscles and Europe dithered before him, a major constitutional crisis engulfed the British Empire and almost brought down the monarchy. It was triggered by a Leeds newspaper: a simple editorial comment in the *Yorkshire Post* precipitated the Abdication Crisis. Whenever the Bishop of Bradford, Alfred Blunt, was to make a major speech, he was in the habit of sending the paper an advance copy. He did so in December 1936, expressing concern about the king's casual attitude towards religion, and that he seemed happy for Nonconformists to take part in the coronation. 'His personal views and opinions are his own,' the bishop mused, but in 'his public capacity at his Coronation he stands for the British people's idea of Kingship'. When Arthur Mann, the *Post's* editor, read this he believed the bishop was referring to Edward VIII's clandestine involvement with Mrs Wallis Simpson. Despite the world's press speculation about it, the British press had been united in refusing to make any mention of the royal love affair. Now Mann publicly reflected on rumours circulating in 'reputable United States journals and even, we believe, in some Dominion newspapers'. The Abdication Crisis was launched. Ironically, Bishop Blunt had never heard of Mrs Simpson!

The crisis was simply a temporary diversion from the grim reality of the large-scale unemployment that bedevilled the nation. In October 1936 the famous Jarrow Crusade arrived for an overnight stop in Leeds. The famous march by unemployed men from Jarrow to Westminster sought to draw attention to the appalling problem of unemployment in the North-East. In Leeds the men were warmly welcomed and given a donation to aid their return journey home by train. The same year also saw the shape of things to come. Fascist demonstrators targeted Jews in the city, and in September that year Sir Oswald Mosley proposed to march his black-shirted British Union of Fascists through the Jewish areas of the city, then demonstrate on Holbeck Moor. The Watch Committee changed the route, but allowed the parade to go ahead and the demonstrators to wear their uniforms. On Sunday 27 September Fascists from across the West Riding marched to the moor, but found themselves confronted by a mass of Communist sympathisers and Jews. The crowd of 30,000 clashed violently, and the police had difficulty in restoring order.

Although the fear of war hung heavy in the air, people still hoped for peace. On 9 March 1936 Leeds men and women reflected on the optimistic view

of the *Yorkshire Evening News*: 'Nobody wants a European war. No, not even Hitler. Not even Mussolini. All over the Continent the nations are preparing for Armageddon but deep down in the souls of the common people there is no desire for conflict. Too many of us still remember the lessons of 1914–18.'[17] Even so, war seemed inevitable, despite Prime Minister Chamberlain's policy of appeasement. The government prepared and in Leeds a Civil Defence force was organised. In 1938 George VI visited the city to see how effective it was. Gas masks were issued, and the council set up a unit trained to decontaminate food that might have been affected in a gas attack. The Leeds system was so highly thought of that it was used as a blueprint for the rest of the country.[18] By 1939 over 14,000 domestic air raid shelters had been erected in the city, and Alderman Bretherick had a brainwave. He suggested using government grants for building shelters to construct an underground monorail tramway system, which, he argued, could double up as air raid shelters when required. But the plan never materialised.[19] On 1 September 18,250 children, 1,450 teachers and a further 1,350 voluntary helpers were evacuated from the city and two days later, on 3 September, war was declared. The political parties in Leeds declared a truce and the people waited. The greatest fear was of air raids. Some had occurred in England during the First World War but none had affected Leeds. Now, however, having seen what German planes did to the town of Guernica during the Spanish Civil War, people waited in trepidation. Across the city eighty-five centres were established to provide food and shelter for families who might be rendered homeless by an aerial attack.

On 14 May 1940 an appeal went out for men to join the Local Defence Volunteers, and by 9 a.m. the next morning 2,600 had volunteered across Leeds. Later that year the LDV became known as the Home Guard. The city was divided into areas, each defended by a battalion, while some local firms formed their own detachments, amongst them Montague Burtons, Greenwood and Batleys, and Kirkstall Forge. Here the women, rather than simply serve in a support role as Nominated Women or Home Guard Auxiliaries, as women supporters were usually known, joined the men in full battle dress and took part in all the training exercises.[20] The Home Guard was called on during air raids to man anti-aircraft batteries and to guard wounded enemy prisoners of war in hospitals. Their main role was to help combat an invasion, which in 1940 remained the major fear. If London fell, Leeds was to be established as the Regional Centre for the Ministry of Defence, with its offices under City Square.

In preparation for an invasion, the Deputy Head of the SS, Reinhard Heydrich, had identified five Leeds men to be apprehended by the Gestapo: Professor Theodor Plaut and Professor Robert Bloch of Leeds University, Professor Selig Brodetsky, a celebrated mathematician and Zionist leader, Herbert Purcel Astbury, a Leeds engineer, who was sought for matters relating to defence and the armed services, and Karl Eschka, wanted for passport offences by the aliens police. There is no evidence that the German army intended using Quarry Hill Flats as its headquarters, but the Luftwaffe had detailed maps of the city, with munitions factories and other targets marked.[21]

The City of Leeds Training College at Beckett Park was again commandeered as a hospital. Two prisoner of war camps were opened in the city, at Post Hill, Farnley, and Butcher Hill, Horsforth. Air raid shelters in City Square and static water tanks in the Headrow were a grim reminder to Leeds people of the ever-present threat of German attacks. But there were moments of light relief. On Thursday 16 May 1940 a barrage balloon broke away from its moorings and drifted over Leeds. It caused havoc. As *The Times* reported, 'It tore up a lamp standard and wrapped itself round the tower of a hospital, demolished a number of chimney stacks and tore the slates off a number of house roofs before it was finally brought down by RAF men and taken away.' Its journey ended in Sheepscar Street North.[22]

Although Leeds was fortunate in that it suffered only nine air raids during the war, serious damage was inflicted. In all 197 buildings were destroyed and between 6,556 and 7,623 damaged; figures vary. The heaviest raid happened on the night of 14–15 March 1941: over 200 people were injured and sixty-five or sixty-six people killed. Despite this, Leeds's support for the war never faltered. In all £72 million was raised, including £9 million during Ark Royal Week, when the city collected to provide a new aircraft carrier to replace the recently sunk *Ark Royal*.

On 16 May 1942 Prime Minister Winston Churchill visited Leeds on a morale-boosting tour. The war dragged on. Then on Tuesday 6 June 1944 the *Yorkshire Evening Post* headline proclaimed, 'Invasion of Northern France Goes According To Plan.' It reported that in Leeds many servicemen passing through the city had not heard the news. When told, five French servicemen at the YMCA shouted 'Vive la France!' but were bitterly disappointed they could not celebrate until 11.30 a.m., when public houses were allowed to open.

On Monday 7 May 1945 Leeds people read the headline they had waited so long to see: 'Surrender. Mr Churchill's "VE" News Expected Any Moment.'

Albion Street was decked out with flags and many shops were decorated with Allied colours in anticipation of the announcement. When it came the council announced it would run 'a Bank Holiday service of trams and buses'. The lord mayor stated that as soon as the end was announced a ceremony of thanksgiving would be held from the Town Hall steps, two hours after the official announcement. The Vicar of Leeds would offer a thanksgiving, and a hymn would be sung followed by the national anthem.

Churchill returned to the city on 26 June 1945, this time campaigning in the general election. When the result of the poll was announced the people of Leeds were amazed to read the *Yorkshire Evening Post* headline: 'Labour wins election; Electoral landslide unseats many famous ministers.' It was contrary to

"*They're all right, Nobby, but for ruins give me Kirkstall Abbey any time.*"

On 4 June 1944, British troops entered Rome. Thack in the *Yorkshire Evening Post* took a decidedly parochial view of the event! (Cartoon courtesy of the *Yorkshire Evening Post*, 6 June 1944.)

what all the pollsters had predicted. Labour was swept to power, offering to radically change society, and Leeds found itself with its first woman MP, Alice Bacon, who captured Leeds North-East for Labour. The party also took control of the city council.

The end of the Second World War saw Britain virtually bankrupt and Clement Attlee's Labour government faced enormous problems, identified by the *Yorkshire Evening Post* as 'demobilisation, resettlement, housing and social progress'.[23] It was a difficult task made even harder in 1947 as blizzards swept across the nation from January to March, inflicting one of the worst winters the country had ever faced. Drifts between 4ft and 6ft deep brought the city to a standstill as an estimated 2¾ million tons of snow fell on Leeds. Coal supplies were disrupted, schools closed as coke supplies ran out and factories either closed or were forced to work part-time. The manager at Grangefield Mills at Bramley summed up the frustration that people felt: 'Yesterday and the day before we were idle for the want of coal and now we have an electricity cut!'

Charles Henry Wilson was a giant of man, figuratively and literally. This 20-stone Conservative leader dominated Leeds politics for thirty years and shaped the city's destiny more than any other politician. A passionate member of the Church of England, a teetotaller and a bibliophile, he began life as an accountant in South Parade. In 1890 he was elected as a Conservative councillor for North Ward and by 1904 he was the leader of the local party. Wilson was made an alderman in 1906 and a year later became leader of the council, a post he held for virtually twenty years, albeit with Liberal support at times.

Wilson saw Socialism as the greatest threat to the stability of the nation, and consequently fought the Labour Party whenever he could. He bitterly opposed the Municipal Workers' Strike of 1913–14 and organised the city's response during the General Strike of 1926. When the female lecturers at the City of Leeds Training College rebelled in 1916, Wilson emphatically backed Walter Parsons, the principal, and James Graham, the Director of Education, against them. During the First World War he played a crucial role in forming the Leeds Pals, and later in the conflict he became commander of the Leeds Group of Motor Transport Volunteers. He was knighted in 1923, and the same year he became MP for Leeds Central – a seat he lost six years later.

He negotiated the purchase of Temple Newsam for the council, and in 1928 pro-posed making Soldiers' Field at Roundhay an aerodrome. That was typical of the man whom the *Yorkshire Post* described as 'a dreamer of dreams'. One dream cer-tainly came true. He prophesied that one day people would be able to 'see face to face friends and relatives who may be thousands of miles away'.

To the *Leeds Weekly Citizen*, however, Wilson's dream was 'to make Leeds the hub of the universe.' His enemies called him the Sultan of Leeds, and there was no doubt he was a devoted municipal imperialist. 'I hope to see Leeds with an area of fifty thousand acres, knowing that some day the area will comprise three million inhabitants,' he wrote. Under his leadership between 1912 and 1927 the city acquired Roundhay, Shadwell, Seacroft, Cross Gates, Middleton, Adel, Temple Newsam, Eccup and part of Austhorpe. It was, however, during Wilson's failed attempt to absorb Pudsey and Farsley through the Leeds and Bradford Extension Bill of 1922 that he made his most famous remark. When asked a question about the city he responded, 'I am Leeds.' Charles Henry Wilson died on 30 December 1930.[24]

Charles Wilson (1859–1930), municipal imperialist. He extended the boundary of Leeds significantly during his time leading the council which he dominated for thirty years. Not for nothing was he known as the Sultan of Leeds.

The *Yorkshire Post* similarly reflected the feelings most people had: 'If ever a people deserved a gentle ... thaw, we do'. The thaw eventually did come, and the slow process of rebuilding the country began. But people grew tired of rationing and the austere way of life they still endured. Inevitably blame fell on the Labour government, so in the general election of 1951 Winston Churchill's Conservative Party regained control at Westminster, and the party control of Leeds City Council.

Three months after the new government had taken office an official announcement was made from Sandringham at 10.45 a.m. on 6 February 1952. King George VI had 'passed away in his sleep'. People in the city, like the rest of the country, were saddened at the news, campaigning in the by-election for Leeds South-East was temporarily halted and the nation prepared itself to face a new Elizabethan Age – and whatever that would bring.

The map shows the original parish boundary and the extended county borough boundary. When Leeds was given Parliamentary representation in 1832 only those people living in the parish could vote. The boundaries of the city were extended extensively under the leadership of Charles Wilson.

eleven

A NEW ELIZABETHAN AGE

oronation Day was Tuesday 2 June 1953. In Leeds bunting decked the city, street parties were arranged and a massive display was planned for Roundhay Park. But it rained! Grey skies hovered above as a blustery cold wind and downpours swept across the country. Nevertheless the people of Leeds celebrated. Street parties relocated to nearby schoolrooms, though at Carnaby Street, near Fenton Street Barracks, women and children wearing red, white and blue hats ignored the rain. On Woodhouse Moor a twenty-one gun salute was fired by the 269th West Riding Field Artillery, a grand firework display was held that evening in Roundhay Park, Meanwood Working Men's Club gave away six pints to each member and the council offered free rides on the two new single-decker trams that had just come into service.

During the day, for much of the time, the streets were unusually silent as most people settled down to listen to the coronation service on the radio or watched it on the new marvel of BBC television. That evening Winston Churchill, the Prime Minister, introduced the newly crowned Queen Elizabeth II, and remarked that 'the present is hard and the future veiled'.[1]

The present *was* hard. Food was still rationed; goods were difficult to come by; there was a housing shortage; and pollution still scarred much of the city. Life in early 1950s Leeds was not so very different from life there in the late 1930s and '40s. People used their corner shops, and the local Co-op or the Thrift stores. Saturday was the day to go shopping in the city centre or watch football or rugby. But there was one difference in post-war Leeds: although shops, theatres and dance halls were closed on Sundays, some cinemas were not. In 1946 the city had voted in a referendum to open cinemas on a Sunday, and those in central Leeds took advantage of this.

But the veiled future that Churchill spoke of hid changes that would transform the city and its people. Its demography would alter beyond all

recognition as New Commonwealth immigrants came to settle in Harehills and Chapeltown, Burley and Beeston. Great events would shape its destiny: it would be in the forefront of the revolution that information technology introduced. In place of the traditional dependence on textiles Leeds would eventually emerge as a major centre for legal and financial services, solicitors' offices, insurance companies, financial houses and call centres, and become a fulcrum for the nation's email traffic.

During the so-called 'Swinging Sixties' it saw greater freedoms being enjoyed in dress, in manners and in morals; people's lifestyles were greatly expanded, while the contraceptive pill ensured greater choice for women, and the austere days of the 1950s were consigned to memory. But the city would also see riots, would be traumatised over the serial killings of the Yorkshire Ripper, and, as in other major cities in the United Kingdom, would be appalled at the increase in crime, drug culture and football hooliganism that shamed society. And for four decades, hovering over Leeds and the rest of the Western World, was the threat of nuclear Armageddon in the shape of the Cold War.

But probably the change that was most immediately noticeable to people in Leeds related to pollution. Pollution manifested itself not simply in buildings disfigured by soot but also in dense, all-invasive fogs that brought the city to a standstill and impregnated the eyes and lungs of the population. In December 1822 the guard on the Kendal Union coach had to lead the horses by hand from Kirkstall Bridge to Leeds because the fog was so dense – and nothing much had changed 140 years later. Between 3 and 6 December 1962 a blanket of smog suffocated the city. Levels of sulphur dioxide eight times above normal were recorded. (According to *The Times* they were even higher than during the famous Killer Fog in London of 1952.) Leeds hospitals were called upon to treat thirty-seven people for respiratory diseases.

For a century or more pollution had occupied the public mind. In 1842, to its credit, Leeds council was the first in the country to take action to reduce noxious and offensive gases in the atmosphere. Even so, in 1844 J.D. Kohl was still able to comment that 'Leeds like all the great manufacturing cities in England is a dirty, smoky, disagreeable town ... perhaps the ugliest and least attractive town in all England.' However, efforts continued to be made to improve matters. Both the Leeds Society for Promoting Public Improvements and the Leeds Smoke Abatement Society drew the subject to public attention, but it was not until 1959 that smokeless zones were first introduced in the city. By 1973 there were 109 such designated areas.

Looking south over Leeds in 1975. Note the distinct lack of multi-storey office blocks. The Civic Hall is on the immediate left.

Looking east over Leeds in 1975. Note the parish church, the roof of the Corn Exchange and in the far distance the large number of multi-storey flats. The railway line on the left was extended through the town in 1869.

Probably the most horrendous example of pollution developed in West Leeds. From the 1870s until 1958 a factory in an area of dense back-to-back housing in Armley, manufactured asbestos mattresses and asbestos boiler linings. By the 1980s it had become apparent that the number of people in the neighbourhood dying from chest disease was significantly higher than in the rest of the city. After breathing in asbestos particles, they were developing mesothelioma, an incurable cancer. The problem was that the disease can take up to fifty years to show, and diagnosis can only occur in its later stages. John Battle, the local MP, raised the issue in the House of Commons in 1988. In 1994, when June Hancock was diagnosed with the disease, she sued the current owners of the business and was awarded damages of £65,000. Although June died shortly afterwards, her example led to many others suing for justice.[2]

If soot and industrial pollution were the main causes of pollution, it became apparent as the twentieth century unfolded that car exhausts were beginning to make a major impact environmentally. It was an issue that Dr Johnston Jervis, the Medical Officer of Health, and J. Goodfellow, Chief Public Health Inspector, brought to the attention of the Leeds authorities. But it was not simply the pollution from cars that caused difficulties; the increase in the number of vehicles itself became a major concern. In 1960 Leeds registered 42,974 cars. Within four years the number had reached 61,690. To solve the problem of parking in the city's streets parking meters were introduced on

5 April 1965 at a cost of 6*d* for forty minutes. By 1975 there were 1,700 such meters in Leeds, and the cost had risen to 10p. But a national strategy was required, and in November 1963 Colin Buchanan published *Traffic in Towns*, a detailed study of the effects that vehicles would have on the environment. Leeds was one of its case studies. Previous surveys of traffic in the town had tried to estimate the impact the increase in cars would have. One in 1951 recommended the building of the Inner Ring Road, and this was commenced in 1966. It took until 2009, however, for it to be fully completed. The Buchanan Report launched what became known as the Leeds Approach, which included proposals to build a series of long-term multi-storey car parks for commuters, to pedestrianise the city centre and to introduce bus lanes.

It was the age of the bus. Some 238 million passengers were carried annually on Leeds trams, but it was becoming obvious that there was a need for the council to rethink its transport policy. Oil was cheap, and the increase in traffic meant that boarding and alighting from trams when they stopped in the middle of the road was becoming more and more dangerous. Most Leeds people thought trams belonged to the past and that buses offered a brighter, better way forward. A phased withdrawal of trams began, and finally, on a cold, damp and foggy Saturday, 7 November 1959, a crowd gathered to watch the last convoy leave Selby Road junction and make its way to Swinegate. At about 7.15 p.m. the last of them, No. 178, clanged into the depot – and the age of the tram in Leeds was over.

With hindsight many people regret that decision today, as they do the failure to build an underground rail system in the town. William Vane Morland, the general manager of Leeds City Transport, had submitted such a proposal in 1944, his routes running from the Woodpecker Junction to Wellington Street; from North Street to Lower Briggate and from Woodhouse Lane to Neville Street via City Square. In October 1945, when the Labour Party gained control of the council, it considered the estimate of £750,000 a mile too much, and shelved the plan until a more propitious financial climate emerged. The scheme has never been officially rejected.[3]

In fairness the council had other major problems to address, and none more so than housing. It was not until about 1964 that the 1934 housing programme was completed. Many of the back-to-backs, those which were considered to be 'unfit for human habitation', were demolished, and in their place permanent post-war council estates were opened at Armley Heights, Cow Close, Ireland Wood, Moor Grange, Spen Lane and Tinshill.

So acute was the immediate problem after the war that some prefabricated homes were erected at Woodhouse, Seacroft, Becketts Park and Cottingley; then the council embarked upon erecting a series of high rise flats. Eventually it decided that such buildings were generally socially undesirable, and concentrated instead on providing houses and maisonettes. Meanwhile private housing at West Park, Adel, Cookridge, Cross Gates and Moortown continued to be built.

One of the truly great breakthroughs in those immediate post-war years was in education. The 1944 Education Act was implemented and that meant all children sat the eleven plus examination. This decided which type of education was most suitable for them: secondary grammar at schools like Lawnswood High, secondary technical at Central High or secondary modern at schools like Brudenell. In 1956 an attempt to introduce comprehensive education was tried at Foxwood School, and by 1967 three other such schools had been opened. To cater for the increase in pupil numbers a new training college was opened at Farnley in 1959, on the site of the old special school. It became known as the James Graham College of Education in 1961.[4]

During the 1960s radical changes in the curriculum were introduced. For example, in 1966 Leeds, working with the Nuffield Foundation, pioneered a revolutionary approach to teach French to children as young as eight. New schools were also essential for the changing population. In 1905 there were 30,000 children living within a mile radius of the city centre, with only 6,700 dwelling on the city outskirts. By 1966 the situation was completely reversed: only 2,400 then lived within a mile of the town centre, while some 30,000 lived in the suburbs.[5]

Dramatic strategies needed to be devised, and the council, irrespective of its political hue – Labour (1945–51), Conservative (1951–53), Labour (1953–67) and Conservative (1967–72) – rose to the occasion. One of its biggest challenges was to deal with the large influx of New Commonwealth immigrants who arrived in the city during the 1950s and '60s. Over the previous century Leeds had absorbed two major immigration influxes: the Irish in the 1840s and Jews in the 1880s. The last two decades of the nineteenth century saw a small Italian community arrive in Leeds, and in the early years of the twentieth century a Polish community was established. But the largest wave of new immigrants, this time from the New Commonwealth, arrived in the 1950s and '60s. They settled in the poorer areas of the city, generally the West Indians in Chapeltown, the Asians in Harehills and Beeston. Burley was multi-racial.

A further group arrived in August 1972, when President Idi Amin expelled 50,000 Asians from Uganda.

Although the new arrivals faced similar difficulties to those that the Irish and Jews had faced, theirs were compounded by other factors. Their religions were very different from that of the indigenous community, their social customs were equally dissimilar and they were visually more noticeable. Certain sections of the English community resented the fact that many immigrants refused to adopt western lifestyles, and claimed that the authorities gave preferential treatment to the newcomers. The newcomers in turn pointed out that they were discriminated against and that unemployment of Afro-Caribbean and Asian people was far higher than that of white people, and frequent allegations were made that the police were racist. An additional problem was that younger members of these communities often faced a dilemma as they found themselves torn between the strict moral traditions of their own communities and the much freer way of life enjoyed in British society generally.

Green Lane Board School. Opened in 1874 in the congested area of New Wortley, it famously housed its playground on the roof. The school closed in 1982.

But despite these difficulties the newcomers settled in, finding employment in heavy industries, the manufacture of surgical boots and shoes, and running garages and corner shops, mini-supermarkets and restaurants. The first gurdwara or Sikh temple opened in a house in Savile Road in 1957. The following year Muslims in Leeds opened their first mosque in a house in Leopold Street. The Hindus opened their temple on Alexandra Road in 1969. In 1965 Albert Johanneson of Leeds United became the first black player to play in an FA Cup Final at Wembley. When Diana Phillips was appointed a JP in 1967, she was the first West Indian to be so honoured. Major efforts were made by both communities to create harmony and understanding, despite tensions arising at times. On August Bank Holiday Monday 1967 a great Caribbean Carnival, attended by 150,000 people, was held in Chapeltown. It is today second only to the Notting Hill Carnival, and has become one of the city's traditions.[6]

If the demography of the city changed, so too did its industries. By 1955 there were only thirty-five firms left in the textile industry. Hunslet, once its centre, had none, and by 1980 only six firms were listed as manufacturing cloth in the town. Ready-made clothing, too, fell into a steep decline. Many of the larger firms failed to respond to changing markets and found it increasingly difficult to compete with imports. Smaller firms began to concentrate on bespoke tailoring.[7]

Shopping, too, underwent a major change. During the 1960s some suburbs in Leeds developed Arndale shopping centres, at Armley, Cross Gates and Headingley. Meantime the *Financial Times* claimed, in March 1961, that the first fully fledged discount store to open in this country was Grandways in Leeds. The city was at the forefront of the supermarket revolution, when one of the big five was founded in the city. In 1920 Hindells' Dairy Farmers Ltd established Craven Dairies in Leeds, changing its name in 1949 to Associated Dairies and Farm Stores Ltd. From the 1920s the Asquith family owned a butcher's shop in Knottingley and a store in Castleford. In 1965 the two companies merged, and so ASquith and DAiries became ASDA. In July 1999 it became part of the American Wal-Mart company, though its headquarters are still in Leeds.

Shopping in the city centre changed. Huge shopping malls were created: Merrion Centre (1964), Bond Street Centre (1974) which became the Leeds Shopping Plaza (1977), St John's Centre (1985), the Headrow Centre (1990) and the Light in the old premises of the Leeds Permanent Building Society (2001). In 1997, on a 76-acre site off the ring road at Beeston, the White Rose Shopping Centre opened, offering free parking space for 4,800 cars and setting a new trend for out-of-town shopping. But these new ventures took a toll on firms that had graced the streets of Leeds for decades. Marshall and Snelgrove, which had opened on Bond Street in 1869, closed in 1971; Schofields, which appeared in Leeds in 1901, finally closed in 1996; Lewis's, which opened in 1932, went into receivership in 1991 and was sold to Allders in 1996.

Cinema-going also changed. The relentless march of television throughout the 1950s and '60s proved too great a challenge. The Odeon in Leeds made an effort by attracting some of the world's best entertainers to perform live on its stage: Ella Fitzgerald (1957), Louis Armstrong (1959), Judy Garland (1960), Cliff Richard (1963), the Beatles (1964) and Shirley Bassey (1965) all came to the city. But it was to no avail. By 2012 Leeds, which once boasted ninety-six cinemas, had four: two old ones, the Hyde Park and Cottage Road, and two new ones, the Vue on Kirkstall Road with nine screens and the Ster Century cinema on the Headrow with thirteen.[8] Many of the old cinemas,

like the Harehills, the Western, the Clock, the Regent on Torre Road and the Gaumont, were converted to bingo halls as the new gambling craze swept the nation. Working men's clubs in the city also offered bingo to their members, and the profits raised made a significant contribution to club running costs.

Television became the great pastime of the people. Initially it came from the BBC, who had long supplied the radio programmes to the nation. When the corporation was established in 1927 it took over the studios in Basinghall Street of the privately owned British Broadcasting Company. In January 1933 it moved to Woodhouse Lane, and broadcast its radio programmes from there. With the advent of television, Leeds people watched BBC programmes beamed from Manchester until 1968, when it began televising programmes from temporary studios in All Souls' church in Blackman Lane. It was a significant year for Leeds. In June that year BBC Radio Leeds began operating, and in July Yorkshire Television began its commercial programmes from its newly built studios on Kirkstall Road. Until then Leeds viewers wanting to watch commercial television had to watch Granada's Manchester output. In 1981 Radio Aire, the Leeds commercial radio station, opened – also based on Kirkstall Road.

If television in the 1950s and '60s changed the lifestyles of many people, the city itself underwent a transformation. The building of the M1 and the M62 motorways placed Leeds at the hub of the nation's transport system and Leeds became known as the Motorway City of the '70s. But in doing so the new highways tore out the heart of the ancient townships of Hunslet and Holbeck. Huge office blocks rose across the city centre – upended glass and concrete shoe boxes, as some referred to them. And in the name of modernisation old buildings were swept away regardless of their historic value. The destruction of Sir Gilbert Scott's Becketts' Bank on Park Row was one demolition too many, and in 1965 the Leeds Civic Trust was established. It determined to protect the city's architectural heritage, and its prompt campaigning saved Thomas Ambler's St Paul's House, the Moorish-style clothing factory and warehouse in Park Square, and the Bank of England building on South Parade. A voluntary body, it still continues its work to influence the planning of the city and preserve the 'beauty, history and character of the town'.

But the character of the town was blighted by a darker side. By the end of the 1960s Leeds United, for so long a mediocre team that hovered between the First and Second Divisions, developed a side under Don Revie, the manager, that became unquestionably one of the finest teams in the world. However, its performances were marred and the name of the city blackened by the behaviour of a group of its supporters. Football hooliganism became a social phenomenon that plagued many English football clubs from the 1960s, and the tribal violence indulged in by some Leeds supporters was typical. Leeds fans gained an international reputation for violence when they clashed with opposition supporters; in particular the bitterness was most marked when Leeds played Chelsea and Manchester United. The vast majority of Leeds supporters were appalled, and the club itself did everything in its power to prevent it. Unfortunately the name of Leeds became synonymous with football hooliganism, a reputation enhanced when the team played Bayern Munich at the Parc de Princes in Paris in the European Cup Final on 28 May 1975. A disallowed goal saw Leeds lose the match, and before a worldwide television audience of millions the Leeds fans ran riot, causing millions of pounds worth of damage. Later the Leeds Service Crew gained a reputation for violence when its members clashed with rival supporters. When Leeds played Birmingham City in 1985 a young supporter died, and then in May 1990 Leeds fans rampaged through the streets of Bournemouth, creating mayhem. Allegations were made that racism aggravated by the National Front was in part to blame. Although the problem has been contained it still occurs from time to time.[9]

Serious race rioting also broke out in the city on occasion. In July 1969, following a murder in Woodsley Road, Burley, rioting broke out between white and non-white youths. Two further serious outbreaks occurred on 4 November 1974, and on the same date in 1975. In the first incident a fire engine called to a fire in Moortown was attacked by youths, and six firemen were injured. The second incident in Chapeltown was more serious: between 150–300 mainly black youths raced through the streets, hurling missiles and fireworks and attacking the police who were sent in to contain them. The worst riots of all, however, were in July 1981 when crowds of mainly black teenagers supported by a large number of white youths attacked the police. They were following a national trend, as similar riots occurred at the time in Blackburn, Blackpool, Bradford, Brixton, Cirencester, Crewe, Derby, Gloucester, Halifax and Hull. The damage in Leeds was estimated as being between £1¾ million and £2 million. Chapeltown saw further serious outbreaks. For two nights in June 1987 rioting occurred in the area: petrol bombs were thrown, buildings burnt and looted and vehicles attacked. In October 1994 a mob attacked police officers, the confrontation lasting for two hours. Harehills saw an outbreak in 2001 involving 200 rioters, and cars and property were destroyed.[10] After each occasion community relations were seriously disrupted, but determined efforts by

community leaders, the council and the police managed to re-establish order and generate communal harmony. Interfaith strategies were devised in the 1970s, designed to bring different religious groups together, and in 1985 the Concord Multi-Cultural Resources Centre was opened to help disseminate ideas about other faiths.

The 1981 outburst of street violence in Chapeltown had started off near the Hayfield public house, a place that became deeply involved in the drug culture in Leeds. The area itself developed a bad reputation for both drugs and prostitution. Drugs were not a new problem in the town. In 1845 James Smith remarked that Leeds people showed 'a desire for spirits and opiates'. During the 1960s, however, a drug culture developed across the western world. The use of cannabis, amphetamines, hallucinogenic drugs such as LSD and 'hard drugs' like heroin became common, and in 1967, in order to combat the deteriorating situation, Leeds City Police formed a drug squad. But the use of drugs increased. The end of the century saw every part of the city affected, and it also began to be a problem in some schools. By then 80 per cent of crime in Leeds was drug-related and drug barons, engaging in turf wars, brought repeated violence to the streets. Gun crime had been rare in Leeds up to the 1960s: of the ninety-two men and one woman hanged at Armley Jail, only three of those executed were men who had shot someone in the city.

As crime rose dramatically in the 1960s the Leeds Sub-Regional Crime Squad, made up of officers from the Leeds, Bradford and West Riding forces, was formed in 1963. With the collapse of the Communist bloc, guns became readily available from Eastern Europe, and criminals in Leeds could purchase or hire them from various public houses in the town, in particular the Hayfield and the Market Tavern, known locally as the Madhouse. Among certain sections of the community guns became almost a fashion accessory, and shootings in the city occurred with unfortunate regularity. Two police officers died as a result of gun crime: Sergeant John Speed was gunned down outside the parish church on 31 October 1984, and PC Ian Broadhurst was shot in the Oakwood area on Boxing Day 2003.[11]

But for the vast majority of Leeds inhabitants crime was simply something they read about in the press. But what of that press? The city was fortunate that it was well served with a wide range of publications. Only twice, however, did it ever host a national newspaper: for seven years it was the home of the Chartists' *Northern Star*, from 1837 to 1844, and then from 1925 to 1930 it published the northern edition of the *Daily Chronicle*. The *Leeds Weekly*

Citizen, the Labour Party's local publication, continued its campaigning from its inception in 1911 until its demise in 1986. It most famously supported the Municipal Workers' strike of 1913–14, and the lesser known rent strikes of 1914, when tenants struck against a proposed increase in rents, and 1934, when council tenants objected to the Labour council increasing rents so that slum dwellers could be housed free.

The *Yorkshire Post* was still popular, but many in the city preferred to take the national newspapers in a morning. The evening market was split between the *Yorkshire Evening Post* and the *Yorkshire Evening News*. The competition was further continued on a Saturday evening, when both papers published sports editions: at the time it was the only way people could find out the football results. The *Post's* was a buff coloured edition while the *Evening News* was green – hence its common name, the *Green 'Un*. In December 1963 the *Evening News* was taken over by the *Post*, and Leeds was left with only one local paper. It was to introduce some opposition to this monopoly that the *Leeds Other Paper* was born in 1974. This left-wing publication continued under that name until 1991, when it became the *Northern Star*. However, like its Chartist predecessor, it was eventually forced to close – and did so three years later. In 1980 a new trend in publishing arrived from the USA. Newspapers, known as free sheets, were given away. Although they were primarily advertising sheets, they contained a considerable amount of editorial copy. That year United Provincial Newspaper Group, which owned the *Yorkshire Post* and *Evening Post*, launched the *Leeds Weekly News*. It publishes separate editions for different areas of the city, and consequently often concentrates on parochial matters that would be ignored by mainstream publications.

Reading habits changed as the century progressed, and newspaper circulations fell. Life in the latter part of the century saw great changes generally. More and more people owned washing machines, fridges and freezers, telephones and cars. Dining out in the vast numbers of restaurants that opened in Leeds became a popular pastime. Holidays took on a different dimension. Instead of the traditional holidays in Bridlington and Scarborough, Morecambe or Blackpool, Leeds people, like the rest of the country, sought more exotic locations abroad. The commencement of international flights from Leeds Bradford Airport accelerated the trend.

Cultural activities in the city saw the Leeds International Pianoforte Competition commence (1961); Opera North established at the Grand Theatre (1978); and the Leeds International Film Festival (1986). The popular music scene, too, was not neglected. Entertainers such as the Rolling Stones (1982) and Michael Jackson (1988 and 1992) performed at Roundhay Park, while from 1999 the city hosted the northern leg of the Reading Festival, known as the Leeds Festival, on August Bank Holiday weekend. By the first decade of the twenty-first century there were some 1,000 local bands in the area, the most famous being the Kaiser Chiefs, one of the most successful bands in the country.

In literature Leeds can claim two of the world's most popular authors. Barbara Taylor Bradford, born in Armley, who commenced work on the *Yorkshire Evening Post* when she was fifteen years old, has gone on to write twenty-five novels – which have sold in excess of 81 million copies worldwide. Alan Bennett, also born in Armley, is one of Britain's most highly acclaimed playwrights. Richard Hoggart, born in Chapeltown but brought up in Hunslet, wrote the seminal work on working-class life in Leeds, *The Uses of Literacy*. He went on to become Assistant Director-General of UNESCO.

Hoggart was a product of the old grammar school system, attending Cockburn High School, but the educational provision in the city was changing. In 1972 Leeds opted for a comprehensive system based on three tiers; first schools catered for five to nine year olds, middle schools nine to thirteen year olds; high schools thirteen to eighteen year olds. The system was changed again in 1991–92, when the council decided to revert to a two tier system; five to eleven year olds and eleven to eighteen year olds. Changes in higher education also occurred. In 1970 Dr Patrick Nuttgens was appointed to amalgamate the colleges of Technology, Commerce and Home Economics, to form Leeds Polytechnic. In 1976 the City of Leeds Training College, Carnegie College of Physical Education and James Graham College were also absorbed, as were some parts of the College of Art and Design. The polytechnic became independent of the council in 1989, and in 1992 became Leeds Metropolitan University.

The year 1974 saw one of the biggest changes Leeds has ever experienced. It had been agreed by many that for some years local government was in need of re-organisation; consequently the Local Government Reorganisation Act was passed in 1972, coming into force two years later. It revolutionised local government in Britain. Leeds became the second largest metropolitan district in the United Kingdom. Its opponents saw the city, like some huge leviathan, devouring all around it. Otley in the north-west, Rothwell in the south east, Wetherby in the north-east, and Morley and Pudsey in the south-west all

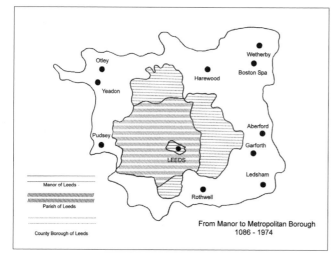

The Metropolitan Borough of Leeds. The manor of Leeds was described in Domesday Book in 1086. It was part of the extensive parish of Leeds which became the Parliamentary constituency in 1832. It became a municipal borough in 1836, a county borough in 1889 and a metropolitan borough in 1974.

From Manor to Metropolitan Borough
1086 - 1974

reluctantly became part of this vast new borough. Alderman Frank Marshall of Leeds dismissed the protesting councils with the simple comment that they should 'broaden their minds'. The population of Leeds now stood at 738,931.

One thing that caused disquiet in the old borough of Leeds was the fact that under the new act the Leeds City Police Force would cease to exist, and was to become part of the new West Yorkshire Metropolitan Police Force (later renamed West Yorkshire Police).[12] The old Leeds force was generally well-respected in the town, tackling the problems of hooliganism at Elland Road intelligently and proudly claiming it never needed to call for support from Scotland Yard. There were, however, allegations of racism levelled against it at times, and it was bitterly criticised in 1969 over the death of David Oluwale, a mentally unstable vagrant. Within a couple of years of its inception the new force was faced with one of the major crimes of the century, and in the opinion of a later government inquiry was guilty of bungling and incompetence, with its senior officers lacking both imagination and flexibility. The serial killings of Peter Sutcliffe, the infamous Yorkshire Ripper, traumatised the Leeds public, and thirty years later people in the city still remember that time with horror. From 1975 to 1980 at least thirteen women, some of them prostitutes, were butchered by Sutcliffe, mostly in the Leeds area. The investigation became bogged down as 250 detectives conducted 21,000 interviews, at a time when sophisticated computer programmes were not available. They were further handicapped when hoax letters and a cassette tape led them astray. The city was gripped with fear and suspicion. Restaurants noted a drop in trade; women attending evening classes and dances were advised to travel in groups; it was noticeable girls no longer went to the cinemas or the local public houses alone; and schools cancelled after-school activities. Sutcliffe was eventually arrested, but initially for a minor motoring offence. He confessed to the Ripper murders, his defence was that 'God was controlling me'. He was tried and found guilty in May 1981. Declared a paranoid schizophrenic, he was held in Broadmoor. The hoaxer who so misled the investigation was eventually arrested and sentenced in March 2006.[13]

By the 1970s a sexual permissiveness was noticeable across society, and Leeds was no different. The red light district of Leeds was now centred on Chapeltown; several sex shops opened in the city; soft porn films were available at the Plaza cinema, Upper Briggate; and the Gaiety public house on Roundhay Road set a new trend by featuring topless waitresses.

The abuse of women became a social issue. Two women's refuges were set up in the Burley area of the city, despite lack of council support. The Salvation Army converted Mount Cross Maternity Home at Bramley into flats for deprived women and children. Feminist movements sprang up across the country. A splinter group, the Leeds Revolutionary Feminists, was set up in the city, in turn forming an action group, Women Against Violence Against Women, which organised attacks on sex shops and condemned pornography. In November 1980 the group held their conference at Royal Park Middle School in the city, the same week as Sutcliffe's last killing, less than a couple of miles away from the school. Furious at the failure of the police to make any arrest, 500 women marched in protest through the city's streets. From City Square to Briggate they went, attacking the Odeon and the Plaza, where soft porn films were being shown, attempted to break into the BBC studios on Woodhouse Lane and assaulted any men they came across on their way. The women claimed, 'We have made our point'; the *Yorkshire Post* loftily responded that they were 'at best second rate men'.

The abuse of women was but one of the major social problems besetting Britain in the latter years of the twentieth century. Social deprivation was widespread, and 20 per cent of the local population in Leeds was affected. In 1986 there were 2,600 houses in the city that still had no bath, inside lavatory or hot and cold water. Certain areas suffered not only from inadequate housing but also from a high crime rate and long term unemployment. The council designated those areas in need of help Urban Priority Areas: Armley, Beeston Hill, Burmantofts, Burley, Chapeltown, Harehills, Holbeck, Osmondthorpe, Stanningley and Woodhouse.

From the 1970s Britain also found itself facing major economic problems, compounded by regular industrial disputes. Politically the country became polarised between a Labour Party moving to the left and a Conservative Party moving to the right. In an attempt to bridge the gap, the Social Democratic Party was founded, with some Labour councillors in Leeds defecting to it. It made little progress in the city, however, and in 1982 had only one councillor. The general election of 1979 swept Margaret Thatcher and the Conservatives to power, although no seat in Leeds changed hands during that election. The new government's policies became known as Thatcherism. This was a radical attempt to reinvigorate the economy by encouraging entrepreneurs to develop new initiatives less handicapped by regulations, to discard old and inefficient industries, and encourage people to be more responsible for their own lives. Its opponents accused it of creating mass unemployment and bitter divisions between rich and poor, as well as placing excessive emphasis on materialism in place of compassion and harmony in society. In Leeds these policies saw housing associations take over the provision of social housing from the council.

In 1985 the council had published a plan for the regeneration of the rundown area of the waterfront, but in 1988 the government superseded the council by appointing an unelected quango, the Leeds Development Corporation, to undertake the work. It was bitterly opposed by the Labour Party and the Chamber of Commerce, while the *Yorkshire Evening Post* ran a vitriolic campaign headlined 'Behind Closed Doors', in which it demanded that the new corporation's board meetings should be open to public scrutiny. Eventually the Labour council and the Development Corporation began to work together, and the dilapidated area of derelict warehouses and run-down docks on the river were converted into expensive apartments, hotels and quality restaurants. Unquestionably its finest achievement was the building at Clarence Dock of the Royal Armouries Museum, which the queen opened in 1996. If that was the positive side of the Development Corporation, its plan to rejuvenate the Kirkstall valley led to charges of corruption. Its members were accused of failing to declare their personal interests, and it was claimed that some members of the corporation had links to the Conservative Party.

Two other controversial policies brought in by the Thatcher government and which affected the city concerned public transport and the poll tax.[14] In 1974, as Leeds became a metropolitan borough, the West Yorkshire Metropolitan Council took over control of public transport in the city and established the West Yorkshire Passenger Transport Executive, with its service known as

Metro. Following privatisation in 1984 it became Yorkshire Rider and from 1995 First Bus. Arriva is its main rival in the city. The introduction of the Community Charge in 1990, usually referred to as the poll tax in England and Wales, was extremely unpopular and led to riots across the country. In March a mob of about 300 clashed with police outside the Civic Hall, protesting at the council's decision to impose a charge of £348. 'Break the poll tax, not the poor' and other such slogans were daubed on the building, and the protesters then led a torchlight procession through the streets. It was argued that two left-wing groups, the Socialist Workers' Party and Militant Tendency, were the principal organisers.

Right Crown Point Bridge and the Port of Leeds *c.* 1970. Run-down warehouses line the waterside.

Below A radical transformation. Crown Point Bridge in 2012 and exclusive apartments now line the waterside.

If the Conservatives held sway at Westminster both major parties held power in Leeds: Conservatives (1976–80) and Labour (1980–2004). Both parties embarked on a policy where councillors became more actively involved in running the corporation. Morale among council employees was affected and certain services suffered. Education was one such service. In 1992 the Office of Standards in Education (Ofsted) was set up, and in 1999 its inspectors found the local authority less than efficient. The council set up Education Leeds in 2001, its remit to provide the service with support from a private company, Capita.[15] In April 2011 Education Leeds was taken over by a new children's services department of the council.

The 1997 general election saw the Conservatives suffer a heavy defeat, and for the first time since 1837 no Conservative was returned for any of the city's constituencies. If Labour could take satisfaction from that, it had little cause for comfort in the by-election for Leeds Central in 1999. When Hilary Benn won it for Labour, the turnout was just 19.6 per cent, the lowest in any Parliamentary election in the United Kingdom since the war.

The Green Party gained its first seat in 1998 when David Blackburn won Wortley ward in the council election that year. In 2004, when Labour lost control of the council they had won in 1980, the Greens joined the other parties in a rainbow coalition. Coalition councils continued for the first ten years of the new century: Liberal Democrats, Conservatives and Greens (2004–07), Liberal Democrats, Conservatives (2007–10), Labour and Greens (2010). Labour regained overall control in 2011.

The last decade of the twentieth century and the first decade of the twenty-first saw Leeds change dramatically. It was now seen as a city of academic prowess; Leeds University catered for 33,323 students and Leeds Metropolitan University for 29,000. Amazing new skyscrapers transformed the landscape.[16] New industries undreamed of a century before blossomed as Leeds became a major European city. It still retained its prominent position in printing, and is the second major centre in the country for paper, printing and publishing. Leeds is the third largest centre for media and communications in the country. There are about thirty national and international banks in the city, as well as accounting firms, insurance companies, law firms and companies offering financial services. It became a place for entrepreneurs. On 22 September 1998 Rob Wilmot and Ajaz Ahmed set up Freeserve, the world's first internet service provider to dispense with a monthly subscription fee. When it sold its shares to Wanadoo, a French Telecom company, in 2001, it had 2 million customers and was worth £1.65 billion.

The last phase of the motorway at Leeds linked the M1 with the A1 and the North.

But if Leeds now played a major part in the international community, it also found itself involved in international crises. During the so-called 'Troubles' that had bedevilled Ireland, the city was occasionally subjected to acts of terrorism. In February 1974, when the Provisional IRA targeted a coach carrying soldiers from Manchester to Catterick, a 50lb bomb exploded at Hartshead Moor, just outside Leeds, killing twelve people. In June 1992 the Irish National Liberation Army struck, detonating bombs in the city centre and causing £50,000-worth of damage. That was followed in April 1997 by an IRA explosion in Leeds City station. Five hotels were evacuated and the centre of Leeds sealed off. Islamic extremism also played its part in the city's story. It was three terrorists from Leeds who took part in suicide attacks in London on 7 July 2005, in which fifty-two people were killed and over 700 injured. Police raided homes in Burley and Beeston, and the moderate Muslim community in the city, like the rest of society, was appalled. They wrote to *The Times* 'to express our deepest anger at the terrible atrocities committed in London. ... These actions are despicable and cowardly in the way they targeted innocent individuals. We strongly and unequivocally condemn these barbaric actions which are an attempt to damage our democracy, freedom and community relations.'[17] But community relations were not seriously affected. Considerable efforts had been made to generate

The end of the Second World War saw the emergence of another kind of war. There were no fighting armies, no cities bombed, no thousands slaughtered. It was the Cold War. As the war against Germany and Japan ended, differences emerged between the Allied powers. The western nations, Britain, the USA, France and the rest feared the threats the Soviet Union posed as it turned its eyes westwards and wanted to spread its Communist beliefs there. The Soviet Union was equally fearful that the western powers were intent on destroying their nation and everything it stood for. And each power, East and West, possessed the newly developed atomic weapons.

If the Soviets did launch such an attack and drop a bomb capable of destroying an entire city, how would the authorities in such places respond? In Leeds plans were drawn up accordingly. It was estimated that if such a bomb were dropped over Leeds Bridge, Woodlesford and Kirkstall bridges, 10 miles apart, would be destroyed in the blast, 90,000 would be killed or seriously injured and 157,000 would be rendered homeless. There were 11,000 council houses and about 11,000 private houses in a 3 mile radius that would be destroyed. Those people would have to be forcibly billeted in properties still standing. Those who could were to be asked to remain in their damaged homes, and encouraged to use open fires to cook. Gas supplies would be completely cut off, as would be electricity supplies in the central areas. Drinking water would have to ferried in from Eccup reservoir to North Leeds. The homeless there were to be guided to the open areas towards Otley, York, Harrogate and Wetherby. In the south of the city survivors were to gather in Middleton Park before being moved to the Wakefield area. They were to be asked to bring a mug and spoon with them. As many as 60,000 would be forced to sleep in the open and plans were drawn up to issue them with heavy overcoats, knee-length boots, and hats with ear flaps. Food stocks that had been stored included 19 tons of sugar, 4 tons of tea, 21 tons of Mexican corned beef, 30 tons of margarine and 96 tons of potatoes. Food convoys were based at Sheffield and Wetherby, each made up of four stores vans, two water tankers, an office van, three motorbikes and eight canteens. Each could serve 7,000 helpings of stew at a sitting.

One other possible problem was considered. If the family of a member of the Civil Defence Corps fled, he may well join them. 'Blood was thicker than water,' the report observed. Fortunately the situation was never put to the test.

harmony in the previous fifty years, and no act of terrorism could be allowed to destroy that. Leeds needed to look to the future – and that was bright.

In 1999 the Leeds City Region Partnership was established to further the development of the region. This private-public partnership involves eleven authorities and various businesses. In 2006 the Partnership's City Region Development Programme was agreed, which included addressing transport, skills, housing, and innovation issues. The region is the largest employment centre both for financial and business services and manufacturing outside the capital.

As the city moved into the second decade of the twenty-first century, its people, viewing the future, can once again consider the words of the *Leeds Mercury* of December 1900 and its observation on what was to come: 'wonders far surpassing anything the wisest among us can foresee or imagine'. For two millennia the history of Leeds and its people have shown that whatever fate thrusts at them, whatever vicissitudes they have had to face, they have borne them with stoicism and forbearance, with determination and strength. Whatever 'wonders far surpassing anything the wisest among us can foresee or imagine' lie ahead, the people of Leeds are ready for them.

NOTES

Chapter One

1. B. Nelson, *The Woollen Industry of Leeds* (Leeds, 1980), pp.3–5.
2. F.G. Dimes and M. Mitchell, *The Building Heritage of Leeds* (Leeds, 2006), pp.65, 27, 80, 79.
3. P. Brears, *Leeds Waterfront Heritage Trail* (Leeds, 1993), p.3.
4. M.L. Faull and A. Moorhouse, *West Yorkshire: an Archaeological Survey to AD 1500*, I (Wakefield, 1981), pp.99–100, 107.
5. D. Cole, *Cookridge: the Story of a Yorkshire Township*, Part 1 (Leeds, 1980), pp.7–9.
6. Faull and Moorhouse, pp.157–59.
7. R. Thoresby, *Ducatus Leodiensis* ed. by T.D. Whitaker (Leeds, 1816), p.159; T.D. Whitaker, *Loidis and Elmete* (Leeds, 1816), p.175.
8. V. Crompton, *History of Adel* (Leeds, 2009), p.19.
9. J. Wardell, *The Antiquities of the Borough of Leeds* (Leeds, 1853), p.8.
10. Bede, *A History of the English Church and People* trans. by L. Sherley-Price, revised by R.E. Latham (Harmondsworth, 1968), p.130.
11. *Ibid.*, p.184.
12. D. Thornton, *Leeds: the Story of a City* (Ayr, 2002), pp.9–10.
13. Adel and Whitkirk were parishes in their own right.
14. G.N. Garmonsway (trans.), *The Anglo-Saxon Chronicle* (1978), p.204.
15. M. Faull and M. Stinson (eds), *Domesday Book; Yorkshire*, I (Chichester, 1986), p.315.
16. S. Burt and K. Grady, *The Illustrated History of Leeds* (Derby, 1994), p.14.

Chapter Two

1. J. le Patourel, 'The Manor and Borough of Leeds, 1066–1400', *P(ublications of the) Th(oresby) S(ociety)*, XLV (1956), pp.35–6. Tonsuring occurred when men became priests.
2. Garmonsway, p. 248.

3. D.E. Owen, *Kirkstall Abbey* (Leeds, 1955), pp.26–31.

4. See Thornton, *Leeds*, Chapter 2.

5. All Cistercian monasteries were dedicated to St Mary the Virgin.

6. Most historians accept this date, though some have disputed it.

7. For a detailed account of the building of the abbey and the life there see B. Sitch, *A Guide to Leeds' Cistercian Monastery* (Leeds, 2000).

8. Owen, pp.69–70.

9. J. Gillingham, 'The Early Middle Ages 1066–1290', in *The Oxford Illustrated History of Britain* ed. K.O. Morgan (Oxford, 1997), p.161.

10. M. Ashley, *The Life and Times of King John* (1984), p.162.

11. J. le Patourel, 'Medieval Leeds', *PThS*, XLVI (1963), p.16.

12. G.C. Forster, 'The Roots of Incorporation and Industrial Leeds', *PThS*, LXIV (2008), p.3.

13. *Ibid.*, p.xix.

14. In October 2007 on the 700th anniversary the Vatican announced their innocence.

15. O.J. Benedictow, *The Black Death 1346–1353* (2004), pp.127, 140.

16. J. Dixon, 'Surprising Survivors of the Black Death in Leeds', *PThS*, 20 (2010), pp.15–18, 20.

Chapter Three

1. For full details of the manor of Leeds see W.T. Lancaster, 'A Fifteenth Century Rental of Leeds', *PThS*, XXIV (1919); J. le Patourel, 'The Manor and Borough of Leeds 1066–1400', *PThS*, XLV (1957); J.W. Kirby 'The Manor and Borough of Leeds; 1425–1662: an Edition of Documents', *PThS*, LVII (1983).

2. Nelson, p.7.

3. J. Ayto and I. Crofton, *Brewer's Britain and Ireland* (2005), pp.153, 277, 600, 823, 1070.

4. M. McKisack, *The Fourteenth Century 1307–1399* (Oxford, 1959), p.353.

5. P. Johnson, *The Life and Times of Edward III* (1973), pp.145–48.

6. H. Heaton, *The Yorkshire Woollen and Worsted Industries* (Oxford, 1920), p.136.

7. Nelson, pp.8–14.

8. See A. Lonsdale, 'The Last Monks of Kirkstall Abbey', *PThS*, LIII (1973).

9. D. Thornton, *Leeds*, p. 56.

10. Anon, *Education in Leeds: A Backward Glance and a Present View* (Leeds, 1926), p.6.

11. Thoresby, *Ducatus*, p.vii.

12. E.K. Clark, 'A Brawl in Briggate', *PThS*, IV (1895), pp.125–38.

13. Heaton, p.139.

Chapter Four

1. Forster, 'Roots', pp.10–11.
2. C.V. Wedgwood, *The King's Peace* (1956), pp.34–5.
3. Nelson, p.18.
4. Burt and Grady, *Leeds*, pp.37–8.
5. Wedgwood, *Peace*, pp.62–3.
6. G.C.F. Forster, 'Leeds in the Civil War and Interregnum', *PThS*, LXIV (2008), pp.25–6.
7. J.W. Kirkby, 'The Aldermen of Leeds (1626–1700)', *PThS*, LXIV (2008), pp.52–69.
8. A.J. Hopper, 'The Clubmen of the West Riding of Yorkshire During the Civil War: "Bradford Club-Law"', *Northern History*, XXXVI (2000), p.65.
9. D.H. Atkinson, *Old Leeds: Its Bygones and Celebrities* (Leeds, 1868), pp.98–103.
10. T. Fairfax, *The Memoirs of Thomas Fairfax* (1776), pp.32–7.
11. It should be borne in mind that documents of the time give the date as 1642 because in the Old Style Julian calendar the year began on 25 March. It was only in 1752 that the New Style Gregorian calendar was introduced and New Year's Day became 1 January. Dates used in this book are all New Style.
12. C.V. Wedgwood, *The King's War 1641–1647* (1958), p.172.
13. J. Wilson, *Fairfax: General of the English Civil War* (New York, 1985), p.30.
14. J. Sprittles, *Links with Bygone Leeds* (Leeds, 1969), pp.37–40.
15. For details of the church see J. Douglas and K. Powell, *St John's Church Leeds; a History* (1992).
16. Thoresby, p.104.
17. Burt, Grady, *Leeds*, pp.46–8; Thornton, *Leeds*, p.74.

Chapter Five

1. Forster, 'Interregnum', pp.31–2.
2. A disease in the glands of the neck.
3. Sprittles, p.74.
4. Kirby, 'Aldermen', pp.69–83.
5. Forster, 'Interregnum', pp.25–36.
6. Later he was stabbed to death in a tavern brawl in London in 1667. See D. Thornton, 'Thomas Danby', *Leeds; a Historical Dictionary of People, Places and Events* (Huddersfield, 2013).
7. For details of the plot see S.J. Chadwick, 'The Farnley Wood Plot', *Thoresby Society Publications*, XV (1909); A. Hopper, 'The Farnley Wood Plot and the memory of the Civil Wars in Yorkshire', *Historical Journal*, 45 (2002).
8. G.C. Forster, 'The Government of Restoration Leeds', *PThS*, LXIV (2008), pp.44-5.

9. For a detailed account see J.E. Mortimer, 'Thoresby's "Poor Deluded Quakers": the Sufferings of the Leeds Friends in the Seventeenth Century', *PThS*, Second Series 1 (1990).
10. A. Heap and P. Brears, *Leeds Describ'd; Eyewitness Accounts of Leeds 1534–1905* (Derby, 1993), p.16, quoting *The Journal of Celia Fiennes*.
11. For details see E. Kitson Clark, 'The Leeds Mace made by Arthur Mangey, 1694' and C.M. Atkinson, 'Trial at York for Counterfeiting of Mr Arthur Mangey',' *PThS*, IX (1899).
12. For more details see F. Williamson and W.B. Crump, 'Sorocold's Waterworks at Leeds, 1694', *PThS*, XXXVII (1945).
13. For further reading see M. Clarke, *The Aire and Calder Navigation* (1999).

Chapter Six

1. Sprittles, p.42.
2. For details of William Milner see Kirby, 'Aldermen', pp.108–10.
3. Details of the Jacobite period in Leeds are graphically covered by Jonathan Oates. See J. Oates, 'Leeds and Jacobite Rebellions of 1715 and 1745', *PThS*, Second Series 14 (2004).
4. Contrary to popular belief, Wade Lane was not named after Marshall Wade. Waide Lane was a thoroughfare as early as 1677.
5. J. Dyer, 'The Fleece' in S. Johnson, *Works of English Poets* (1779).
6. For details of the Leeds press see D. Read, *Press and People 1790–1850; Opinion in Three English Cities* (1961). Several *Publications of the Thoresby Society* produced extracts from both the *Leeds Mercury* and the *Leeds Intelligencer* for the eighteenth century. Editions of the *Leeds Mercury* for 1718 and 1719 can be seen in the Special Collections at the University of Leeds.
7. See J. Oates (ed.), *The Memoranda Book of John Lucas 1712–1750* (Leeds, 2006).
8. R.W. Unwin, 'Leeds Becomes a Transport Centre' in *A History of Modern Leeds* ed. D. Fraser (Manchester, 1980), pp.120–24.
9. The best account of coaching in Leeds is to be found in T. Bradley, *The Coaching Days in Yorkshire* (Leeds, 1889).
10. Bradley, p.142.
11. Oates, *Lucas*, p.90.
12. Thornton, *Leeds*, pp.96–7.
13. For a detailed account see G. Stead, *The Moravian Settlement at Fulneck, 1742–1790* (Leeds, 1999).
14. P. Forsaith, *A Kindled Fire: John and Charles Wesley, and the Methodist Revival in the Leeds Area* (Leeds, 1988).
15. Sprittles, pp.66–9.
16. See J. Bushell, *The World's Oldest Railway* (Sheffield, 1975) and S. Bye, *A History of Middleton Railway* (1994).

Chapter Seven

1. For further details see C. Hadfield, *British Canals: an Illustrated History* (Newton Abbot, 1969).
2. *Leeds Mercury*, 26 October 1816.
3. For further details see W.G. Rimmer, *Marshalls of Leeds, Flax-Spinners 1788–1886* (Cambridge, 1960).
4. Burt and Grady, *Leeds*, pp.91–2. For further details of Mathew Murray's life see E. Kilburn Scott, *Matthew Murray; Pioneer Engineer Records from 1765–1826* (Leeds 1928).
5. For further details see J. Goodchild, 'The beginnings of Gott's mill', in *Aspects of Leeds*, ed. L.M.S. Tate, I (Barnsley, 1998).
6. For further details see H. Pemberton, 'Two Hundred Years of Banking in Leeds', *PThS*, XLVI (1963).
7. Mayhall, p.155; Sprittles, pp.61–2.
8. Thornton, *Leeds*, pp.104–5.
9. Burt and Grady, *Leeds*, p.78.
10. For further details see F. Beckwith, *The Leeds Library* (1994).
11. The most detailed account of housing in Leeds is to be found in M.W. Beresford, *East End, West End; the Face of Leeds During Urbanisation, 1684–1842*
12. Sprittles, pp.93–8; J. Copley, 'The Theatre in Hunslet Lane I', *PThS*, LIV (1974); J. Copley, 'The Theatre in Hunslet Lane II', *PThS*, LIV (1976).
13. Burt and Grady, *Leeds*, pp.78–84.
14. Wilberforce to Hey, 12 June 1787 and quoted in W. Hague, *William Wilberforce; the Life of the Great Anti-Slave Trade Campaigner* (2007), p.105.
15. Thornton, *Leeds*, pp.112–13.
16. For the most detailed information about the Leeds Volunteers see E. Hargrave, 'The Formation of the Leeds Yeomanry, 1817' and 'The Leeds Volunteers, 1820', *PThS*, XXIV (1919), 'The Early Leeds Volunteers', The Gentlemen Volunteer Cavalry, 1797', 'Leeds Volunteers 1803–1808', 'Leeds Local Militia 1808–1814', *PThS*, XXVIII (1928).
17. For further details see M. Parsons, *The General Infirmary at Leeds* (2003).

Chapter Eight

1. *Leeds Mercury*, 16 January, 14 August 1802, 22, 27 July, 17 August 1805.
2. D. Thornton, *Mr Mercury; the Life of Edward Baines 1774–1848* (Chesterfield, 2009), p.54.
3. J. Ryley, *The Leeds Guide Including a Sketch of the Environs and Kirkstall Abbey* (Leeds, 1806), pp.134–36.
4. D. Thornton, *Great Leeds Stories* (Ayr, 2005), pp.184–95.
5. R. Reed, *Land of Lost Content; the Luddite Revolt of 1812* (1986), p.113.

6. *Ibid.*, p.105.

7. Nelson, p.42.

8. The most detailed account of the battles for control of the vestry is to be found in D. Fraser, 'The Leeds Churchwardens 1828–1850'; *PThS,* LIII (1971).

9. K. Grady, 'Commercial, marketing and retail amenities, 1700–1914' in *A History of Modern Leeds*, ed. D. Fraser (Manchester, 1980), p.183.

10. *Leeds Mercury*, 11 June 1825.

11. *Leeds Mercury*, 17 December 1825.

12. Thornton, *Mr Mercury*, pp.162–64.

13. Burt and Grady, *Leeds*, pp.128–29.

14. A.S. Turberville and F. Beckwith, 'Leeds and Parliamentary Reform, 1820–1832', *PThS*, 12 (1954), p.13.

15. Two of the best books on Hook are W.R.W. Stephens, *Life and Letters of Walter Farquhar Hook* (1878) and H.W. Dalton, *Anglican Resurgence under W. F. Hook in Early Victorian Leeds; Church Life in a Nonconformist Town, 1836–1851* (Leeds, 2002).

16. The story of Beckett Street Cemetery is told in S.M. Barnard, *To Prove I'm Not Forgot; Living and Dying in a Victorian City* (Manchester, 1990).

17. *Leeds Mercury*, 4 January 1840.

18. The most detailed account of Chartism in Leeds is by J.F.C. Harrison, 'Chartism in Leeds' in *Chartist Studies* ed. A. Briggs (1958).

19. A comprehensive account of the epidemic is to be found in H. Kennally, 'Famine, Typhus and the Poor Law Irish Families in Leeds', *PThS*, Second Series 20 (2010). The story of William Stanley Monck, the curate who died, is to be found in G. Figures, 'Typhus, two windows and a gold chain' in the same volume.

20. The definitive life of Richard Oastler is C. Driver, *Tory Radical; the Life of Richard Oastler* (Oxford, 1946).

Chapter Nine

1. A. Briggs, *Victorian Cities* (1990), pp.139–83; *Leeds Mercury*, 7 September 1858; Victoria, vol. 46 *Queen Victoria's Journals*, RA VIC/MASIN/QVJ/1858: 6 and 7 September, pp.114–17.

2. For the most recent books on the architecture of the city see S. Wrathmell, *Pevsner Architectural Guides: Leeds* (2005) and C. Webster (ed.), *Building a Great Victorian City; Leeds Architects and Architecture 1790–1914* (Huddersfield, 2011). For Brodrick's work in particular see D. Linstrum, *Towers and Colonnades: the Architecture of Cuthbert Brodrick* (Leeds, 1999).

3. M.W. Beresford, 'The face of Leeds, 1780–1914', in *A History of Modern Leeds*, ed. D. Fraser (Manchester, 1980); E. Bradford, *Headingley, this Pleasant and Rural Village* (Huddersfield, 2008), pp.195–215; Burt and Grady, *Leeds*, p.146.

4. B.J. Barber, 'Aspects of municipal government, 1835–1914', in *A History of Modern Leeds*, ed. D. Fraser (Manchester, 1980). The most comprehensive history of transport in Leeds is to be found in J. Soper, *Leeds Transport; 1830–1902*, 1 (Leeds, 1985); *1902–1931*, 2 (Leeds, 1996); *1932–1953*, 3 (Leeds, 2003); *1953–1974*, 4 (Leeds, 2007).

5. *Leeds Mercury*, 3 November, quoting a report of 1870.

6. For details of education in Leeds see Thornton, *Dictionary*, 'School Board', 'Leeds Church Middle Class School', 'Leeds Girls' High School', 'Education Committee'.

7. For details of Leeds libraries see M. Shipway, 'The Adoption of the Public Libraries Act in Leeds 1861–1868, *PThS*, Second Series 8 (1998).

8. For further information about the clothing industry see K. Honeyman, *Well Suited: a History of the Leeds Clothing Industry, 1850–1990* (2000).

9. The best account of Leeds theatres is in R.E. Preedy, *Leeds Theatres Remembered* (Leeds, 1981).

10. *Leeds Mercury*, 7 November 1878.

11. *Leeds Mercury*, 22 June 1891, 19 November 1886.

12. For details of both Irish and Jewish immigration into Leeds see T. Dillon, 'The Irish in Leeds 1851–1861', *PThS*, LIV (1974) and M. Freedman, *Leeds Jews: the First Hundred Years* (Leeds, 1992).

13. For details of the politics of Leeds see D. Fraser, 'Politics and society in the nineteenth century' and E.D. Steele, 'Imperialism and Leeds politics 1850–1914' in *A History of Modern Leeds*, ed. D. Fraser (Manchester, 1980).

14. The *Daily Mail* first used the term on 6 January 1906.

15. D. Thornton, *Stories*, 'New Year Horror'.

16. The Victorians argued that 1900 completed the hundred years from 1801. The end of the twentieth century was celebrated officially in 1999 but many argued that 2000 was the correct date.

17. *Leeds Mercury*, 31 December 1900.

18. *Leeds Mercury*, 23 February 1865; *The Times*, 23 February 1865.

Chapter Ten

1. *The Times*, 23, 24, 25, 26, January 1901.

2. *The Times*, 17 September 1903.

3. See Thornton, *Dictionary*, 'Diet'.

4. For further details see S. Bayliss, *Leeds Babies' Welcome Association; a Memoir* (Leeds, 1991).

5. See H. Benn, *James O'Grady Member of Parliament for Leeds East 1906–1918 and Leeds South-East 1918–1924* (2005).

6. See J. Lidington, *Rebel Girls: Their Fight for the Vote* (2006).

7. J.M. Haggerty, *Leeds at War; 1914–1918, 1939–1945* (Wakefield, 1981), pp.2–48.

8. Anon, *British Labour and the Russian Revolution. The Leeds Convention: A Report from the* Daily Herald (Nottingham, 1974).
9. For detailed accounts of the incident see various editions of the *Leeds Mercury, Yorkshire Evening Post* and *Yorkshire Evening News* June 1917 and *The Times*, 5 June 1917.
10. Thornton, *Stories,* 'A Year of Pestilence'.
11. Burt and Grady, pp.216–18.
12. See E.M. Sigsworth, *Montague Burton: the Tailor of Taste* (1990).
13. See T. Woodhouse, 'The General Strike in Leeds', *Northern History,* XVIII (1982).
14. See A. Heap, *The Headrow; a Pictorial Record* (Leeds, 1990).
15. *Yorkshire Evening Post*, 23 August 1933.
16. *The Times*, 9 July 1936.
17. *Yorkshire Evening News*, 9 March 1936.
18. R. Freethy, *Yorkshire; the Secret War, 1939–1945* (Newbury, 2010), p.76.
19. For further details of the Second World War see Thornton, *Leeds,* pp.205–9; Hagerty, pp.50–100.
20. For further reading see Thornton, *Stories,* 'The Home Guard in Leeds'; F.R. Cowell, *Citizen Soldiers: Being the Story of the Kirkstall Forge Home Guard, 1940–1945* (Leeds, n.d.).
21. The map can be seen in the Local and Family History Library, Leeds.
22. *The Times*, 17 May 1940; Freethy, pp.34–6.
23. *Yorkshire Evening Post*, 26 July 1945.
24. See W.R. Meyer, 'Charles Henry Wilson: the Man who was Leeds', *PThS*, Second Series 8 (1998); Thornton, *Stories,* 'The Sultan of Leeds'.

Chapter Eleven

1. *Yorkshire Post*, 3 June 1953; *The Times*, 3 June 1953.
2. G. Tweedale, 'The Armley asbestos tragedy', *Journal of Industrial History*, p.2.
3. Soper, vol. 3, pp.816, 823.
4. O. Hartley, 'The Postwar Years and after' in *A History of Modern Leeds*, ed. D. Fraser (Manchester, 1980), pp.447–53.
5. G. Taylor, 'Education in Leeds' in *Leeds and Its Region*, ed. M.W. Beresford and G.R.J. Jones (Leeds, 1967), pp.288–98.
6. M. Zulfiquar (ed.), *Land of Hope and Glory? The Presence of African, Asian and Caribbean Communities in Leeds* (1993).
7. Nelson, pp.45–7.
8. For further reading see R.E. Preedy, *Leeds Cinemas* (Leeds, 2005).
9. See Thornton, *Stories,* 'The Hooligans of Elland Road'; C. Gall, *Service Crew: the Inside Story of Leeds United's Hooligan Gangs* (Preston, 2007).

10. For further reading see M. Farrer, 'Towards a History of Harehills and Chapeltown: Riot and Revolution: the Politics of an Inner City', *Revolutionary Socialism* (Winter 1981–82).
11. See Thornton, *Stories*, 'Crime and the City'.
12. See E.W. Clay (ed.), *The Leeds Police 1836–1974* (Leeds, 1974).
13. See M. Bilton, *Wicked Beyond Belief: the Hunt for the Yorkshire Ripper* (2006).
14. Burt and Grady, *Leeds*, pp.246–49.
15. Thornton, *Leeds*, p.225.
16. See J. Stillwell and R. Unsworth, *Around Leeds: a City Centre Reinvented* (Leeds, 2008).
17. *The Times*, 14 July 2005.
18. *Yorkshire Post*, 26 April 2001.

BIBLIOGRAPHY

Anon, *British Labour and the Russian Revolution. The Leeds Convention: A Report from the* Daily Herald (Nottingham, 1974)

Anon, *Education in Leeds: A Backward Glance and a Present View* (Leeds 1926)

Ashley, M., *The Life and Times of King John* (1984)

Atkinson, C.M., 'Trial at York for Counterfeiting of Mr Arthur Mangey', *Publications of the Thoresby Society*, IX (Leeds, 1899)

Ayto, J. and Crofton, I., *Brewer s Britain and Ireland* (2005)

Barber, B.J., 'Aspects of municipal government, 1835–1914', in *A History of Modern Leeds*, ed. D. Fraser (Manchester, 1980)

Barnard, M., *To Prove I'm Not Forgot; Living and Dying in a Victorian City* (Manchester, 1990)

Bayliss, S., *Leeds Babies' Welcome Association; a Memoir* (Leeds, 1991)

Beckwith, F., *The Leeds Library* (1994)

Bede, *A History of the English Church and People* trans. by L. Sherley-Price, revised by R.E. Latham (Harmondsworth, 1968)

Benn, H., *James O'Grady Member of Parliament for Leeds East 1906–1918 and Leeds South–East 1918–1924* (2005)

Beresford, M.W., 'The face of Leeds, 1780–1914', in *A History of Modern Leeds*, ed. D. Fraser (Manchester, 1980)

Benn, W., *More Annals of Leeds* (Leeds, 2005)

Benedictow, O.J., *The Black Death 1346–1353* (2004)

Bilton, M., *Wicked Beyond Belief: the Hunt for the Yorkshire Ripper* (2006)

Bradford, E., *Headingley, this Pleasant and Rural Village* (Huddersfield, 2008)

Bradley, T., *The Coaching Days in Yorkshire* (Leeds, 1889)

Brears, P., *Leeds Waterfront Heritage Trail* (Leeds, 1993)

Briggs, A., *Victorian Cities* (1990)

Burt, S. and Grady, K., *The Illustrated History of Leeds* (Derby, 1994)

Bushell, J., *The World s Oldest Railway* (Sheffield, 1975)

Bye, S., *A History of Middleton Railway* (1994)

Chadwick, S.J., 'The Farnley Wood Plot', *Publications of the Thoresby Society*, XV (Leeds, 1909)

Clark, E.K., 'A Brawl in Briggate', *Publications of the Thoresby Society*, IV (Leeds, 1895)

Clarke, M., *The Aire and Calder Navigation* (1999)

Clay, E.W. (ed.), *The Leeds Police 1836–1974* (Leeds, 1974)

Cole, D., *Cookridge: the Story of a Yorkshire Township* Part 1 (Leeds, 1980)

Copley, J., 'The Theatre in Hunslet Lane I', *Publications of the Thoresby Society*, LIV (1974)

Copley, J., 'The Theatre in Hunslet Lane II', *Publications of the Thoresby Society*, LIV (1976)

Cowell, F.R., *Citizen Soldiers: Being the Story of the Kirkstall Forge Home Guard, 1940–1945* (Leeds, n.d.)

Crompton, V., *History of Adel* (Leeds, 2009)

Dalton, H.W., *Anglican Resurgence under W.F. Hook in Early Victorian Leeds; Church Life in a Nonconformist Town, 1836–1851* (Leeds, 2002)

Dillon, T., 'The Irish in Leeds 1851–1861', *Publications of the Thoresby Society*, LIV (Leeds, 1974)

Dimes, F.G. and Mitchell, M., *The Building Heritage of Leeds* (Leeds, 2006)

Douglas, J. and Powell, K., *St John s Church Leeds; a History* (1992)

Driver, C., *Tory Radical; the Life of Richard Oastler* (Oxford, 1946)

Dyer, J., 'The Fleece in S. Johnson', *Works of English Poets* (1779)

Fairfax, T., *The Memoirs of Thomas Fairfax* (1776)

Farrer, M., 'Towards a History of Harehills and Chapeltown: Riot and Revolution: the Politics of an Inner City', *Revolutionary Socialism* (Winter 1981–1982)

Faull, M.L. and Moorhouse, A., *West Yorkshire: an Archaeological Survey to AD 1500*, 3 vols (Wakefield, 1981)

Faull, M. and Stinson, M. (eds), *Domesday Book; Yorkshire*, I (Chichester, 1986)

Figures, G., 'Typhus, two windows and a gold chain', *Publications of the Thoresby Society*, Second Series 20 (Leeds, 2010)

Forster, G.C.F., 'The Roots of Incorporation and Industrial Leeds', *Publications of the Thoresby Society*, LXIV (Leeds, 2008)

Forster, G.C.F., 'Leeds in the Civil War and Interregnum', *Publications of the Thoresby Society*, LXIV (Leeds, 2008)

Forster, G.C.F., 'The Government of Restoration Leeds', *Publications of the Thoresby Society*, LXIV (Leeds, 2008)

Fraser, D., 'Politics and society in the nineteenth century' in *A History of Modern Leeds* ed. D. Fraser (Manchester, 1980)

Freedman, M., *Leeds Jews: the First Hundred Years* (Leeds, 1992)

Freethy, R., *Yorkshire; the Secret War, 1939–1945* (Newbury, 2010)

Gall, C., *Service Crew: the Inside Story of Leeds United's Hooligan Gangs* (Preston, 2007)

Garmonsway, G.N. (trans. and ed.), *The Anglo-Saxon Chronicle* (1978)

Gillingham, J., 'The Early Middle Ages 1066–1290', in *The Oxford Illustrated History of Britain*, ed. K.O. Morgan (Oxford, 1997)

Grady, K., 'Commercial, marketing and retail amenities, 1700–1914' in *A History of Modern Leeds*, ed. D. Fraser (Manchester, 1980)

Haggerty, J.M., *Leeds at War; 1914–1918, 1939–1945* (Wakefield, 1981)

Hague, W., *William Wilberforce; the Life of the Great Anti-Slave Trade Campaigner* (2007)

Hargrave, E., 'The Formation of the Leeds Yeomanry, 1817' and 'The Leeds Volunteers, 1820', *Publications of the Thoresby Society*, XXIV (Leeds, 1919)

Hargrave, E., 'The Early Leeds Volunteers', The Gentlemen Volunteer Cavalry, 1797', 'Leeds Volunteers 1803–1808', 'Leeds Local Militia 1808–1814', *Publications of the Thoresby Society*, XXVIII (Leeds, 1928).

Harrison, J.F.C., 'Chartism in Leeds' in *Chartist Studies* ed. A. Briggs (1958).

Hartley, O., 'The Postwar Years and after' in *A History of Modern Leeds*, ed. D. Fraser (Manchester, 1980)

Heap, A., *The Headrow; a Pictorial Record* (Leeds, 1990)

Heap, A. and Brears, P., *Leeds Described; Eyewitness Accounts of Leeds 1534–1905* (Derby, 1993)

Heaton, H., *The Yorkshire Woollen and Worsted Industries* (Oxford, 1920)

Honeyman, K., *Well Suited :a History of the Leeds Clothing Industry, 1850–1990* (2000)

Hopper, A., 'The Farnley Wood Plot and the Memory of the Civil Wars in Yorkshire', *Historical Journal* 45 (2002)

Johnson, P., *The Life and Times of Edward III* (1973)

Kennally, H., 'Famine, Typhus and the Poor Law Irish Families in Leeds', *Publications of the Thoresby Society*, Second Series 20 (Leeds, 2010)

Kirby, J.W. (ed.), 'The Manor and Borough of Leeds; 1425–1662: an Edition of Documents', *Publications of the Thoresby Society*, LVII (Leeds, 1983)

Kirkby, J.W., 'The Aldermen of Leeds (1626–1700)', *Publications of the Thoresby Society*, LXIV (Leeds, 2008)

Kitson Clark, E., 'The Leeds Mace made by Arthur Mangey, 1694', *Publications of the Thoresby Society*, IX (Leeds, 1899)

Lancaster, W.T., 'A Fifteenth Century Rental of Leeds', *Publications of the Thoresby Society*, XXIV (Leeds, 1919)

Lidington, J., *Rebel Girls: Their Fight for the Vote* (2006)

Linstrum, D., *Towers and Colonnades: the Architecture of Cuthbert Brodrick* (Leeds, 1999)

Lonsdale, A., 'The Last Monks of Kirkstall Abbey', *Publications of the Thoresby Society*, LIII (Leeds, 1973)

McKisack, M., *The Fourteenth Century 1307–1399*

Mayhall, J., *Annals of Yorkshire* (Leeds, 1860)

Mortimer, J.E., 'Thoresby's Poor Deluded Quakers: the Sufferings of the Leeds Friends in the Seventeenth Century', *Publications of the Thoresby Society,* Second Series 1 (Leeds, 1990)

Nelson, B., *The Woollen Industry of Leeds* (Leeds, 1980)

Oates, J., 'Leeds and Jacobite Rebellions 1715 and 1745', *Publications of the Thoresby Society,* Second Series 14 (Leeds, 2004)

Oates, J. (ed.), *The Memoranda Book of John Lucas 1712–1750* (Leeds, 2006)

Owen, D.E., *Kirkstall Abbey* (Leeds, 1955)

le Patourel, J., The Manor and Borough of Leeds 1066–1400', *Publications of the Thoresby Society*, XLV (Leeds, 1957)

le Patourel, J., 'Medieval Leeds', *Publications of the Thoresby Society*, XLVI (Leeds, 1963)

Pemberton, H., 'Two Hundred Years of Banking in Leeds ', *Publications of the Thoresby Society*, XLVI (Leeds, 1963)

Preedy, R.E., *Leeds Theatres Remembered* (Leeds, 1981)

Preedy, R.E., *Leeds Cinemas* (Stroud, 2005)

Reed, R., *Land of Lost Content; the Luddite Revolt of 1812* (1986)

Ryley, J., *The Leeds Guide Including a Sketch of the Environs and Kirkstall Abbey* (Leeds, 1806)

Shipway, M., 'The Adoption of the Public Libraries Act in Leeds 1861–1868', *Publications of the Thoresby Society*, Second Series 8 (Leeds, 1998).

Sigsworth, E.M., *Montague Burton: the Tailor of Taste* (1990)

Sitch, B., *A Guide to Leeds Cistercian Monastery* (Leeds, 2000)

Soper, J., *Leeds Transport; 1, 2, 3, 4* (Leeds, 1985, 1996, 2003, 2007)

Sprittles, J., *Links with Bygone Leeds* (Leeds, 1969)

Stead, G., *The Moravian Settlement at Fulneck, 1742–1790* (Leeds, 1999)

Steele, E.D., 'Imperialism and Leeds politics 1850–1914' in *A History of Modern Leeds*, ed. D. Fraser (Manchester, 1980)

Stephens, W.R.W., *Life and Letters of Walter Farquhar Hook* (1878)

Stillwell, J. and Unsworth, R., *Around Leeds: a City Centre Reinvented* (Leeds, 2008)

Stratton, J.M., *Agricultural Records AD 220–1977* (1978)

Taylor, G., 'Education in Leeds' in *Leeds and Its Region* ed. M.W. Beresford and G.R.J. Jones (Leeds, 1967)

Thoresby, R., *Ducatus Leodiensis* ed. T.D. Whitaker (Leeds, 1816)

Thornton, D., *Leeds: the Story of a City* (Ayr, 2002)

Thornton, D., *Great Leeds Stories* (Ayr, 2005)

Thornton, D., *Mr Mercury; the Life of Edward Baines 1774–1848* (Chesterfield, 2009)

Thornton, D., *Leeds; a Historical Dictionary of People, Places and Events* (Huddersfield, 2013)

Turberville, A.S. and Beckwith, F., 'Leeds and Parliamentary Reform, 1820–1832', *Publications of the Thoresby Society*, 12 (Leeds, 1954)

Tweedale, G.,'The Armley asbestos tragedy', *Journal of Industrial History*, 2

Victoria, vol 46 Queen Victoria's Journals, RA VIC/MASIN/QVJ/1858: 6 & 7 September

Wardell, J., *The Antiquities of the Borough of Leeds* (Leeds, 1853)

Webster, C. (ed.), *Building a Great Victorian City; Leeds Architects and Architecture 1790–1914* (Huddersfield, 2011)

Wedgwood, C.V., *The King's Peace* (1956)

Wedgwood, C.V., *The King's War 1641–1647* (1958)

Whitaker, T.D., *Loidis and Elmete* (Leeds, 1816)

Williams, J.E., 'The Leeds Corporation Strike in 1913' in *Essays in Labour History 1886–1923* ed. A. Briggs and J. Savile (1971)

Williamson, F. and Crump, W.B., 'Sorocold's Waterworks at Leeds, 1694', *Publications of the Thoresby Society*, XXXVII (Leeds, 1945)

Wilson, A.N., *The Victorians* (2003)

Wilson, J., *Fairfax: General of the English Civil War* (New York, 1985)

Wrathmell, S., *Pevsner Architectural Guides: Leeds* (2005)

Zulfiquar, M. (ed.), *Land of Hope and Glory? The Presence of African, Asian and Caribbean Communities in Leeds* (1993)

Leeds Intelligencer
Leeds Mercury
Leeds Other Paper
Leeds Weekly Citizen
The Times
Yorkshire Evening News
Yorkshire Evening Post
Yorkshire Post

www.theinsider.org.

THE THORESBY SOCIETY

Most of the illustrations in this book are from the archives of the Thoresby Society. On Monday 13 May 1889 a meeting was held in the hall of the Leeds Philosophical and Literary Society to form a society dedicated to the history of Leeds. One of the leading lights of the society, Colonel Edmund Wilson, was elected its president. In July that year it was decided to change the name from the Leeds Historical and Antiquarian Society to the Thoresby Society, after Ralph Thoresby, the town's first historian.

Its object was to establish a society devoted to the history of Leeds and its neighbourhood through lectures, visits and regular publications of academic material. But another of its aims was 'the collection and preservation of books, pamphlets, MSS, deeds, engravings, drawings, coins, antiquities and other objects relating to the town and neighbourhood of Leeds or bearing in any way upon the past or present history of the inhabitants'.

Thus was built up over 123 years the society's archive, held in its library at Claremont and now containing an extensive collection of books on the history of the city and thousands of photographs, as well as watercolours, pencil and pen-and-ink sketches, lithographs, and, until recently, oil paintings, which are now held by the Leeds City Art Galleries. The 'other objects' it referred to now include, among other things, woodwork from Ralph Thoresby's house, advertising posters, election bills, old bus tickets and a large collection of old newspapers, in particular the *Leeds Mercury* and the *Leeds Intelligencer*.

The archive is available for consultation by both members of the society and students of local history. The Librarian may be contacted at the Thoresby Society, Claremont, Clarendon Road, Leeds LS2 9NZ; by telephone 0113 247 0704; by email at library@thoresby.org.uk. The society's website is www.thoresby.org.uk.

INDEX